Sic Buchananus ora sic vultum tulit,
Pete, scripta et astra nosse si mentem cupis.

GEORGE BUCHANAN (1506–1582)
Reproduced from a painting in Elphinstone Hall, King's College, by kind permission of
the University Court, University of Aberdeen

GEORGE BUCHANAN

Prince of Poets

PHILIP J FORD

---

with an Edition
(Text, Translation, Commentary)
of the
Miscellaneorum
Liber

by
PHILIP J FORD

W S WATT

ABERDEEN UNIVERSITY PRESS

First published 1982
Aberdeen University Press
A member of the Pergamon Group

© Philip J Ford 1982
Miscellaneorum Liber: Translation and Commentary
© Philip J Ford and W S Watt 1982

The financial assistance of the Scottish Arts Council,
the Carnegie Trust for the Universities of Scotland,
and the University of Aberdeen, in the publication of this
book is gratefully acknowledged

British Library Cataloguing in Publication Data
Ford, Philip J.
  George Buchanan
  1. Buchanan, George, *1506-1582*—Criticism and
  interpretation
  2. Latin poetry, Medieval and modern—History
  and criticism
  I. Title
  871'.04'09   PA8051

ISBN 0 08 028458 2

PRINTED IN GREAT BRITAIN
AT THE UNIVERSITY PRESS
ABERDEEN

Contents

To my parents

Preface

When a Scotsman once asked Dr Johnson what he would have said of George Buchanan had he been English, he received the reply: 'Why, Sir, I should *not* have said of Buchanan, had he been an *Englishman,* what I will now say of him as a *Scotchman,*—that he was the only man of genius his country ever produced.'[1] Although not everyone may now (for whatever reason) share that view, it is indicative of Buchanan's standing in the eighteenth century, and even during his own lifetime he received the well known description by the printer and scholar Henri Estienne of 'poeta sui saeculi facile princeps'. Until recently in this century, however, Buchanan's reputation as a poet has been somewhat eclipsed by his other activities, but with the renewal of interest in Renaissance Latin Literature, his literary status is once again being fully realised.

Buchanan is too diverse a poet to be handled within the confines of a single book, and he will always offer new perspectives to those who read and study his works. My aim in this book has been to indicate some of his achievements in the field of Neo-latin versification by seeing him in the context of Renaissance verse theory and practice; to follow his poetic development over the years and his connections with vernacular poetry; and to estimate his success as a poet. Neo-latin poetry often comes under fire from both classicists and Renaissance scholars for not adhering strictly to Golden Latin usage in prosody, versification, and language, or for failing to be an authentic work of art because it is written in a dead language for which the poet can have no instinctive feel. I hope that this study and the poetry of Buchanan itself will help to meet these objections in some degree.

It is unfortunate that no complete modern edition of Buchanan's poetic works exists, although in the case of the secular poems and the sacred tragedies, this situation will eventually be remedied.[2] Meanwhile, the *Opera omnia* edited by Thomas Ruddiman (Edinburgh, 1715) and the revised version with Burman's additions (Leiden, 1725) are the most convenient editions to consult. The last few years have also witnessed the appearance of a number of anthologies of Neo-latin poetry, and Buchanan will be found with English translations in some of these.[3]

However, in order to fill in the existing gap in some measure, I have included at the end of this study Buchanan's *Miscellaneorum liber,* together

[1] Notes start on p. 115.

vii

with a translation and explanatory notes. There are several reasons for this decision, rather than the alternative possibility, a personal anthology of Buchanan's verse. In the first place, the Miscellaneous poems offer contributions from almost the whole of the Scottish poet's creative life, in a wide range of metres and genres. Moreover, a personal anthology might run the risk of showing only the best examples of a writer's works, while this ready-made collection will enable the reader to judge a whole gamut of Buchanan's poetic output. Finally, while many of Buchanan's other works have been translated into English, I am not aware of the existence of a complete translation of the Miscellaneous poems.[4]

It is a pleasure to record my very deep gratitude to Professor Ian McFarlane, who supervised the Cambridge doctoral dissertation out of which this book has grown. His boundless energy, meticulous scholarship, enthusiasm, and *humanitas* are a constant source of inspiration, while my bibliography bears witness to what he has achieved on behalf of Buchanan and Neo-latin literature in general. I should also like to express my great appreciation and thanks to Professor W. S. Watt of the University of Aberdeen, whose collaboration was invaluable in preparing the texts, translations, and notes of the *Miscellaneorum liber*.

Of course, this study would not have seen the light of day without the good offices of Aberdeen University Press, and I am most grateful to them, and in particular to their publishing director, Mr Colin MacLean, for their confidence and encouragement at a time when the *respublica litteraria* is under attack from all sides. Grateful thanks are also due to the Scottish Arts Council, whose generous support has made possible the production of this book in its present form, as well as to the Carnegie Trust for the Universities of Scotland and the University of Aberdeen for their financial assistance. Finally, I should like to thank Allan Doig for his help in reading and correcting the proofs, and for his constant encouragement at an earlier stage of the proceedings.

Aberdeen   P.J.F.

Abbreviations

BHR   *Bibliothèque d'Humanisme et Renaissance*

BN   Bibliothèque Nationale, Paris

CSP   *Calendar of State Papers relating to Scotland*

DNB   *Dictionary of National Biography*

O.O.   *Opera omnia* of Buchanan, edited by Thomas Ruddiman and Peter Burman, 2 vols (Leiden, 1725). This has been used as the basis of all references to Buchanan's writings, with minor changes to the punctuation and spelling for the sake of clarity.

CHAPTER 1

Introduction

The sixteenth century in France saw the rise of an extremely copious body of literature written in Latin, whose importance and pervasive influence are only now beginning to receive the attention which they deserve.[1] For Latin was far from being the dead language which it has since become. It was spoken extensively in the schools where the vernacular was generally banned, and formed an international language amongst humanists, diplomats, and churchmen all over Europe. Even as late as the 1550s, there was a grudging recognition by the most ardent supporters of the vernacular, such as du Bellay, that French was still deficient and in its infancy, whereas classical Latin literature represented in many people's minds the summit which they were striving to attain. As a literary language, Latin was familiar to the humanist and offered him models in accord with his ideals and aspirations, while the vernacular was still associated with the obscurity of the Middle Ages. For the poet, in particular, Latin provided an established diction, form, and background which were totally consonant with his ideals. Moreover, Latin poetry had stood the test of time and therefore seemed more likely to some poets to ensure their posthumous renown. As the Renaissance humanist was frequently an exile from his own country, living among friends from all over Europe, he would naturally turn to the universal language of humanism in which to express himself. In this way, Latin transcended both temporal and geographical boundaries.

The explanation for the sheer number of Neo-latin poets in France—one estimate puts the figure at over seven hundred for the sixteenth century[2]— should perhaps be sought in the schools and universities. The d'Estouteville reforms of the University of Paris in 1452 had laid great emphasis on Latin versification as a means of improving the general standard of Latin, and even if their influence required time to take effect, it was at least being felt in the closing decades of the fifteenth century. It is then perfectly natural for people to continue to practise after their formal education a subject for which they find they have some aptitude. Through verse, the humanist expressed his aspirations, prejudices, petty grievances, religious and political opinions. He vied with the Romans—and the Italians—for supremacy in the realms of poetry, and while publicly denigrating his *nugae* and *juvenilia*, secretly felt a Horatian pride in the outpourings of his Muse. In addition, there was a growing feeling amongst certain humanists that the

1

divinely-inspired poet or *vates* had a unique role as mediator between the human and the divine worlds, acting as a repository for certain important philosophical or religious truths.

These feelings of national pride and of the prophetic role of the poet were something which closely linked the Neo-latin poet with his vernacular colleague, and indeed, there was a considerable band of poets like Mellin de Saint-Gelais, Jean Dorat, and Joachim du Bellay who composed in both French and Latin. However, until the middle of the century, it was primarily the Neo-latinists who led the way. They helped to establish the currency of certain poetic styles, themes, images, and philosophical attitudes, and produced a body of literature which raised the status of French poetry. Of the French vernacular writers, on the other hand, du Bellay remarks:

> qu'ilz ont bien ecrit, qu'ilz ont illustré notre langue, que la France leur est obligée: mais aussi diroy-je bien qu'on pouroit trouver en notre langue (si quelque scavant homme y vouloit mettre la main) une forme de poësie beaucoup plus exquise, la quele il faudroit chercher en ces vieux Grecz et Latins, non point és aucteurs francoys.[3]

It was the Neo-latin writers who had been turning to the Ancients, and their treatment of the classical poets served as a model to the Pléiade poets who wished to elevate French poetry by similar methods, and whose influence, *pace* Malherbe, lasted into the seventeenth century.[4]

Of the Neo-latin poets living in France during this period, George Buchanan is amongst the most successful. He was a man of great breadth of vision, whose activities encompassed all branches of literature, including poetry, drama, history, and political thought. At the same time, he managed to bridge the gap between the ancient and the contemporary worlds by establishing a dialogue between the two civilisations and helping his fellows to assimilate the cultural heritage of their predecessors, which they so greatly desired to emulate but seldom fully comprehended.

Since the appearance of Professor McFarlane's magisterial biography of Buchanan, which draws together for the first time the many new facts to have emerged over the years while correcting previous inaccuracies, there is no need to deal at length with the Scottish humanist's life.[5] Areas of his biography must in any case remain rather shadowy, for if the Portuguese Inquisition has repaid its debt to Buchanan by the preservation of many of the surviving details about his middle years, the ravages of time and con-flagrations have not been so kind to other likely sources, such as the records of the Scots College in Paris or the Bordeaux archives. However, it is hoped that the following summary will be of use in setting the Scottish humanist in his cultural context and in indicating some of his achievements.

Buchanan was born at the beginning of February 1506 near the village of Killearn in Stirlingshire. At the age of seven, he moved from his birthplace to Cardross in Menteith, two farms in the neighbourhood being granted by Robert Erskine to Buchanan's mother and her three elder sons, Patrick, Alexander, and George. From 1520 to 1522 he was sent by his maternal uncle James Heriot to Paris to continue his studies, but was forced to return home because of his uncle's death and his own poor health. After a period of convalescence, he joined the forces of the Duke of Albany who, at the end of 1523, led an abortive attack against the English. Another period of illness ensued, and Buchanan turns up next in the following spring at St Andrews University where he matriculated in 1525. In October 1527 he incorporated as a BA in the University of Paris, and by March 1528, he had his licence and was thus qualified to teach. His reputation and popularity are demonstrated by the fact that in June 1529 he was elected Procurator of the German Nation, an office which involved looking after financial matters, presiding over meetings, and reporting decisions to the University council.[6]

Buchanan's early education would have been centred on the study of Latin. Scotland had not been slow to recognise the importance of correct Latin in education, and in 1496 an Education Act was passed, encouraged by James IV, which made provisions for students, especially the sons of the nobility, to achieve 'perfite latyne'. So, Scottish secondary education in the early part of the sixteenth century continued to centre on the *trivium*, with particular emphasis on grammar and rhetoric (which included the increasingly important study of Latin versification). Dialectic, on the other hand, was for the most part ignored at this stage. Medieval practices died hard, and Alexander Villa-Dei's *Doctrinale*, as edited by John Vaus of Aberdeen, continued to form the basis of Latin instruction for some time before finally being replaced by Despauterius.[7] There were few people in Scotland, on the other hand, who were qualified to teach Greek, and this state of affairs was to continue far into the century. It was while he was in Paris for the first time that Buchanan really became involved in writing poetry, 'partly through natural bent, and partly out of necessity, as this was the only form of school work offered to the young' (*O.O.* I, fo. g2^r). The d'Estouteville reforms were obviously taking effect.

It was probably during his second period in Paris, which began in 1526, that Buchanan had the opportunity of studying Greek, perhaps aided in this by the public lectures which Jacques Toussaint instituted around this time, and supplemented by Clenardus' *Institutiones in linguam graecam*, which had first appeared in 1521 and had largely supplanted earlier grammars. Greek literature was to have a lasting effect on Buchanan's poetic output, and as early as 1530 he could be described by Robert Wauchope as 'cet homme capable, le doctissime en grec et en latin'.[8] An interest in Hebrew may also have grown up then. Florentius Volusenus (Florens Wilson), a fellow-countryman and graduate of Aberdeen University who was in Paris from around 1526 until 1534, presented Buchanan with a copy of Sebastian Münster's *Dictionarium hebraicum* (Bâle, 1523) which is now in Edinburgh University Library.

Towards the end of 1528, Buchanan obtained his first teaching post at the progressive Collège de Sainte-Barbe, where he was engaged to teach Latin grammar and literature, and subsequently (probably in 1532) he became the private tutor of Gilbert Kennedy, the young Earl of Cassilis, who had gone to Paris to pursue his studies. In teaching Latin to Kennedy, Buchanan made use of Thomas Linacre's *Rudiments* because of its concision and accuracy, and in fact he was sufficiently impressed by the manual to publish a Latin translation of it in 1533 for international use. It seems probable that Buchanan returned to Scotland with Kennedy in the first half of 1534, settling until 1535 on the young Earl's country estate in Ayrshire. However, his pupil was now growing up and no doubt Buchanan's reputation as a pedagogue was becoming established. At any rate, by February 1536, he was employed by James V to teach his illegitimate son, Lord James Stewart. While at Court, Buchanan was involved in a series of controversies with the Franciscans in which the King played a distinctly ambiguous role, apparently encouraging Buchanan to produce increasingly bitter satires against them.[9] On the whole, Buchanan seems to have been on good terms with James, and no doubt his experiences in France were particularly welcome in the Scottish Court after James's marriage to Madeleine de Valois early in 1537. Madeleine arrived in Scotland in May of that year bringing with her an entourage which included, amongst others, the young Ronsard, whom it is quite possible that Buchanan met at this time.

Any favour which Buchanan had with the King could not prevent his arrest in a wave of religious persecutions at the beginning of 1539, since by this time he was in bad odour with the Franciscans, because of the satirical poems he had directed against them, and certain others of rank, both at Court and in the Church. However, it may have been thanks to the King that he escaped from custody so easily, and made his way to England where, after various adventures and mishaps, he arrived in London in February. The political and religious climate in England was not to the Scotsman's liking, and by August of the same year he was in Paris once again.

However, he was shortly to leave the French capital for Bordeaux where many of his former colleagues from Sainte-Barbe were now established in the Collège de Guyenne. The next eight years of his life would be shared between Bordeaux and Paris, but despite his moving away from Aquitaine, his loyalties and affections seem largely to have centred around his friends at the Collège de Guyenne, and indeed, it is now clear that there was no clean break with Bordeaux after his initial period of teaching there which ended in 1543. On his arrival, Buchanan was offered the *primus ordo*, or rhetoric class. The study of rhetoric itself was based on the theoretical works of Quintilian and Cicero, along with some of the latter's speeches; poetry lessons included the reading of such classical poets as Virgil, Lucan, Persius, Juvenal, Horace, and Ovid, and the composition of epigrams on set subjects, for which Despauterius' *Ars versificatoria* served as a textbook; the other main subject was history. Buchanan seems to have been happy in Bordeaux: he was with like-minded friends, appreciated by his pupils (if Montaigne's opinion is anything to go by),[10] and productive in the literary field. The reasons for his leaving may well concern the adverse effects on his health of the Bordeaux climate, and indeed, for the next few years, his health continued to cause him problems. However, he seems to have remained in contact with his friends and colleagues at the Collège de Guyenne.

On reaching Paris towards the end of 1543, the Scottish humanist took up a teaching post at the Collège du Cardinal Lemoine, lodging with the printer Michel Vascosan. It was probably through Vascosan that Buchanan made the acquaintance of other scholars who were either seeing their books through the press with him, or who used his house as a meeting place. These would have included Jacques Peletier du Mans, who in 1547 also lived at Vascosan's house, and who did so much to encourage the efforts of the future members of the Pléiade, and Théodore de Bèze, with whom Buchanan remained on good terms until the end of his life.

The bad health of which Buchanan had complained in Bordeaux continued to dog him in Paris, and in the summer of 1544, he fell seriously ill. It was not until the end of the year that he recovered, when he probably travelled to Toulouse, perhaps in order to convalesce. Some time after this, he made his way to Bordeaux, where he was teaching again in 1545, although he seems to have returned to Paris later on in the year, probably on business connected with the Collège de Guyenne. No doubt, he went back to Bordeaux after this.

It was during these years that Buchanan made the acquaintance of a number of influential figures in French life, who were to stand him in good stead in later years. For example, he appears to have lived with Lazare de Baïf for some time, and this connection would have made him known to many of those poets who were later to form the Pléiade. Lazare de Baïf, as well as being a keen hellenist, was also interested in the translation of Greek tragedy, and in 1544 his French version of the *Hecuba* was published. Lazare's house in the faubourg Saint-Michel was an important centre for humanists and patrons of the arts in Paris, and many of the people whom Buchanan knew in the 1540s were connected with the French diplomat.

For example, it was probably Baïf who introduced Buchanan to the Guise family. In 1544, Jean Dorat went to live with the Baïfs to act as tutor to the young Jean-Antoine, then aged twelve, whose fellow student, also living with the family, was the twenty-year-old Ronsard. Of the other members of the Pléiade, Joachim du Bellay almost certainly came to know Buchanan at this time. Du Bellay met Jacques Peletier in 1546 after studying law in Poitiers, and Peletier, who as well as frequenting the Vascosan *officina* also attended the Baïf *cénacle*, encouraged him in his poetical enterprises. Du Bellay was certainly acquainted with Buchanan's poetry, as his 'Adieu aux Muses', closely based on the Scotsman's first Elegy, was published in 1551, before Buchanan's return from Portugal.[11] Other poets with whom Buchanan was on good terms in the Paris of the 1540s include Mellin de Saint-Gelais, who was to exercise a certain amount of influence on Buchanan's poetry in the 1550s and who was a close friend of Bèze. The Neo-latin poet Salmon Macrin also moved in the same humanist circles in Paris, although he goes unmentioned by Buchanan. Finally, although principally a theologian and not a poet, there is Jean de Gagnay who, like Lazare de Baïf, provided a roof over Buchanan's head in Paris. A protégé of Jean, Cardinal de Lorraine, he published in 1547 seventy-five paraphrases of the Psalms, and could thus have awakened Buchanan's interest in a genre which was to earn him the admiration of both his contemporaries and of future generations.

Despite his increasing reputation, Buchanan chose not to remain in France, but to follow a number of his Bordeaux colleagues to Portugal, where they were to set up the Real Colégio das Artes in Coimbra. Negotiations for the founding of the college had been going on for a number of years between André de Gouveia, the principal of the Collège de Guyenne, and the Portuguese king, before the Bordeaux teachers actually set off in March 1547. Dom João III was extremely keen to improve the standard of education in his country and his efforts centred around the University of Coimbra. He had already embarked upon a reform of the University, but many of the students of the higher courses lacked a solid basic education in the humanities, with which the Colégio de Santa Cruz seemed unable to provide them. Therefore, he decided upon the foundation of the Colégio das Artes, whose aim would be the teaching of Latin, Greek, Hebrew, mathematics, logic, and philosophy. Towards the end of 1542, the King sent for André de Gouveia, but the final arrangements for the college do not appear to have been completed before the end of 1546 when Gouveia, accompanied by one of his teachers, Diogo de Teive, was summoned again to Portugal. By March 1547, the final details were settled and the future staff of the Colégio das Artes was ready to leave Bordeaux. The official opening of the school took place on 21 February 1548, and soon the thousand or so students who enrolled for courses must have kept the Bordeaux teachers extremely busy. As at the Collège de Guyenne, Buchanan was in charge of the *primus ordo*, teaching both Latin and Greek.

On 10 August 1550, his academic peace was to be shattered when he, together with two colleagues, was arrested by the Inquisition, suspected of heterodox views and practices. Held in custody in Lisbon, Buchanan was interviewed a number of times about his religious beliefs and habits, but soon made a written confession of his past errors and, in July 1551, he was sentenced, made an abjuration, and was afterwards sent to the monastery of San Bento in Xabregas 'where he is to busy himself with pious exercises and things necessary for his salvation'.[12] He spent less than six months here, being granted a conditional release in December 1551. Finally, on 29 February 1552, he was freed unconditionally. Despite being condemned by the Inquisition, he still seems to have retained the King's esteem, receiving royal financial assistance until such times as he could find employment. However, a suitable post seems to have been long in coming, and so Buchanan left Lisbon in a Cretan ship bound for England. When he arrived there is not known, but it seems unlikely that he remained for long. The political situation under the infant King Edward VI was far from stable, and in any case, Buchanan had few friends there. However, it is possible that he made his way to Scotland in order to gain dispensation for his earlier crimes against the faith, before returning to France.

The years in Portugal were fertile ones for Buchanan as regards poetry. It is principally to this period that we owe the Psalm paraphrases and, in distinct contrast, the twenty or so erotic poems composed about Leonora and her mother Peiris. Many of this second group of compositions were written in the iambic metre, which also served for a number of vituperative satires against Beleago, a colleague of Buchanan's in Coimbra. Satirical epigrams also flowed from the Scotsman's pen, along with the very fine poem *Silvae* 3, the 'Desiderium Lutetiae', a nostalgic address to Paris in the form of an eclogue.

By November 1552, Buchanan was back in France. After an absence of almost six years, he quickly slipped back into French society, picking up the threads of old acquaintances and forming new ones. In terms of the reputation which he enjoyed and his position in society, Buchanan's final extended sojourn in France was highly successful.

His first post was at the Collège de Boncourt which, under its principal Pierre Galland, was to witness a considerable interest in French tragedy in the early 1550s, thanks to a large extent to the presence there on the teaching staff of Buchanan and Muret. Marc-Antoine Muret, whose Latin tragedy *Iulius Caesar* had been performed at the Collège de Guyenne, started teaching at Boncourt in 1551. He was soon to come into contact with a number of members of the Pléiade, and his lectures on Catullus had a considerable impact on them.[13] The liminary verses for his *Iuvenilia* (Paris, 1552) attest his links with Dorat, Jean-Antoine de Baïf, Jodelle, as well as Buchanan, who must have composed his own offering shortly after returning to France. It can be no coincidence that the Collège de Boncourt counted amongst its students at this time future dramatists such as Belleau, La Péruse, Jodelle, Jean de la Taille, and Grévin. Jodelle staged his *Cléopâtre captive*, France's first regular vernacular tragedy, in the courtyard of the Collège de Boncourt in 1553.

As usual, it was not long before Buchanan attracted private patronage and, probably in 1554, he became attached to the household of the comte de Brissac, Marshal of France, as private tutor to his son Timoléon. Buchanan would have been mostly based in Paris during his period as tutor until 1560, since Timoléon spent much of his time at Court, being made in 1556 a page of the duc d'Orléans, the future Charles IX. However, his father often arranged for his family to visit him in Piedmont, where he was governor, he himself only having leisure to visit the French court for a time in 1556 and 1558. Buchanan evidently enjoyed his life at Court, and seemed fully intent on remaining in France, since in August 1557, 'lettres de naturalité' were granted to him, and in May of the following year, he received the living of Mulleville-sur-Mer, thanks to the good offices of Brissac who was patron of the Bishop of Coutances.

Throughout the 1550s, Buchanan was closely associated with a number of humanist *cénacles* in Paris. The home of Jean Brinon, for example, provided the scenario for meetings of poets and humanists associated with the Pléiade from 1550 until Brinon's death in 1554. It is to him that Muret addressed the preface of his *Iuvenilia*, and he is also mentioned a number of times in the poetry of Ronsard and du Bellay. He was connected with Buchanan's former patron the Cardinal de Lorraine, to whom he gave away much of his land in 1553. A circle composed of similar members also formed around Henri de Mesmes, who was later to expend considerable energy on the collection and printing of Buchanan's verse. De Mesmes, whose friends overlapped to some extent with those of Michel de l'Hôpital, probably attracted to his *bibliothèque* amongst others Turnèbe, Pierre de Montdoré, Thomas Sebillet, Dorat, António de Gouveia, and Denis Lambin, and it is possible that it was through this circle that Montaigne became re-acquainted with Buchanan.[14] But for the Scottish humanist, perhaps it was the house of Jean de Morel near the church of Saint-André-des-Arcs which proved to be the most congenial intellectual centre. The Morel family was closely connected with many members of the Pléiade, and especially du Bellay who addressed a number of his *Regrets* to Jean de Morel; but the house in the rue Pavée was concerned with humanism and education as much as with poetry. It was frequented by Salmon Macrin, Nicolas Bourbon, Jean Dorat, and Michel de l'Hôpital who, by his careful machinations, seems to have advanced the career of more than one habitué of the Morel *cénacle*, and who himself was a protégé and chancellor of the king's sister, Marguerite de France, to whom Buchanan dedicated his *Alcestis*. Buchanan's connections with the Morel circle lasted for the whole of his time in Paris in the 1550s, and it was there, in 1558, that he must have met Charles Utenhovius, the new tutor of the precocious ten-year-old Camille de Morel. Utenhovius was to teach the Morel children Latin, Greek, and Hebrew for about four years, before being dismissed from their service. He then crossed the Channel to England, where he was a protégé in the early 1560s of William Cecil, and around 1568, he produced an edition of the poetry of Buchanan and several other poets who had been connected with the Morel circle, including, apart from himself, du Bellay, Turnèbe, Michel de l'Hôpital, and Dorat.[15]

Buchanan's decision to return to Scotland may appear to be somewhat surprising, considering the extent to which he was settled in France. Two main reasons may be adduced: the deteriorating political and religious climate in France, and the Scotsman's connections at Court with Mary Stuart. The 'Epithalamium' composed for her marriage with the dauphin François (*Silvae* 4), in which the Scottish nationalist in Buchanan, even after twenty years of exile, cannot be stifled, and *Silvae* 5 on François's death both attest Buchanan's links with Mary. Moreover, his connections with the Guise family and, on a very different level, with Ronsard would bring him closer to the young queen. And so, when she was compelled to return to the Scotland which she had hardly ever known, what could have been more natural than that she should be accompanied by a Scottish scholar, acquainted with the Scots people as she could never be, yet at the same time imbued with the manners and wit of the French Court? And what could have been more natural than that Buchanan, after years of absence from his homeland, seeing his period of service with the Brissacs drawing to a close, growing increasingly interested in the education of the influential, and committed against tyranny, should accept an offer to return with Mary? Certainly, by the end of 1561 he was back in Scotland and in Mary's service.

In many ways, Buchanan's career until 1561 was a preparation for the last twenty years of his life, when he started to take an active part in the government of the country from which he had so long been an exile, and when the publication of his works ensured his international fame. On returning to Scotland, he embraced the Protestant faith, and from 1563 to 1566 he was a member of the General Assembly of the Reformed Church.

To begin with, his duties at the Scottish Court do not seem to have been particularly arduous: he acted at first as a kind of tutor to Mary, perhaps not always telling her what she wanted to hear. One passage of Livy which they studied together (mentioned in a letter from Randolph to Cecil dated 7 April 1562) contains an attack on extravagance of dress in women along with a condemnation of their wielding any political power (Livy 34, 1 sqq.). In 1563, Buchanan was to be engaged as official translator of Spanish documents for the Court, but later on, his appointment as principal of St Leonard's College in St Andrews (1566–1570) would have kept him away from Court life to a certain extent. This did not prevent him from visiting France in the winter of 1565–1566, partly on government business, and partly to see an edition of his poems through the press.

It was not until after the death of Darnley that Buchanan's influence really seems to have spread, as official propagandist of the anti-Mary faction and an important member of the ruling party. Thus, he was involved in the examination of a number of prisoners who were concerned with the murder of Darnley at the Kirk of Fields (and who were not always treated in the gentlest of fashions). In 1570, he was appointed guardian of the privy seal, a post which he held until 1578, although he continued to be a member of the Privy Council until his death. 1570 also saw his appointment as tutor to the four-year-old James VI, a position which would keep him in Stirling Castle for much of the remainder of his life.

A concern for politics in the broadest sense seems to have marked these years. As tutor to James, he would have seen himself in a unique position to influence future events by his moulding of the young King (although classical precedents for the success of such a venture did not augur well), a crucial role as James had to be weaned away from his mother and won over definitively to the Protestant faith. It was no doubt with this project partly in mind that Buchanan became a strong supporter of a close alliance with England rather than France, and his connections with notable Englishmen during the final decade of his life, expecially the group associated with Sir Philip Sidney, underline these new preoccupations.[16] At the same time, he was in close contact with scholars and Protestant churchmen all over Europe, who were following the progress of his education of the Scottish king with interest.

As perhaps the most distinguished scholar in Scotland at this time, his services were also of use in the realm of education, and as early as c.1563, he produced proposals for the government for the re-organisation of the teaching of the humanities at St Andrews University. He would again be asked to investigate the conduct of affairs at St Andrews in 1579. Another project with which he became involved at the beginning of 1576 was the production of a Latin grammar to be used throughout Scotland, and it is in connection with this that his own *De prosodia libellus* was written.[17]

But Buchanan's literary achievements contained more ambitious projects than this. Although he continued to write verse, largely of an occasional nature, it was to more serious matters that he directed his attention, notably his *Rerum scoticarum historia*, a comprehensive history of Scotland dedicated to, and for the instruction of, James VI. Similarly, the *De iure regni apud Scotos*, a dialogue on the rights and duties of the prince, was intended for the young king's edification. One other ambitious project begun in France, the *De sphaera*, was never completed by Buchanan, however.

One important aspect of Buchanan's personality which is apparent more in his poetry than in his more serious prose writings is his capacity for friendship, and it was from his friends, colleagues, and patrons that he derived much of the inspiration for both his verse compositions, and more generally for the evolution of his thought. Elie Vinet, a lifelong friend, had developed an interest in cosmology some time before the inception of the *De sphaera*; Nicolas de Grouchy's views on the position of the ruler in society seem likely to have helped to shape Buchanan's own opinions on the subject; while on a less elevated plane, Buchanan's friends and colleagues provided him with the material for countless epigrams. Buchanan could not live in a social vacuum. For renewed inspiration, he relied heavily on the stimulus derived from those around him, but having received that stimulus, he was capable of progressing far more rapidly than they, so that he frequently outstripped his original inspirers.

This ability to continue learning and to respond to new ideas seems to have been coupled with fundamental attitudes which were strongly rooted in the opening decades of the sixteenth century. Buchanan retained throughout his life the open-mindedness which those early years of humanism had heralded, so that he was able to adapt when necessary to new situations. As far as poetry is concerned, this quality was a particular advantage since, throughout his poetic career, he continued to develop, constantly moving on into new genres and new styles.

CHAPTER 2

Neo-latin Poetry:
the Theoretical Background

Before taking a closer look at Buchanan's poetry, it will be useful to consider the standards which governed the composition of Neo-latin verse. And it should perhaps be emphasised at this point that, although Renaissance humanists attempted to elucidate the principles of classical Latin poetry, they in fact arrived at a set of criteria which differed in certain essentials from those of their models. This in itself is not surprising. Even today, classicists do not fully understand every aspect of Latin prosody and metre. What is surprising is that scholars should continue to evaluate Neo-latin poetry according to classical rules rather than according to its own, verifiable standards. It is as if one were to judge a Palladian villa according to the criteria of a classical temple; for Palladio, no less than the Renaissance poet, based his works on classical precedent and theory. This chapter, then, will attempt to establish the areas where basic differences between classical and Renaissance practice are found.

Any author who wrote in Latin during the Renaissance was faced with a number of problems arising from the nature of his chosen vehicle of expression; and for the poet in particular, these problems were even greater. Neo-latin was in a peculiar twilight zone, midway between a dead language, in that it had not enjoyed an uninterrupted development as a single recognisable entity since the days of the Roman Empire, and a living one, since for many people in Renaissance Europe it was the normal language for everyday communication. From this duality springs the first main problem. A language is normally a dynamic phenomenon, constantly undergoing small, perhaps imperceptible changes in semantic, syntactic, and phonetic processes. It is in its ability to extend and adapt that much of its potential strength lies, and to deprive it of this is to limit severely its powers of expression. At the same time, significant linguistic development normally channels itself in a particular direction, otherwise the result would be confusion, a state which language seeks to avoid. The Neo-latin author was therefore forced to choose between the anarchy of a hybrid Latin based upon no particular writer or period but developed along his own lines, and the possible sterility of writing in the style of a Cicero or a Virgil. From this dilemma arose the protracted debate on Ciceronianism.[1] In prose writing, of course, the problem is not too acute. The wide range of genres practised by Cicero—forensic, philosophical, philological, epistolary writing, etc.—covered most of the needs of the Renaissance humanist. On the other hand, Virgil was far from fulfilling all the poet's needs.

Following the linguistic practices of one particular author does have a certain logic and in some measure ensures unity of style, but it produces a circumscribed language and omits an essential element of good writing, linguistic creativity and flexibility. When this language is applied to situations dramatically different from anything envisaged by its creator, it can only cope by becoming excessively long-winded and periphrastic, or simply obscure. This is particularly the case in matters of vocabulary. Moreover, from the literary point of view, as most critics pointed out, the purist is unlikely to outdo his model. The opposing point of view also entails difficulties. Most sixteenth-century theoretical writers recommend the reading of basically classical Roman authors. For example, Despauterius in the preface to his *Ars versificatoria* writes: 'For we should not trust all writers indiscriminately, but only those who flourished in the period of about 250 years from the birth of Cicero to Antoninus Pius.'[2] However, this period covers important changes in matters of syntax and vocabulary so that mixtures of archaic and novel usages might easily result, objectionable to the purist.

These problems are particularly acute in verse where not only syntactic and semantic, but also phonetic changes come into play. In classical times, the quantity-based metre was reflected not only in vowel length but also in the quality of any given vowel. So, in the infinitive *cēdĕrĕ*, the first *e* would probably have been pronounced like the modern French *é*, while the two short *es* would have the value of French *è*. In the sixteenth century, although national differences in pronunciation existed, these quantitative and phonetic distinctions were almost universally ignored; moreover, the diphthongs *ae*, *oe*, and *ei* were all pronounced like a simple *e*.[3] This meant that Neo-latin poetry was, at least in the early part of the century, only quantitative in theory, and that the poets were applying rules of prosody which no longer had any practical significance but which would have been second nature to a Roman schoolboy. Further complications existed. In the course of time, even in the classical period of Roman poetry, pronunciation changed. For example, the final *o* of the first person singular of verbs which had been long in all except one or two cases (e.g. *scio, puto, volo*), at the time of Ovid began to be shortened in a number of verbs. This gave rise to the Renaissance idea that final *o* was common which, reflecting a synchronic approach to classical Latin, tries to view it as an unchanging entity, ultimately reducible to definite rules. A further difficulty sprang from the inaccuracy of early printed texts which could also lead versifiers into making errors of quantity, especially as such faith was placed in the authority of classical writers in matters of prosody. Until the second half of the century and the appearance of the work of men such as Muret, Lambin, and J. J. Scaliger, very few critical texts existed.

Humanist writers of prosody were not unaware of all these problems, although quite often they viewed them back to front. Micyllus, for example, remarks in the preface to his *De re metrica* that poetry can help with correct pronunciation. However, where poets treated a syllable in the same word differently, it was considered common, no account being taken of changes in pronunciation, as is demonstrated by Rodolphus Gualtherus, *De syllabarum et carminum ratione*, fo. 8^v: 'But those syllables are common which by their nature are such that they may be shortened or lengthened at different times; or which are treated in this way on the authority of the Poets.' This attitude is for the most part followed by other theorists, but it was not unknown for French poets to justify their treatment of a syllable by an appeal to Italian Neo-latinists like Petrarch or Mantuan.

The Herculean task attempted by the Renaissance theorists of reducing the practice of the Roman poets to a comprehensible and comprehensive set of rules was at least partly facilitated by the survival of the works of several late Roman grammarians. They provided useful foundations for the Neo-latinists to build on, along with a basic working vocabulary, although they did not deal with a number of issues, especially in the realms of prosody, which were vital to later generations.[4]

Amongst the first writers on metrics published in the fifteenth century were Priscian and Rufinus, who were both printed in Venice in 1470. Priscian, the sixth-century author responsible for the encyclopedic *Institutiones grammaticae*, also produced a short treatise entitled *De metris fabularum Terentii*, while Rufinus, a grammarian of the fifth century, wrote a *Commentarium in metra Terentiana*. Both works deal exclusively with the iambic and trochaic metres of Roman comedy with some reference to tragic writers, and would not therefore have been directly relevant to the needs of the majority of Neo-latin versifiers. More important than their actual teaching, perhaps, is their *modus operandi*, which was to be followed to a large extent by Renaissance theorists. Both writers include numerous quotations from previous grammarians—Charisius, Caesius Bassus, Terentianus Maurus, Asmodius etc.—and having established a particular point, they provide copious illustrations taken from the writings of classical authors. This method tends inevitably to lead to a consensus view of the subject and to ignore historical matters: what was sauce for Ennius may not necessarily be sauce for Seneca. Nevertheless, they both indicate the most correct usage while explaining any deviations from it. A device used by Rufinus, but not by Priscian, which was taken over by a number of

Renaissance manuals is the use of mnemonic verses to sum up a rule, followed by examples drawn from ancient writers.

Thus, the method they established was to elaborate the usage of previous writers, both Greek and Latin, to provide a comprehensive catalogue of deviations from normal practice, with corroborative *exempla,*and to fix the rules in an easily memorisable form.

Of more direct relevance to the early Neo-latin versifiers was the *Centimetrum* of Virgil's famous commentator, Servius. Appearing in print for the first time in Venice in 1475, this work, as its name suggests, contains a description of a wide range of metres, classifying them as iambic, trochaic, dactylic etc. It enjoyed considerable success, being included in book V of the highly influential *Ars versificatoria* of Despauterius, and no doubt proving useful to early theorists such as Niccolò Perotti. Before tackling the various metres, Servius has a brief introduction in which he defines and explains basic terms and principles such as resolution, the caesura, the naming of metres. In doing so, he helped to establish the technical vocabulary in matters of prosody and metre (largely Greek), and to set out a method for dealing with the various metres. After his intro-duction, he proceeds to describe in turn the various metres, along with a miscellaneous chapter 'de diversis metrorum generibus'. He points to differences between normal usage and the usage of the comic poets in iambic and anapaestic metres, an important distinction since it is a step towards the understanding of metrical *decorum*. Each kind of line is named and described, and is followed by one example, but what Servius fails to do is to give any of the usual combinations of these lines to form metres like the elegiac couplet or the lyric metres.

Diomedes, the next theorist to be published, was much fuller in his treat-ment of the subject. This grammarian of the latter half of the fourth century had produced a lengthy Latin grammar, unremarkable for its originality but useful in preserving the thoughts of earlier writers on the subject. The *Liber tertius* deals exclusively with matters concerning poetry and metre, relying heavily, according to Sandys, on Suetonius' lost work *De poetis.*[5] The *editio princeps* appeared in Venice around 1476. Like Servius, Diomedes begins with some basic definitions, but his greater interest in theory soon becomes apparent. He has a descriptive, structuralist approach to his subject, is extremely comprehensive in his definitions, many of which are taken over from earlier theorists, and shows an interest in etymology which often leads him into the realms of mythology. Chapter 5 deals with the various feet at some length (up to combinations of five syllables). Many of his definitions would be taken over *verbatim* by the Renaissance, and indeed, much of the opening nine chapters would find its way into J. C. Scaliger's *Poetices libri septem* of 1561. Chapter 10 deals with a practical problem of obvious benefit to Neo-latin writers, the quantity of the different case endings of nouns and adjectives. The remaining twenty-eight chapters are concerned with the various metres, first the dactylic hexameter at considerable length, then the remaining metres more succinctly. Although Diomedes includes many useful details on caesura, elision, the effect of various foot combinations, and other points, he frequently falls prey to a mania for sterile classification, a legacy which the Renaissance in less discriminating moods took over. The last five chapters of the work deal with all the metres employed by Horace in his *Odes* and *Epodes*, a notable advance on Servius' method.

Of the other Roman writers on verse printed in the Renaissance, Caesius Bassus had nothing new in his *Ars de metris* (Milan, 1504), while Atilius Fortunatianus covered much the same ground as Diomedes, with the addition of some definitions in the second part of his *Ars de metris* concerning vowels, consonants, and syllables and their quantity. However, none of these works deals more than briefly with the question of quantity. For this, the poet or grammarian would have to consult Servius' *De ratione ultimarum syllabarum*, *Probus' Artium instituta ad Caelestinum*, or Terentianus' *De literis, syllabis et metris Horati liber*.[6] These books provide useful rules for the final syllables of various declension and verb endings, although they seldom go beyond this.

Such were the classical works at the disposal of the Renaissance theorists. One other pre-Renaissance book on Latin verse must also be mentioned: the 'pars tertia' of Alexander Villa-Dei's *Doctrinale*.[7] Written in mnemonic verse and probably dating from the twelfth century, this work sets out to describe in simplified form the rules of Latin versification, concentrating almost exclusively on quantity. Alexander is not interested in exceptions, just in the general rules. It is sufficient, he writes in lines 1560 sqq., to know six feet (dactyl, spondee, trochee, anapaest, iambus, and tribrach); by line 1584 he has dealt with the hexameter (which always has a dactyl in the fifth foot and never in the sixth), and the pentameter. He forbids the elision of *m* before another vowel (line 1603), and then goes on to deal with syllable quantity, covering in fact a number of rules which find their way into the humanist handbooks. For example, he discusses prepositional prefixes (lines 1616–20), derived words (which in most cases have quantities identical to the root words), reduplicating perfects (lines 1637–45), dissyllabic supines and nine exceptions to the rule, before approaching verb endings in lines 1663 sqq.:

> a crescens verbum producere debet ubique,
> ex *do* fit *a* brevis cum primae compositivis.
> *e*, nisi cum subit *r*, debes producere semper;
> cum subit *r* curtam dant plurima, plurima longam.[8]

He then treats the medial syllables of words, covering briefly all the possible vowel and consonant combinations, and finally end-syllables. Alexander was rather despised by the early humanists for his oversimplification, his refusal to confront anomalies, and his omission of any appeal to classical precedents. In spite of this, he was very popular in France, certainly until the 1520s and even later, judging by the numerous editions which were produced; and it seems that his absence from the curriculum in some schools in the 1530s occasioned complaint on the part of the students, as is suggested in Buchanan's first *Elegy*, lines 69–70:

> Et queritur nullis onerari compita chartis,
> Esse et Alexandrum nullo in honore suum.

Buchanan himself probably made his first acquaintance with Neo-latin verse through Alexander, for his *Doctrinale* as edited by John Vaus continued to form the basis of Latin instruction for much of the sixteenth century in Scotland. Alexander certainly simplifies things, but perhaps he does not deserve all the strictures he received. Many of the rules which he gives on quantity are taken over by the humanists, admittedly in expanded form, and his discussion of syllable length according to vowel/consonant combinations in the middle of words finds its way into most sixteenth-century verse manuals. But his attitude was medieval, and this fact could not be forgiven by the early humanists.

It is not until the second half of the fifteenth century that any emphasis was placed on verse composition in France. However, a number of reforms of the University of Paris, especially those of cardinal d'Estouteville in 1452, began to attach some importance to the teaching of the rules of Latin versification, and when their effects eventually made themselves felt, it was realised that the old manuals were no longer sufficient for the needs of the day. Robert Gaguin, the pupil, friend, and successor of Guillaume Fichet as professor of canon law in the University of Paris, was one of the first to fill the gap. His *Ars versificatoria* was probably written in the 1470s and ran to more than fifteen editions, now quite rare.[9] The influence of both the Roman grammarians and of Alexander Villa-Dei is apparent in this book, and it contains in embryo many of the elements which were to be included in later works. Book I begins with definitions and etymological discussions of terms like *carmen, metrum,* and the division of the alphabet into vowels, semi-vowels, and consonants. Gaguin emphasises the importance of knowing the quantity of syllables, and then sets out certain rules which help in this. One important difference from the *Doctrinale* emerges: Gaguin is happy to give exceptions, and to stress the general but not absolute nature of his observations, although they are as yet somewhat disordered. Like Alexander, he deals with the quantity of various combinations of vowels and consonants in initial as well as middle and final syllables, again including a number of exceptions, and he illustrates his precepts with quotations from classical poets. Book II concerns the different kinds of feet (up to four syllable combinations), their names and derivations. Gaguin writes about poetic licence with relation to syllable length, referring mainly to Virgil, about the use in poetry of rhetorical figures and tropes like metonymy and synecdoche, and about elision of vowels and of *m* before other vowels (synaloepha and ecthlipsis). Book III, on metre, opens with the distinction between three kinds of verse: *dramaticon, exegeticon,* and *commune* (cf. Diomedes, ed. cit., p. 440). He speaks of the general principles of naming metres, deals with the caesura, and briefly describes the more important metres.

The work is far from ideal. Its format is not very clear, it deals with the different aspects of versification rather haphazardly, and the material under discussion is often too compressed to result in perfect clarity. Its claims to a 'classical' approach to the subject seem to reside in its superficial resemblances to the Roman grammarians, typified by the delight in definitions, categorisation, and often somewhat dubious historical explanations. However, it goes some of the way to meeting the needs of the Renaissance by combining a relatively detailed exposition of the laws of prosody (as Alexander had attempted to do) with many of the theoretical elements to be found in the Roman manuals, thus helping to establish a working vocabulary in the field of versification. In addition, Gaguin provides the reader with a wealth of illustrative quotations taken from classical poets, especially Virgil and Statius. In this way, he prepares the path for the next important verse manual, probably the most influential in sixteenth-century France.[10]

Despauterius' *Ars versificatoria* first appeared in 1511 or 1512 with an introduction (omitted in some later editions) by Josse Bade, who sets out in brief many of the rules which Despauterius himself will discuss. As a student in the early 1520s in Paris, Buchanan would almost certainly have been taught from this work, whose use was to continue far into the next century, when it was still being employed by the French Jesuits. The book is intended for both teachers and students, and this is reflected in its format. The work is divided into five books, of which the first two are particularly useful for school use, while the last three go into much greater detail about points which could only interest the serious connoisseur.

Josse Bade's introduction is a miniature handbook in itself. He sets out the general rules for syllable quantity, produces rules for the length of final vowels in sufficient detail for most students' needs, as well as giving in simplified form the rules for quantity in initial and middle syllables. In many ways, this is as useful as Despauterius' much longer treatment of this subject. Bade also describes some of the more important metres (hexameter, pentameter, sapphic pentameter, and asclepiad).

Despauterius' general preface is an interesting treatment of the history of Latin poetry and the dangers to be avoided by the Neo-latin writer. As has already been said, Despauterius limits the poets to be read and imitated to the period from 100 BC to AD 150, although (according to him at any rate) this includes writers as diverse as Lucretius and Ausonius, Catullus and Claudian (see fo. I'). He claims that the Goths were responsible for the destruction of Roman culture, the Church was opposed to poetry, and a barbaric state of affairs reigned until about 1340 and the advent of Petrarch. 'Post hunc coepit lingua latina mirum in modum instaurari' (fo. II'). However, he warns that there are still corrupt texts in circulation which lead people astray. Other dangers lurk in the indiscriminate mixing of Greek and Latin poetry, which even Horace had warned against.

Book I, after expressing the wish that Alexander Villa-Dei should be swept away, begins with some definitions of *carmen, versus, metrum* (fo. V') followed by a description and names of the twelve simple metrical feet, and some compound feet. After speaking of the tempus of a short or long syllable, and resolution, he moves swiftly on to the hexameter (fo. VI'). He provides the basic rules (i.e. that dactyls or spondees may be used at will in all but the fifth and sixth feet) and goes on to give exceptions (mainly from Virgil) to these rules, speaks of synaeresis, the caesura, and finally the number of syllables which the last word of a hexameter should contain (two or three are both acceptable, four or five are not generally permissible, nor is a monosyllable unless it is the name of an animal [sic], an enclitic, or coupled with another monosyllable). The pentameter is next described and scanned (fo. IX'). This should end, writes Despauterius, in a dissyllable, occasionally in words of four, five, or even six syllables, but never in three or one (again unless the monosyllable is an enclitic or is joined to another monosyllable). The elegiac couplet, he writes, should normally be a self-contained unit and, concerning adjectives, 'the elegiac poem delights in pairs of epithets, adjectives which are not inflated, or pompous, or recherché', illustrated by a couplet from Propertius:

> Sic me nec solae poterunt avertere sylvae
> Nec vaga muscosis flumina fusa iugis. (fo. IX')

Despauterius then describes the asclepiadic metre and the sapphic and phalaecian hendecasyllable before coming on to ecthlipsis (which he calls 'ellipsis'), and synaloepha, where he incidentally disagrees with the *Doctrinale*, saying that elision is perfectly permissible (fo. XII') and adding 'euphony in writing is sometimes more important than analogy or teachers' rules'. Finally, he deals with synaeresis and diaeresis.

Book II is concerned with syllable quantity and contains twelve general rules with numerous exceptions and subdivisions for discovering syllable length. Since these rules would find their way into practically all the verse manuals printed after Despauterius, it will be useful to summarise them here. They are:

(a)   a syllable containing a short vowel but followed by two consonants or a double consonant (*x, z,* or consonantal *i*) is long by position   (fo. XVI^r)

(b)   when a short vowel is followed by a mute (*b, c, d, f, g, p, t*) and a liquid (*l, r* and in Greek words *m* and *n*) the syllable is anceps   (fo. XVII^r)

(c)   diphthongs are long, but may be short if in hiatus   (fo. XVIII^r)

(d)   a vowel before another vowel is short in Latin words, with five exceptions:
  (i)   *fio* has a long *i* unless the verb contains an *r*
  (ii) genitives and datives of fifth declension nouns are long when preceded by *i* (*speciēi*, but *spĕi*)
  (iii) *-ius* genitives of pronouns are anceps except *alterius* (always short) and *alius* (long by contraction)
  (iv) *ohe* is anceps
  (v)   vocatives of words like *Caius, Pompeius* are long (*Cāi*)
  Greek words are then treated in some twenty pages   (fo. XIX^r)

(e)   a syllable has the same quantity in a derived word as it does in the root. At this point, the author stresses the importance of etymology.

(f)   in compound words, even if a vowel or diphthong changes, the quantity remains the same, e.g. *lūdo, collūdo; laēdo, illīdo; tăceo, retĭceo*   (fo. XXXII^v)
There are exceptions to this, like the *-dĭcus* ending from *dīco*. Under this heading, Despauterius also includes prepositional prefixes, giving particular attention to the prefix *pro*.

(g)   dissyllabic preterites have their first syllable long except for *bibit, scidit, fĭdit, tulit, dedit, stetit*   (fo. XXXVI^r)

(h)   the first two syllables of a reduplicating perfect are short (except that the second syllable may be long by rule (*e*), e.g. *cecīdit < caēdo*)

(i)   the first syllable of a dissyllabic supine is long with the exception of *satum, citum, statum, situm, datum, rutum, quitum, itum, ratum*

(j)   the syllable preceding a supine in *-tum* is long, e.g. *amātum, petītum*

(k)   in verb endings, *a* is long (*amāmus*)
                          e is long except before *r* (but N.B. *-rēris, -rēre* as 2nd person singular verb endings)
                          i is long in 4th conjugation verbs except in perfect tenses
                          o is long
                          u is short

(l)   this section concerns syllable length in imparisyllabic third declension nouns

Book III, the longest in the work and comprising some two hundred pages, gives the special rules for the quantity of all possible vowel/ consonant combinations in initial, middle, and final syllables of a word. Despauterius deals with this systematically and exhaustively, setting out the numerous exceptions to each empirical rule in alphabetical order, and listing them in the margin. He is fully aware of the problems which poets experience with regard to prosody and admits that 'the matter is so difficult that more time must be spent on searching for quantities than on writing poetry' (fo. XLIIᵛ), a statement which indicates the corrupt pronunciation of Latin in the early stages of the sixteenth century, even amongst quite accomplished teachers. As it stands, the principal use of book III must be as a reference book, a dictionary of Latin prosody. Book IV, on stress accents and punctuation, begins by emphasising the importance of correct Latin pronunciation (fo. CXLIIʳ). He may be derided for this, he says, 'but if we all fight shy of it, there is no hope for the restoration (*instauratio*) of the Latin language, which I so passionately long for'. Finally, book V deals with the various types of metre, reproducing Servius' *Centimetrum* and adding further observations to this.

The advent of Despauterius' *Ars versificatoria* is a significant event in the history of versification in sixteenth-century France, for it was not only influential in its own right, but affected the format and contents of many subsequent *artes*. It is difficult to ascertain how quickly it found its way into the school curriculum, but judging by the number of early editions (it was printed in Paris alone in *c*.1512, 1515, 1517, 1520, 1526 and 1529) its use probably spread rapidly. It was certainly one of the prescribed texts for Buchanan's classes at the Collège de Guyenne, and would have been used at the Colégio das Artes in Coimbra. It was a work belonging to the early part of the rebirth of French interest in the humanities (we have seen Despauterius speak of the hoped-for 'instauratio' of the Latin language) and it acted as the principal midwife for Neo-latin poetry. However, its influence on people's conception of Latin poetry must have taken some turns which may have surprised the author. For example, a very large proportion of the work is taken up not so much with rules as exceptions to rules, along with copious corroborative *exempla* taken from a wide range of Latin poets, both classical and modern, *exempla* which would be repeated time and again in later manuals, and easily assimilated. The rule might be dealt with in a couple of lines, the exceptions occupied far more space, receiving more apparent emphasis than, statistically speaking, they deserved. Also, Despauterius does not adopt a diachronic approach to Latin poetry. If, for example, he sees that a final *o* in Catullus is long, but short in Ovid or Statius, he concludes that *o* is common. Even the important appeal to classical usage as exemplified in the poetry of Rome entails certain dangers. Uncommon usages gained currency providing that they could be supported by at least one quotation from a reputable poet, notwithstanding the corrupt state of many classical texts circulating at this time. The results of these attitudes are obvious. The student writing Neo-latin verse would develop a distinct awareness of the apparent flexibility in the rules of prosody and versification, and a false quantity by all generally accepted criteria might be justified by an appeal to the exceptional usage of one or other of the Roman, or even Italian, poets. Thus, the rules of Neo-latin versification are really distinct from those of classical Latin, being a composite of 250 years of Roman verse experience. Moreover, Despauterius provided a canon by which modern Latin verse could be judged, and any cases not covered by him could be deduced analogically, a process likely to lead to still further breaches of normal classical usage. In conclusion, it is not an exaggeration to say that in attempting to establish classical Latin practice in versification, Despauterius in fact helped to formulate the rules for Neo-latin poetry by which the writings of the sixteenth-century humanists and poets must be evaluated. Often they are quite different in spirit from classical norms.

Despauterius' was exhaustive, accurate for the most part, but frequently tedious. The way lay open for shorter works on Latin versification, and the Swiss Henricus Glareanus was one of the first people to try to supply this need. His *De ratione syllabarum brevis isagoge* first appeared in Bâle in 1516, where another edition was printed in 1527. He treats his subject succinctly, but goes to the opposite extreme of Despauterius, preferring to pass over difficulties and anomalies. It is a work best suited to the beginner, being quite well set out, but it would have had to be supplemented at a later stage of a student's development. The same could be said for a number of other works written at this time. The next verse manual to be printed which enjoyed any popularity in France was by Ulrich von Hutten whose *Rudimenta poetices*, written in hexameters, was first produced in 1523, although it appears from the full title that it had been written a number of years previously.[11] Then, in 1530, comes Murmellius, who approaches his subject by means of tables and explanatory notes. The number of editions to which this manual ran bears witness to its usefulness and its sensible approach to the subject.[12] Murmellius covers the basic rules of prosody in detail, including exceptions, but he is careful to warn his readers that certain licences should not be copied, as, for example, the use of a spondee in the fifth foot of a dactylic hexameter. He does not waste time giving the vowel/consonant combinations in initial and middle syllables, pointing out that there is no need for this if Latin is correctly pronounced and learnt from competent teachers: 'Therefore, take care that, being well taught under the best teachers in a grammar school, you grow accustomed to the pure speech of Rome, and that you do not defile your tender little tongue with solecisms, insanely struggling under barbaric schoolmasters.' Further on, he names and describes nine feet together with the dactylic hexameter and pentameter, and breaks them down into their components for students to practise. He includes rules regarding the number of syllables that the final words of these metres should contain. Although this manual was written by 1530, less than twenty years after Despauterius' *Ars versifica-toria*, it reflects considerable changes in attitude to Neo-latin verse and in the teaching available. Despauterius was concerned to aid the 'instauratio' of Latin, but by 1530 this was well on the way to being accomplished. Certain principles are no longer questioned, like the idea of imitation, which now includes the best Italian Neo-latin poets as possible models. Murmellius writes: 'I am of the opinion that you should imitate poets who are neither too ancient, nor born after the Muses were expelled from Italy, apart from those who, being endowed with divine genius and ennobled by outstanding learning, seem to come closest to the Ancients, and the most excellent of them at that.' Thus, Virgil, Ovid, Horace, and Catullus are joined by poets such as Poliziano, Mantuan, Pico della Mirandola, Pontano, Filelfo, and Petrarch as worthy models to follow. There are also warnings against certain faults which were becoming apparent in Neo-latin verse and which sprang from an excessively stereotyped approach to the subject. Bad Latin, confused word order, obscurity should all be avoided; he quotes Bigus Pictorius' advice to shun words which are superfluous but which conveniently supply gaps in hexameters and pentameters:

> Dic mihi, cur ponis toties in carmine *nunc, sed,*
> *Ipse, puer, frater, quippe, profecto, rogo?*
> Scilicet ut magnum possis absolvere versum?
> O vir praecipua calliditate vafer.

Stupid imitation should be eschewed, but invoking Quintilian he says 'the best poets should regularly and constantly be read and imitated'. Murmellius always emphasises the importance of a correct education conducted by competent and enlightened teachers. 'Also, they are no less stupid who entrust their children to pathetic little private tutors. These people teach the same thing to twenty or thirty boys of differing intellect and very unequal rates of progress, taking no notice of anything just as they ignore the parents' complaints.' This implies, however, that good progressive schools were available by now and that educational techniques were indeed changing. Another important advance is the development of a critical attitude to the Roman grammarians, who are no longer accepted as unerring oracles of the truth. In conclusion, this is an extremely useful school book which summarises in a graphic form with mnemonic verses and copious examples the principal rules and exceptions of Latin versification, including warnings where necessary regarding the best usage, but generally avoids burdening the student with a plethora of only marginally useful information. Many other works were written in the first half of the century, but after Murmellius they did not have much new to offer.[13]

If there was no lack of manuals on the art of versification in this period, the same cannot be said for works devoted to poetics, although references to the subject are to be found scattered throughout the *artes versificatoriae*, as well as in the introductions to editions of classical authors. One principle which was established early on, however, was the idea of imitation. It is well-known that for the sixteenth century, *imitatio* had two distinct meanings: Aristotle's *mimesis* or imitation of Nature, which is the function of all art; and literary imitation of a model or models. The first of these concepts was important for the status of poetry in the Renaissance. Against Plato's thesis that poetry, being an imitation of the physical world which is itself an imitation of the true world of ideas, is three steps removed from Truth[14] could now be set in opposition Aristotle's views on *mimesis* and its educational properties.[15] However, it is the second of these phenomena, literary imitation, which was to have more tangible effects on poetic style. Classical Roman poetry owed a considerable debt to Greek models, a fact which was being realised more and more in the Renaissance as knowledge of Greek literature increased. Horace had advised the use of traditional themes in poetry, treated in an individual manner so as to become an original work of art:

> difficile est proprie communia dicere; tuque
> rectius Iliacum carmen deducis in actus,
> quam si proferres ignota indictaque primus.
> publica materies privati iuris erit, si
> non circa vilem patulumque moraberis orbem,
> nec verbo verbum curabis reddere fidus
> interpres, nec desilies imitator in artum,
> unde pedem proferre pudor vetet aut operis lex.
>
> *(Ars poetica* 128–35)

(It is hard to express universals in a particular manner; and so you are wiser to reduce the *Iliad* to dramatic poems, than if you were the first to bring out unknown and untold subjects. Popular subject-matter will be your private property, if you do not linger on the vulgar, well-beaten round, or, as a faithful translator, worry about rendering word for word, or, as an imitator, throw yourself into difficulties from which timidity or the laws of the art prevent you from proceeding.)

Although elsewhere (*Epistulae* 1.19.19) he rails against the 'imitatores, servum pecus', he sees his own originality as lying in his adaptation of Greek metres to Latin verse. In a more generally rhetorical context, Quintilian had also produced some specific advice on the subject of literary imitation.[16] The best authors were to be read assiduously, and 'from these writers and others who are worth reading are to be acquired a rich vocabulary ('verborum copia'), a variety to figures of speech, and the principles of verbal arrangement' (10.2.1). With this idea of imitation, however, is a warning on the sterility of simply copying: 'it is also shameful to be content to copy what you are imitating' (10.2.7). The writer must improve upon his model, for all previous authors have some deficiency. At the same time, the greatest qualities of an author are quite inimitable, 'innate talent, the faculty of discovering arguments, force, fluency, whatever art cannot provide' (10.2.12). Thus, on Horace's division of *ars* and *natura*, only *ars* can be achieved through imitation.[17] Quintilian also warns on the dangers of imitating only one style, since this would be unsuitable for certain subjects, and on the need for subtlety in avoiding mere pastiche so as not to be like those who 'become pompous instead of grand, inadequate instead of concise, heedless instead of bold, affected instead of copious, diffuse instead of elaborate, careless instead of straightforward' (10.2.16).

One of the only theorists to write on the subject of imitation at length in the early sixteenth century was Marco Girolamo Vida.[18] He bears in mind the precepts of the Roman theorists in his exposition of imitation in book III of the *Ars poetica*, although there is inherent in his theories a contradiction: Virgil is the poet above all others who is worthy of imitation, but at the same time the possibilities of surpassing his achievements are quite remote. However, Vida does give a number of practical hints on the process of imitation. When a writer has decided on the subject of his poem, he should choose the best exponent of the genre and follow him closely (*A.P.* 3. 188 sqq.). Even mediocre writers have something to offer. Choice expressions ('aurea dicta') may be taken from their original context and utilised elsewhere. There is nothing to be ashamed of in taking over the words of an ancient poet, expecially if they are disguised and providing that they add something new to the poem concerned.

> Atque ideo ex priscis semper quo more loquamur
> Discendum, quorum depascimur aurea dicta,
> Praecipuumque avidi rerum populamus honorem.
> Aspice ut exuvias veterumque insignia nobis
> Aptemus; rerum accipimus nunc clara reperta,
> Nunc seriem, atque animum verborum, verba quoque ipsa.
> Nec pudet interdum alterius nos ore locutos.
> Cum vero cultis moliris furta poetis,
> Cautius ingredere, et raptus memor occule versis
> Verborum indiciis, atque ordine falle legentes
> Mutato: nova sit facies, nova prorsus imago.
> Munere (nec longum tempus) vix ipse peracto
> Dicta recognosces veteris mutata poetae.
>
> (*A.P.* 3. 210–22)

(And so, we must always learn how to express ourselves from the Ancients, on whose golden words we feed, and whose outstanding ornaments of style we greedily plunder. See how we adapt for ourselves the spoils and trappings of the Ancients. At one time we take over their brilliant subject-matter, at another word order and meaning, even their very words. At times, there is nothing to be ashamed of in speaking with another's lips. But when you are attempting thefts from the refined poets, proceed with caution and, remembering what you have stolen, conceal it by changing the form of the words, and deceive the readers by changing their order. There should be a new appearance and a completely new form. Once the job is completed (and it will not take long), you yourself will hardly recognise the altered words of the ancient poet.)

Often, words can be borrowed and used in an entirely different context (*A.P.* 3, 257–8), and far from being ashamed of his borrowings, he glories in them, and attacks the arrogance of those poets who refuse to do like-wise:

> Infelix autem (quidam nam saepe reperti)
> Viribus ipse suis temere qui fisus et arti,
> Externae quasi opis nihil indigus, abnegat audax
> Fida sequi veterum vestigia, dum sibi praeda
> Temperat heu! nimium, atque alienis parcere crevit.
>
> (*A.P.* 3.245–9)

(But he is unfortunate (for there are often some to be found) who rashly relying on his own powers and skill, as though in no need of outside help, boldly refuses to follow the trustworthy steps of the Ancients, being too moderate in taking booty, and having decided to spare other people's property.)

Expressed in such terms, this view is perhaps somewhat extreme, but it reflects the opinions and practice of many other humanists. From Vida and the other theoretical works of the sixteenth century there emerge certain principles concerning imitation. First of all (and this is hardly surprising) copious and careful reading of the ancient writers is a *sine qua non* of Neo-latin poetry. The second principle is the careful choice of model. Here the sixteenth century was divided, with some critics (like Vida) proposing one author in particular, normally Virgil, while others (probably the majority) allowed a far wider choice. All agreed that the style of the author should be in accord with the subject being treated;[19] and all agreed too that something new should proceed from imitation. The simile of the bee, who converts pollen into honey, occurs time and again in this context.

There was general agreement on the legitimate objects of imitation, certain of which went without saying. The classical Latin verse forms and their use in various genres of poetry were to be copied, as was the style appropriate to each poetic kind.[20] Certain themes might also be taken over and reworked, originality deriving from the combination of *topoi* and *exempla* used to illustrate them. Somewhat less unanimity existed concerning the use of 'tags' in a poem. We have seen that Vida highly recommended them, although Josse Bade (in Despauterius, ed. cit., fo. Avii^r) did not altogether agree with Vida's position. While admitting that imitation did serve a useful purpose, he nevertheless warned that 'obvious thefts are shameful'. This opinion is shared by Nausea (*In artem poeticen, carminumque condendorum primordia* (Venice, 1522), fo. 40^r), while von Hutten expresses the view that a tag may be enhanced in a new context: 'often, when you repeat something in your poem, it comes out more beautiful.' Generally speaking, it is considered best to disguise a classical borrowing in some way by changing the word order or substituting synonyms, and the context must normally be different from the original one. This process is taken a step further when an image or anecdote is reworked in different words altogether.

Although memory played a considerable part in Renaissance education, the poet was not expected to rely solely on this. The use of the notebook containing *exempla* and *sententiae* culled from the poet's reading is recommended in many manuals of poetry,[21] and the poet was expected to read from a very wide range of writers. Murmellius gives clear indications on which models to follow, and his list includes, alongside Virgil, epic writers such as Lucan, Statius, Claudian, Poliziano, Mantuan, Pico della Mirandola, and Pontano; elegiac poets like Fausto Andrelini and Pamphilus Saxus; lyric poets such as Boethius, Prudentius, Marullus, and Filelfo; and epigrammatists like Ausonius, Mantuan, and Pontano.

However, the Neo-latin author did not have to rely entirely on his own personal anthology for the adornment of his style. The modern reader, when faced with the extensive knowledge displayed by such Renaissance writers as Rabelais, Montaigne, and Ronsard, tends to wonder at their erudition. Their works are illustrated with a wide range of *exempla*, quotations, and allusions taken from some of the most obscure classical authors, and they are seldom at a loss to produce apposite parallels between the contemporary and the ancient world. However, in addition to his own notebook of quotations, the writer also had at his disposal printed works which provided a similar service, and judging by the number of editions which some of them reached, they must have enjoyed considerable popularity.

As far as the poet is concerned, three dictionaries seem to be particularly successful in France: Torrentinus' *Elucidarius carminum et historiarum* (Deventer, 1500); Calepinus' *Dictionarium* (Paris, 1518); and Robertus Stephanus' *Dictionarium propriorum nominum*.[22] These works all ran to a number of editions in the first half of the century and provided in varying degrees of complexity information on aspects of the ancient world. In addition to these general works, there were also specialist dictionaries such as Joannes Ravisius Textor's *Specimen epithetorum*, a work which ran to many editions in the sixteenth century and whose *editio princeps* appeared in Paris in 1518.[23] The work is in the form of noun headings followed by a list of adjectives which could be attributed to that noun, taken from classical and, in many cases, Neo-latin poets. For some nouns, Textor writes an article, giving the history and facts about it, citing relevant passages from Latin writers, and finally giving the original contexts of the epithets quoted. Nouns treated in this way include such topics as *amor*, Babylon, Dipsas, *equus*, *mors*, *pax*, *tenebrae*, Zoilus. In later editions of the work, the articles are missing, but for each epithet quoted, the original context is given along with the author's name, as in the 1558 Bâle edition. The number of Neo-latin poets cited, especially Italians such as Petrarch, Mantuan, and Pontano, is striking. This dictionary of epithets proved to be very popular and does indeed explain the frequency of certain adjectives used by the French Neo-latin poets but which in classical writers figure comparatively rarely.[24]

Two further influential but greatly differing sources of knowledge in the sixteenth century were the Greek Anthology and the Stobaeus Anthology, both extremely important in the transmission of Greek thought to the Renaissance. The significance of the Greek Anthology for sixteenth-century France has long been recognised. James Hutton suggests that Danès and Toussaint used the Anthology to teach their students,[25] and certainly the practice of translating the Greek epigrams into Latin (and sometimes back into Greek) became common in Renaissance schools. The 1540s and 1550s in France saw a considerable interest in the Anthology amongst a number of poets, both Neo-latin and vernacular, and as well as numerous translations, encouraged later on by Henri Estienne, the thinking of the Anthology influenced the sentiments expressed by many a French poet.

The Stobaeus Anthology, on the other hand, has received comparatively little scholarly attention. The *editio princeps* of this work appeared relatively late in Venice in 1535 (*Ioannis Stobaei collectiones sententiarum*) although partial editions, often with Latin translations, had been printed in 1515 (Strasbourg), 1517 (Rome), and 1521 (Strasbourg). However, the best and most popular edition was the parallel text version of Conrad Gesner, who translated the work himself into Latin as well as collating the Greek text wherever possible with other manuscripts and printed works, suggesting emendations and adding a comprehensive index. Entitled the Κέρας 'Αμαλθαίας (or Cornucopia), it appeared in Zürich in 1543, and further editions were printed in 1549 (Bâle), 1559 (Zürich), and 1581 (Frankfurt). Gesner's Latin text was also printed separately (Paris, 1552 and 1557). The value of this work for Renaissance writers is incontestable. It was arranged in chapters or λόγοι, each one dealing with a single subject and followed in many cases by a chapter on the opposite of a particular virtue, or providing the contrary point of view on a given topic. For example, the opening chapter 'On Virtue' is followed by one 'On Vice'. Later on, there is a whole series of chapters on women and marriage, for example 65, 'That Marriage is Very Fine', 66, 'That Marrying is not a Good Thing'; on democracy and tyranny, and other questions, with sections on general common-places like 'On Self-knowledge'. Each chapter groups together without comment verse quotations followed by prose passages taken from Greek authors to illustrate each subject. In his preface, Gesner speaks of the many writers who 'regularly quote aphorisms collected by Stobaeus, some acknowledging him, others concealing their source', and goes on to discuss the importance of the work:

> Moreover, there is not much reason for me to deal at length with the usefulness of his work, since all those who have greeted literature even from the threshold realise how extensive the use of common-places is. . . . Who, pray, is there among scholars who does not collect for himself, or wishes to collect, all the common examples, sayings, and judgments about virtues, vices etc. which he has noted amongst writers in his daily reading? For this too is one reason why we read and peruse books, in order to extract their fruit like the kernel of a nut.[26]

It is only people's vanity, he says, which makes them rely on their own collections of *loci communes* rather than on Stobaeus', which is infinitely superior.

Such are the basic principles underlying Neo-latin versification and poetics. As we have seen, the Renaissance's attempt to reconstruct the edifice of classical Latin poetry led to a somewhat different structure from the one they intended. Exceptions began to take on the status of rules, the rationale behind some principles was not understood, while some areas of versification remained unexplained (for example, areas concerned with elision or the avoidance of short vowel endings before words beginning with *s* plus consonant). Nevertheless, the verse manuals do not in themselves tell the whole story. The individual poet often had an understanding of the demands of a particular genre despite the fact that this subject received no attention in the *artes versificatoriae*, and it is this intuition which distinguishes the poet from the mere versifier. This sense of poetic *decorum* was an important aspect of versification, as we shall see in the next chapter.

However, it would be wrong to consider only the relationship between Neo-latin poetry and classical literature, for the Neo-latin poet existed side by side with the vernacular poet. Indeed, the two roles were often united in the same individual. Neo-latin poetry, then, looks forward as well as back, and evolves in a direction which is very frequently parallel to the progress made by vernacular poetry, both bestowing and receiving influence. As we examine Buchanan's poetry in detail, these connections will become apparent.

CHAPTER 3
George Buchanan and
Neo-latin Poetic Theory

While Buchanan's insight into classical Latin poetry was undoubtedly more profound than that of the majority of his contemporaries, he was nevertheless a man of his times, and consequently his theory and practice in versification are to be judged by sixteenth-century criteria. We know something of his approach to the subject from the *De prosodia libellus* which he wrote after his return to Scotland but which was not printed until the 1590s. One striking aspect of the book is that it is short (ten quarto pages in the 1725 edition of the *Opera omnia*). Buchanan evidently felt that, while it was useful to summarise the principal rules of Latin verse along with important exceptions, there was little point in delving into a host of empirical rules which could best be learnt through experience. Like other sixteenth-century theorists, he begins with a description and definition of the letters of the alphabet, but then goes on to reverse the order of most handbooks. 'This natural order seems to require that first syllables, then feet, and finally the line of verse are dealt with; but in this case, an analytical order seems to me to be more convenient than the order of composition. So, let us start with the line of verse and analyse it into its constituent parts' (*O.O.* II.710). He then proceeds to scan a line of Virgil, and speaks of the various feet. Of four or more syllable feet, he says that they are 'more common with orators than poets', with the exception of the proceleusmatic and the choriambus. Buchanan is unwilling to burden the learner with useless information, but at the same time he does not wish to give him a false, oversimplified impression which would later have to be corrected. Each definition is illustrated with a range of examples occasionally, as in the case of synizesis, taken from Buchanan's own poetry:

> Dum Papa omnipotens Capitolii immobile saxum
> Accolet, imperiumque pater coleatus habebit.

On unusual usages in poetry, he writes that 'there is a certain poetic licence which should not be entirely rejected, seeing as it was used by the most learned poets; but it should not be allowed to beginners, until their judgement is more sound and they have achieved some skill through the practice of writing' (*O.O.* II.711). These licences, which may help to explain Buchanan's practice at times, are that:

(a) a diphthong or long vowel preceding another vowel may become short by corruption

(b) a single syllable may form two syllables (*terrāi* < *terrae*)

(c) an extra syllable may sometimes be added (*induperator* for *imperator*)

(d) a short syllable may stand for a long one at a caesura, e.g. 'omnia vincit amor,/et nos cedamus amori'.

Buchanan moves on to consider syllables. 'Syllable quantity is known through examples or rules. Examples should be sought in the writings of the learned poets.' He then produces nine rules, which are more or less the same as those provided by Despauterius. Buchanan owned a copy of the works on prosody of Terentianus and Probus which he presented to St Leonard's College in St Andrews, and no doubt his indications are partly based on them.[1] For the most part, he follows the practice of his contemporaries, allowing a fair degree of licence in a number of cases where classical usage tended to be somewhat stricter. For example, he seems to consider adverbs ending in *o* as common (and in his own verse he sometimes has the final syllable of *subito, denuo,* and *imo* as short). He also considered that the final *i* of *uti* was common ('communem habent ultimam mihi, tibi, sibi, uti . . . ') although it is normally long, and that the final *a* of many indeclinable words (e.g. *supra, praeterea, frustra, antea*) is sometimes short. In many cases where Buchanan has prosodic abnormalities, corroborative examples may be found amongst classical Roman poets. He probably relied to a large extent on his own pronunciation of Latin, which was almost certainly as correct as could be expected according to sixteenth-century criteria. James VI himself, the Scottish humanist's pupil, claimed to pronounce Latin correctly, and learnt his pronunciation from Buchanan.[2]

After considering prosody, Buchanan goes on to stress-accents, which are summarised in three short rules, while the final section of the book names and gives the metrical patterns for eight metres along with examples for each one. His scheme for the glyconic metre is not altogether correct since, whereas classical usage invariably made the last syllable long, Buchanan considers it to be anceps; and short syllables were permissible in the first foot for which Buchanan prescribes a spondee. His iambic dimeter allows far more alternative feet than was permitted by normal classical usage, compare Buchanan's scheme:

$$
\begin{array}{c|c|c|c}
- \; - & & - \quad - & \\
\cup \; - & \cup \; - & \cup \quad - & \cup \quad - \\
\cup \; \cup\cup & \cup \; \cup\cup & \cup \quad \cup\cup & \cup \quad \cup\cup \\
- \; \cup\cup & & - \quad \cup\cup & \\
\cup\cup \; - & & \cup\cup \quad - &
\end{array}
$$

with Postgate's:[3]

$$
\left.\begin{array}{cc} \cup - \\ - - \end{array}\right| \left.\begin{array}{cc} \cup - \\ \cup \ \cup\cup \end{array}\right| \left.\begin{array}{cc} \cup - \\ - - \end{array}\right| \begin{array}{cc} \cup \ \ \bar{\cup} \\ \ \end{array}
$$

and similarly, his iambic trimeter admits greater licence, especially in the fifth foot, where tribrachs, dactyls, and anapaests make an appearance.

Naturally, these ideas on prosody and metre are reflected in Buchanan's poetry, and he has on occasion been attacked for his lapses, especially regarding false quantities.[4] Except for certain poetic licences which Buchanan allows himself, it is sometimes difficult to tell whether he is adopting an unusual quantity in a word, or whether he has in mind a different metre plan from the generally accepted kind. He certainly makes use of synizesis at times, for example *dēhīnc* in *Fratres fraterrimi* 34.10; *dēīnde* in *Epigrams* II.26.7; *vĭētum* in *Silvae* 3.53; and *dēēsset* in *Fratres fraterrimi* 30.31. Other licences include allowing a short syllable in place of a long one before a main caesura, for example *De sphaera* 2.244: 'Ambitus aequalis/omni qua parte coercet.'

Thus, Buchanan's treatise on the subject of versification was short and concise. But while his work, in common with other Renaissance verse manuals, legislated on many aspects of prosody and metre, there remained an area of penumbra in versification, seldom if ever discussed by the theorists, through which the best Neo-latin poets nevertheless managed to find their way. Of considerable importance in this area is the question of elision.[5] Despauterius admittedly devotes several pages to this where, in addition to the basic rules, he also cites some notable exceptions and peculiarities. On a related subject, he says that *s* can sometimes be disregarded in scansion (as in 'montibŭs mortalibus'); hiatus is sometimes found in the ancient poets, a practice to be noted rather than followed (and in this context, he quotes Virgil, *Eclogues* 3.79, 'vale, vale inquit' and Ovid, *Metamorphoses* 4.535, 'Ionio immenso'); single monosyllabic vowel words (e.g. *heu, o*) are not elided; elision between lines (hypermetric elision) is sometimes possible. However, he ultimately takes refuge in the vague statement 'quicquid doctis auribus placet, bonum est'. Not every poet possessed this intuition, and Neo-latin verse can at times sound rather clumsy and ponderous; but Buchanan seems to have understood better than most the conventions of the Roman poets, and to have been guided in this, as in other fields, by the principle of *decorum*.

Buchanan's skill in versification can be verified by a study of his poetry. A comparison of the first hundred lines of the satirical hexameter poem *Franciscanus* and of *Silvae* 4, the epithalamium on the marriage of Mary Stuart and François II, yields some interesting results. Whereas the number of elisions in the *Franciscanus* is quite high (45), in the epithalamium we find only 19, conforming with the classical tendency to allow more elisions in colloquial and satirical verse.[6] The Roman tendency to avoid the elision of long syllables before short ones is followed: there is only one example of this in either sample (*Franciscanus* 69), while the majority in both cases follow the pattern ∪ — or — —. Connected with this point is the classical Latin dislike of eliding monosyllables, which are often long, and easily swallowed up in elision. Again, there is a tendency to allow greater licence in colloquial verse, and if we compare the whole of the *Franciscanus* (936 lines) with the serious hexameter poems of the *Silvae* (738 lines), we find 12 examples of elided monosyllables in the *Franciscanus*, but only 3 in the *Silvae*. Moreover, those monosyllables which are elided are generally among the most readily elided ones in classical Latin usage.[7]

Buchanan therefore seems to be very well acquainted with classical practice on elision, conforming to Roman norms concerning its admissibility and frequency of use in the various genres of poetry. However, one point of which he does appear to be unaware is the Roman poets' repugnance for allowing a short final vowel to precede a word beginning with *s* plus consonant or z. Thus, the *Franciscanus* contains 14 examples of this collocation, and the *Silvae* contain a like number.

As far as individual metres are concerned, Renaissance familiarity with classical usage varied, although knowledge of the hexameter was quite extensive, embracing many of its licences and peculiarities. We may therefore expect any liberties which Buchanan takes to be totally conscious, and as in the case of elision, it is in the *Franciscanus* that the majority of anomalies are to be found. For example, there are 17 lines ending in monosyllables (as opposed to 7 in the *Silvae*) of which 4 are particularly unusual (lines 180, 517, 813, 892), probably aiming at particular sonorities. Thus, there is the quick, darting sound of line 892:

> Langius, umbrarum poenas, flammae rapidam vim

heightened by the preceding long syllables, and perhaps suggested by Virgil, *Georgics* 2.321 'prima vel autumni sub frigora, cum rapidus Sol'; and the more sombre ending to line 517:

> Infelix frater turbae sese insinuans clam.

Words of four and five syllables are also found at the end of hexameters (*Franciscanus* 873, *Silvae* 4.269), while other sound effects are achieved by the inclusion of the occasional spondaic line, e.g. *Franciscanus* 114:

> Donec blanditiis, fabellisque admirandis.

Buchanan's hexameters are in general extremely accomplished, and to a large extent this is due to his careful handling of rhythm through the skilful interplay of word-accent and long and short syllables, the position of the main caesura, and the use of elision. By way of illustration, there is the staccato line 44 of *Silvae* 3, in which the alliteration of the *c*, the predominance of dactyls, and the unusual coincidence of word accent with the opening syllable of each foot conjure up the beat of the drum and Lycisca's movements:

> Ēt mē | tȳmpănă | dóctă cĭ | érĕ că | nóră Ly̆ | cĭscă;

or the rather more gloomy line 8 of the same poem:

> Ēt cūm | iām lōn | gās prāe | cēps nōx | pōrrĭgĭt | ūmbrās.

As we have noted, Buchanan employs elision sparingly and does not abuse it, like many of his contemporaries, simply in order to fit the necessary words into a line. He is careful to vary the position of the caesura, often highlighting certain words by placing them in prominent parts of the line; and he achieves further variety by the mixture of end-stopped and non-end-stopped lines.

The elegiac couplet was also well-known in the sixteenth century, being particularly common amongst the epigrammatists. Although in Ovid the pentameter almost invariably ends in a dissyllabic word, observance of this rule was much less strict in earlier and subsequent poets (like Catullus, Propertius, and Martial).[8] Buchanan does tend to avoid monosyllabic endings here, and the one example in line 200 of *Elegy* 3 is only apparent as the *e* of *est* would disappear by prodelision:

> Quo tibi (sed lenae munere) facta via est.

However, endings of three, four, and five syllable words are not uncommon in the satirical epigrams, although in the more serious *Elegies*, there is only one abnormal ending (in *Elegy* 4.32):

> Cum petitur dubii criminis indicium.[9]

On this evidence, it is clear that Buchanan, as in his use of the hexameter, made a distinction between serious and colloquial verse, following a similar tendency to be found in the Roman poets. He avoids elision in the second hemistich of the pentameter (but for one exception see *Elegy* 4.50), and in general there are fewer elisions than in his pure hexameter verse (for example 25 cases in the 110-line early satirical *Elegy* 1.13 in the 100-line *Elegy* 4). The hexameter of the elegiac couplet, which in Ovidian verse tended to be somewhat stricter than normal hexameter verse, contains fewer anomalous endings in the *Elegies* than in the epigrammatic poetry.

So once again, Buchanan exhibits a good grasp of the subtleties of this metre, preserving the distinction between serious and colloquial verse, and using the compression resulting from the self-contained couplets to good effect.

When we enter the realm of the iambic and lyric metres, however, we are presented with a different picture, and Buchanan tends to exhibit a rather more flexible approach to metre scheme than that of the strictest classical exponents. We have already seen that his scheme for iambic dimeters and trimeters is somewhat freer than Horatian practice permitted, and not unnaturally this is reflected in his verse. For example, anapaests are usually avoided by Golden Age writers in the odd feet of an iambic trimeter, but Buchanan prefers to follow later Roman usage, as in *Iambi* 2.23:

$$\text{Pă}\overline{\text{rĭtĕr}} \mid \text{vŏr}\overline{\text{ā}} \mid \text{c}\overline{\text{ēs}}, \text{pă}\breve{\text{rĭ}} \mid \text{tĕr } \overline{\text{īn}} \mid \text{să}\overline{\text{tĭā}} \mid \text{bĭl}\overline{\text{ēs}}.$$

Again, resolution in the iambic dimeter is rare in Horace (there are but two examples)[10] but occur several times in Buchanan, for example *Iambi* 2.4:

$$\overline{\text{Ō}} \text{ scŏr} \mid \text{tă trĭŏ} \mid \text{bŏl}\overline{\text{ā}} \mid \text{rĭă}.$$

It is also unusual to end a line with two iambic words, but Buchanan does this in *Iambi* 10.53:[11]

$$\overline{\text{Ēt cŏn}} \mid \text{iŭg}\overline{\text{ā}} \mid \text{lĭs n}\overline{\text{ēg}} \mid \text{lĭg}\overline{\text{ēns}} \mid \text{tŏr}\overline{\text{ī}}, \mid \text{vĭr}\overline{\text{ō}}.$$

These divergences from Horatian usage are to be encountered in poets like Seneca and Petronius, and as in other matters of prosody and metre, Buchanan is here following a consensus view of versification, approaching the subject diachronically rather than synchronically.

Of the lyric metres, Buchanan makes greatest use of the hendecasyllable, the alcaic stanza, and the sapphic stanza. In the case of the phalaecian hendecasyllable, his practice is closer to Catullus' than to that of the later poets like Martial in that, while keeping a preponderance of spondees in the first foot, he does, unlike later poets, vary the opening. (Of 400 lines of hendecasyllables in the secular poems, 76.75 per cent start with spondees, 15.5 per cent with trochees, and 7.75 per cent with iambi.) Elision is also quite common (151 elisions in 400 lines), although this too was generally avoided by later poets.[12]

In accordance with Horatian usage, Buchanan does tend to avoid elision in the alcaic and sapphic stanzas. Out of a total of 428 lines in the secular poetry, there are 74 cases of elision, or 17.52 per hundred lines.[13] On the other hand, his practice tends to be less strict than that of Horace in the metrical schemes which he follows, occasionally allowing a short fifth syllable in the third line of the alcaic stanza, for example:

Fī | dūcĭ | ā pă | rī tŭ | mēntēm
(*Misc.* 1.23)

but see also *Fratres fraterrimi* 5.23, 27; *Miscellany* 1.35, 95. In the scheme
which he gives for the sapphic hendecasyllable in the *De prosodia libellus*,
he allows a trochee in the second foot instead of a spondee, although there
is no case of this happening in the two secular poems written in this metre.
Greek usage had originally allowed these alternatives in both cases,
however.

A certain pattern emerges from this brief consideration of Buchanan's
versification. The Scottish humanist writes Neo-latin poetry largely in
accordance with contemporary teaching on the subject, while at the same
time exhibiting an awareness of the stylistic and metrical differences
between the various genres, and an appreciation of the sonorities of the
Latin language rare in other Neo-latinists. In matters of prosody, he does
not aim at any kind of historical unity in his verse; if necessary, he will
make a syllable long or short contrary to normal classical usage, provided
that some precedent can be found. As far as metrical considerations are
concerned, he obviously possesses an understanding of many of the subtleties of Roman verse, especially in the dactylic metres, while at the same
time being unaware of other aspects of classical versification. Thus, his use
of elision conforms very closely to Roman usage, but he is not at all
conscious of the Roman avoidance of short final vowels before *s* plus
consonant. Moreover, in the lyric metres, he is largely content to follow
Greek and early Roman usage, rather than the stricter forms evolved by
Horace. In conclusion, it may be said that Buchanan represents one of the
summits of the Renaissance in matters of versification, and that it is fair to
judge other Neo-latin poets by the standards which he himself achieved.

The tendency which we have observed in Buchanan to follow the
metrical peculiarities of individual kinds of poetry is also extended to other
aspects of his verse, and derives from the wish to preserve poetic *decorum*
in his writing. He considers that if he is writing in a particular genre, the
lexical, metrical, and stylistic habits of the best exponents of that genre
should be followed. However, he does not limit himself strictly to using only
what has been written before, but frequently broadens a tendency which
he has observed. This is illustrated most simply in the field of vocabulary
where he will coin new words or take over Greek words in his satirical
poetry, in the manner of Juvenal or Martial. Stylistic imitation goes much
further than this, however. In his iambic poems on Leonora (*Iambi* 2, 3, 4,
and 5), Buchanan's style owes a great deal to Horace, especially the Horace
of the *Epodes*. Both poets seem to delight in vituperative description, word
order plays an important role in the overall effect of the poems, while other

devices shared with Horace include apostrophe, rhetorical questions, and alliteration. This Horatian effect is further strengthened by phrases and motifs modelled on Horace. For example, the opening of *Iambi* 2, 'Matre impudica filia impudicior', is reminiscent of *Odes* 1.16 'o matre pulchra filia pulchrior'. Thus, Buchanan takes over not only the metre, but also the diction, style, and themes of Horace, and yet manages to produce poems which are relevant to his own situation (this is particularly true of the Leonora poems) and contain strong elements of originality. Another example of stylistic imitation is to be found in the poems addressed to Neaera, where Catullus and the Neo-latin poets Marullus and Joannes Secundus are influential. Buchanan exhibits all the characteristics of the Neo-catullan style, which was also popular amongst the Pléiade poets in the early 1550s: the diminutives, indefinite constructions, use of repetition and abstract nouns, and general familiarity of tone. Many other examples could be mentioned: the influence of Virgil's *Eclogues* on *Silvae* 2 and 3, of Lucretius on the *De sphaera*, of Martial on the epigrams. However, in spite of composing in the style of another poet, Buchanan normally manages to inject something of his own style and personality into his poetry, and to preserve some degree of originality.

Apart from stylistic imitation, Renaissance poets frequently reworked themes which had already been treated by another poet. Originality of ideas and novelty are not so important in this case as the elegance of expression achieved by the poet. Obviously, the simplest form of such imitation.is the translation or paraphrase. In such a process, the possibility existed either of improving upon the original or of making it applicable to a new situation, and it is a form of imitation of which Buchanan made extensive use. One of his earliest extant poems, the 'Somnium', is a free paraphrase of a Scots poem by William Dunbar, although the details are changed or expanded, and the *pointe* of the poem is different in the Latin version. His longer translations include the *Medea* and *Alcestis*, in which he tries to preserve as far as possible the meaning, metre, and general flow of Euripides' plays; and the Psalm paraphrases, where his aim, apart from producing a more elegant version than was available in the Vulgate, is to provide the reader with a text whose sentiments reflect more accurately the original Hebrew. Greek verse also provided a number of poems for translation, with the Greek Anthology figuring prominently. At least twelve of Buchanan's epigrams are from that source, and with the possible exception of *Epigrams* I.10 and I.44, the translations are mostly very close to the originals.[14] He generally preserves the same number of lines and metre as the original, except for *Epigrams* I.30 where the first two lines of the Greek poem are omitted and the metre is changed, and *Epigrams* I.44, where two lines are added at the beginning. However, the order of the ideas is altered at times and there is a tendency towards greater elegance and explicitness in Buchanan's versions. This is also apparent in his choice of more picturesque epithets, or indeed, the inclusion of adjectives for which there is no Greek equivalent. Apart from Greek Anthology poems, Buchanan also translated some pieces by Simonides. In fact, although the sixteenth century rarely distinguished between them, there are two Simonides: Simonides of Ceos and Simonides (or Semonides) of Amorgos. Buchanan translated most of the latter's hardly substantial extant work, together with four poems of Simonides of Ceos.[15] Like his versions of the Greek Anthology epigrams, his translations are very close in meaning to the originals, preserving the same metre and the same number of lines. Buchanan also translated from vernacular languages, and apart from Scots, made use of French originals. *Epigrams* I.31, for example, is almost certainly based on a French epigram by Mellin de Saint-Gelais,[16] while I. D. McFarlane traces the interesting source and later history of *Miscellany* 29 in his article on the *Franciscanus*.[17]

More generally, a common classical theme may be taken over, like the 'carpe diem' theme so popular in the Renaissance. Buchanan incorporates a number of classical *topoi* into his poetry, and indeed, at times they form the principal theme of a poem, for example *Hendecasyllables* 3, based on the Catullan 'odi et amo' theme. Sometimes, a particular idea will be reworked several times, as is the case with the poet's criticism of Leonora's use of cosmetics. This theme is found in Tibullus 1.8.9–16 (addressed to a boy) as well as in the Greek Anthology (*Anthologia palatina* 11.408):

> μὴ τοίνυν τὸ πρόσωπον ἅπαν ψιμύθῳ κατάπλαττε,
> ὥστε προσωπεῖον, κ' οὐχὶ πρόσωπον ἔχειν.

(Do not therefore completely plaster your face with white-lead, so that you have a mask instead of a face.)

In Buchanan, it forms the subject of *Elegy* 8, and also occurs in *Epigrams* I.16,17,22,28, and *Miscellany* 6. Buchanan also uses a number of other traditional themes: the 'carpe diem' motif (*Elegy* 2.131 sqq.), a girl's illness (*Elegy* 6), the *lena* (throughout the Leonora cycle). In many instances, the new context is able to revitalise a fairly well worn common-place.

The use of tags taken from other poets (whether straight quotations or hidden by word changes) was, as we have seen in the previous chapter, another fundamental feature of Neo-latin poetry whose origins may be traced to the classical Roman poets and before. These tags fulfilled a number of functions. We have already seen that they helped to establish the diction and style of any given genre of poetry, and it is striking that a particular classical author will supply large numbers of textual reminiscences in a specific poem or group of poems, but not figure at all in others.

This is only partially explained by metre and context. For example, in Buchanan's case, the *Silvae* have numerous allusions to Virgil, while proportionally the *Elegies* are more reliant on Ovid.[18] It is also clear that humour, or at least wit, is one of the reasons for the use of many of the more recognisable allusions. The reader sees a quotation, recalls its original context, and feels pleasure or amusement at the new use to which it has been put. For example, Virgil's famous 'omnia vincit Amor' from *Eclogues* 10.69 (particularly well-known in the Renaissance because it figures in many of the verse manuals as an example of the caesura lengthening a preceding short syllable) turns up in *Elegy* 6.48 as 'Atque hunc, qui vincit omnia, vincit Amor'. Lines like Ovid's self-pitying *adynaton*:

> in caput alta suum labentur ab aequore retro
> flumina, conversis Solque recurret equis
> (*Tristia* 1.8)

are used in an ironic context in Buchanan's Lucianic mock encomium, the 'Pro lena' (*Elegy* 3.3–4):

> Idem posse suos in fontes flumina labi
> Credat, et aversis astra redire rotis.

In some other cases, an almost proverbial expression may be taken over, simply because of its appositeness, without any allusion to the original context being intended; for example, 'aniles fabellae' (cf. *Franciscanus* 879–80 and Horace, *Satires* 2.6. 77–8); 'ponat perfricta fronte ruborem' (cf. *Fratres fraterrimi* 34.21 and Martial, 11.27.7); 'frons caperata minis' (cf. *Franciscanus* 2 and Nonius Marcellus) and ἐς κόρακας (cf. *Franciscanus* 324 with Aristophanes, who uses the expression a number of times, and Erasmus' *Adages*). At other times, the poet recognises a close parallel between the situation or events which he is describing and a similar event in classical literature, and so he includes a textual reminiscence to underline this. Thus, the picture in *Silvae* 3.21 sqq. of the poet looking out to sea for his beloved Amaryllis reminds us of the similar scene in Catullus 64. 50 sqq.:

> Saepe super celsae praerupta cacumina rupis
> In mare prospiciens, spumantia caerula demens
> Alloquor, et surdis iacto irrita vota procellis

and these lines do, in fact, contain an allusion to Catullus 64.59 'irrita ventosae linquens promissa procellae'. Similar parallels may be seen between *Silvae* 4.49–50 and Claudian, *Epithalamium* (10), 23–7; *Silvae* 4.254–5 and Catullus 61.34–5; *Iambi* 5.13–20 and Horace, *Odes* 1.25; and *Hendecasyllables* 2.1–2 and Joannes Secundus, *Elegies* 1.5. Alternatively, periphrases or epithets may be taken over which refer to particular mythological or historical occurrences, for example:

Ipse Deus vatum vaccas pavisse Pheraeas
Creditur, Aemonios et numerasse greges
(*Elegy* 1.99–100)

an oblique reference to Apollo, is taken from Ovid, *Heroides* 5.151 almost
verbatim, while the mythological allusions in *Elegy* 3.93–8 all refer to
specific classical contexts.[19] An entire image from a classical poem may be
taken over and incorporated in a new context, as at the beginning of *Elegy* 7:

Qualiter ut Phrygii crepuit tinnitus aheni
Cymbala mellificas rauca morantur apes

which is borrowed from Lucan 9.284 sqq.:

haud aliter . . .
quam, simul . . . Phrygii sonus increpat aeris,
attonitae posuere fugam studiumque laboris
floriferi repetunt et sparsi mellis amorem.

Compare also in the same poem the war-horse simile (lines 7–12) with
Lucan 4.750–2, and the phoenix simile of *Silvae* 7.27–35 with Claudian, *De
consulatu Stilichonis* 2.414 sqq. Numerous examples could be cited, but the
above give an indication of the uses to which such allusions could be put. In
Buchanan at least, such allusions are seldom purely gratuitous, and generally have a specific reason for their inclusion.

It is not always certain, however, if Buchanan has taken a particular
theme or tag directly from its author, or if he has seen it elsewhere in an
anthology or dictionary such as those mentioned in the previous chapter.
However, there are some indications that they exercised a certain amount
of influence on his writing. Even if he appropriated little directly from
contemporary dictionaries, they nevertheless helped to establish the
currency of certain mythological, legendary, and historical facts, and to
give respectability to words which had found but little favour with classical
writers but which appealed to the Neo-latinists. Some poems show the
marks of books of reference quite clearly, such as *Fratres fraterrimi* 14, 'In
Romam', whose humour derives from the association of Rome with words
based on the *lup-* stem, as in the closing lines:

Nihil comperies nisi LUPERCOS,
LUPERCALE, LUPOS, LUPAS, LUPANAR.

Some details in this epigram could well have come from such an entry as
the following by Calepinus on Lupercal:

Lupercal a lupa dicitur locus sub palatino monte sacratus ab Evandro Pani deo
arcadiae qui lycaeus vocatur. Quamvis quidam ita appellatum velint: quod lupa ibi

Remum & Romulum nutriverit. Ovid. in fast. Illa loco nomen fecit: locus ille lupercal. Magna dati nutrix praemia lactis habet.[20]

Compare this with *Fratres fraterrimi* 14.4–6:

> Donec per freta vectus Arcas exul
> Pani, pelleret ut lupos, Lycaeo
> Lupercalia festa dedicavit

and lines 17–18:

> Et qui moenia prima condidere
> Nutrivit lupa, Romulum Remumque.

Other epigrams may also owe something to dictionaries, for example *Fratres fraterrimi* 20 which concerns the gender of *cucullus*. Buchanan accuses a Franciscan of wrongly using the feminine form *cuculla*, a theme which may have been suggested by a definition of *cucullus* such as the following by Calepinus:

Cucullus etiam genus vestis est. Iuve. Sumere nocturnos meretrix augusta cucullos. Unum constat fratres nostros Eremitanos male uti hoc vocabulo cuculla foe. ge.[21]

Further down, he cites a line from Juvenal, 'Contentusque illic veneto duroque cucullo', to which Buchanan alludes in line 6, 'Et durum et venetum poeta dixit'.

There are also indications in Buchanan's verse that he had his own notebook of *exempla* which he used to illustrate his poems. Lists of similar events are quite common, especially in the longer poems, like the examples of spontaneous generation in *Elegy* 3.93–8:[22]

> Nam neque Partheniis nunc quercubus editur Arcas,
> Curetes pluvio nec geniti imbre cadunt;
> Nec gravida fratres funduntur nube bimembres,
> Nec vivunt Pyrrhae saxa animata manu;
> Myrmidonas nusquam gignit formica, nec usquam
> Ficta Prometheo spirat imago luto.

(For nowadays, the Arcadian is not produced from oak-trees on Mount Parthenios, the Curetes do not fall born from rain showers; the twin-shaped brethren [the Centaurs] are not poured forth from pregnant cloud, and stones do not come to life from Pyrrha's hand; nowhere does an ant bring forth Myrmidons, nor is there anywhere breath in models made from Promethean mud.)

Similar lists are to be found in *Elegy* 7 on the influence of *aes*, *Fratres fraterrimi* 35.23–6 on periphrases for the colour grey, *Elegy* 1.93–102 on the poverty of poets.

Ravisius Textor's *Specimen epithetorum* also seems to have influenced

Buchanan's choice of adjective on occasion, or perhaps even to have suggested many of the elements for a particular poem. An example of this second process may perhaps be seen in *Silvae* 6, the 'De equo elogium', whose text is as follows:

> Caetera rerum opifex animalia finxit ad usus
> Quaeque suos, equus ad cunctos se accommodat unus:
> Plaustra trahit, fert clitellas, fert esseda, terram
> Vomere proscindit, dominum fert, sive natatu
> Flumina, seu fossam saltu, seu vincere cursu   5
> Est salebras opus, aut canibus circundare saltus,
> Aut molles glomerare gradus, aut flectere gyros,
> Libera seu vacuis ludat lascivia campis.
> Quod si bella vocent tremulos vigor acer in artus
> It, domino et socias vomit ore et naribus iras,   10
> Vulneribusque offert generosum pectus, et una
> Gaudia, moerores sumit ponitque vicissim
> Cum domino. Sortem sic officiosus in omnem,
> Ut veteres nobis tam certo foedere iunctum
> Crediderint mixta coalescere posse figura,   15
> Inque Pelethroniis Centauros edere silvis.

(The Creator of the universe made all other animals each for their own individual purposes, but the horse alone adapts itself to all purposes. He draws wagons, bears pack-saddles, and bears chariots, he cleaves the ground with the plough-share, and bears his master, whether he must swim across rivers, or leap ditches, or gallop over ruts, surround woodlands with the hounds, gently trot, or wheel round, or whether unrestrained frolicking disports on the open plain. But if war summons, a keen force enters his trembling limbs, he breathes out rage from his mouth and nostrils in common with his master, he offers his brave breast to wounds, and together with his master takes on or loses in turn joy and sorrow. So dutiful in every task is he that the Ancients believed that, as he is united to us in such a definite bond, he can mingle in a hybrid form, and produce Centaurs in the Pelethronian woods.)

Many of the elements making up this *icon are to be found in the article by* Textor on *equus* in the 1518 edition. For example, line 3 may owe something to Silius Italicus (fo. 128[r]) 'aut molli pacata celer trahit Esseda collo'. Lines 4–5 probably take their idea from Columella 7.27 (fo. 126[v] in Textor) 'si fossam sine contactione transilit, pontem flumenque transcendit'. Compare also line 7 with Virgil's line (quoted fo. 126[r]) 'insultare solo et gressus glomerare superbos'; lines 9–10 with Virgil, *Georgics* 3 (quoted fo. 126[v]–127[r]):

> . . . Tum si qua sonum procul arma dedere:
> Stare loco nescit, micat auribus, et tremit artus,
> Collectumque fremens voluit sub naribus ignem.

There are further similarities between lines 11–13 and Lactantius, cited fo. 126ʳ, 'in equis gloriae cupiditas experimento deprehenditur: victores enim exultant, victi dolent'. Finally, the *pointe* in lines 14–16 may be suggested by Sabellicus, quoted fo. 127ᵛ:

> . . . Frenumque induxit et ipsa
> Strata Peletronius domitor, Martemque ciere
> Thessalus usus equo est primus: quem pura vetustas
> Semiferum spectasse virum sibi visa, vocavit
> Centaurum.

There are also many examples in Buchanan's poetry of the use of adjective/noun combinations found in the *Specimen epithetorum* and attributed to non-classical authors. For example, as McFarlane has indicated, in *Elegy* 4.54–6 'terrificae mortis' and 'ore/Suaviloquo' both have their origins in Mantuan who is quoted in each case by Ravisius Textor. For other examples, see 'ignigenae facis' (*Epigrams* I.29.3) and Textor's example by Remâcle d'Ardenne 'ignigenae flagra domare facis'; *Miscellany* 6.8 'vafris . . . dolis' and Textor's 'dolisque pectora fert sua plena vafris' (by Celtis); *Silvae* 2.2 'horrida tesqua' and Textor (quoting Mantuan) 'si modo sola queunt cum montibus horrida tesqua'; *Silvae* 2.88 'Boreae nivali' and Pontanus 'affatus cave Threicios boreamque nivalem'; *Miscellany* 1.72 'pegasea penna' and Ludovicus Bigus 'Paegaseis divina sequi vestigia pennis'; and *Miscellany* 1.39 'algenti sub Arcto' and Pontanus 'partem algentem festinat in arcton'. In all these cases (and there are many more) it is possible that Buchanan chose the epithet independently, or saw the various combinations in their original contexts. However, since Textor's dictionary was intended to help in poetic composition, it is quite probable that Buchanan did make use of it.

In this chapter, we have examined a number of the general principles governing Buchanan's poetry, and seen that in technical matters of prosody and metre, we must expect less consistency than we find in the poetry of Rome, especially of the Golden Age of Latin literature. However, Buchanan was clearly aware of the differences in diction, style, and metrical usage of the Roman poets, and we shall see in a closer examination of his poetical works that he was firmly guided by the principle of *decorum*, even in his choice of vocabulary. We shall also see the ways in which he was indebted to other writers, and how he transformed and assimilated his borrowings. All these considerations are essential for the appreciation of Neo-latin poetry, along with an awareness of parallel currents in contemporary vernacular verse, for it is only when everything is taken into account that Neo-latin poetry can be fairly judged.

CHAPTER 4

Poetry and Drama before 1547

1547, the year that Buchanan left France to teach in Portugal, marks a convenient break in his poetic career for the purposes of this study. By this time, he had tried his hand at a wide range of genres, including satire, tragedy, occasional poetry of various kinds, and epigrams (of which many, however, are difficult to date precisely). The inspiration for these works reflects to a certain extent his somewhat unsettled life throughout these years, which happen to coincide with the first really important period of Neo-latin writing in France: his fellow poets included such men as Salmon Macrin, Nicolas Bourbon, Jean Visagier, and Théodore de Bèze.[1] Moreover, the falling-off of poetic composition in France during the 1540s seems to be matched by a similar slump in Buchanan's output, at least in the middle years of the decade.[2]

In the previous chapters, we have noted the rapid progress made by Neo-latin poetry during this period, not only in the field of versification, but also in more literary domains. The systematic exploitation of classical themes, and imitation of classical style, guided by the principle of *decorum*, were strongly recommended in the verse manuals, and as familiarity with the ancient writers increased, so too did the range and achievements of the French Neo-latin poets. Emulation, both of the classical poets and of the Italians, proved to be an effective goad to spur on the French Neo-latinists just as it would urge on the Pléiade poets a generation later. Moreover, many of du Bellay's injunctions in the *Deffence et illustration* simply echo, *mutatis mutandis*, what had been Neo-latin practice for some years.

This does not mean, however, that the Neo-latin writers acted uniquely as torchbearers for the vernacular poets, and just as in the 1550s there would be a fruitful interaction between the Pléiade and their Neo-latin colleagues, so the earlier vernacular and Neo-latin writers proved to be mutually stimulating and to share common sources of inspiration in the classical heritage. This is illustrated, for example, by the various *sodalitia* with which Salmon Macrin was associated, and which, in addition to Neo-latin poets like Michel de l'Hôpital, Théodore de Bèze, Etienne Dolet, and Jean Visagier, also included some of the most important vernacular writers of the period such as Clément Marot, Mellin de Saint-Gelais, and Maurice Scève.[3]

Throughout this early period of Neo-latin composition, Buchanan seems to have been associated not so much with specifically poetic circles as with humanist *milieux* in general. Indeed, his frequent changes of residence between Paris, Scotland, and Bordeaux ensured a diversity of poetic stimuli: for, while he constantly looked to the Ancients in all literary matters, he was far from shunning themes suggested by vernacular writers, whether they were French or Scots. Nevertheless, he cannot easily be fitted into any school of poets, despite his acquaintance with Salmon Macrin, Bèze, Saint-Gelais, Etienne Dolet, and others. Rather, it is his humanist colleagues from Sainte-Barbe, many of whom were later to be found at the Collège de Guyenne, who probably provided Buchanan with his principal source of inspiration.

Unfortunately, although Buchanan must have produced a number of Latin compositions during his days at Sainte-Barbe, few of them have survived, and what has reached us has, in all likelihood, been considerably revised at a later stage. With this reservation in mind, *Elegy* 1, 'Quam misera sit conditio docentium literas humaniores Lutetiae', seems on balance to apply best to the end of Buchanan's teaching period in the Paris college.[4] As far as his other extant poetic compositions are concerned, it is impossible to attribute any of them with a reasonable degree of certainty to this early period, although the 'Adieu aux Muses' motif contained in the first Elegy implies that he was spending a significant amount of time on poetic compositions, juvenilia which he must later have consigned to oblivion.

If Buchanan did give up poetry at this time, his 'saeva indignatio' after returning to Scotland soon impelled him to take up his pen once more. The 'Somnium', which was composed in the course of 1535 while he was still resident tutor with Gilbert Kennedy, is loosely based on William Dunbar's poem 'How Dunbar was Desyrit to be ane Fryer'. Some time later, this paraphrase caused offence with the Franciscans so that they started to spread abroad rumours about Buchanan's orthodoxy which eventually reached the ears of the King, Buchanan's new patron. However, James, far from censuring his tutor's conduct, actually encouraged him to write an even more biting satire, and so, probably at some time in 1536, Buchanan produced the 'Palinodes' (*Fratres fraterrimi* 35 and 36). Although he claims that their meaning is ambiguous, it would be a very dull mind that was taken in by this apparent recantation. This was not sufficient for the King, who eventually commissioned the *Franciscanus*, a poem 'de vita, moribus et institutis' of the Franciscans. Quite what state it was in when James received it is difficult to assess, although it probably ended as it does now with the story of William Lang, James's Franciscan confessor, and the Dysart exorcism. This incident happened in 1538, and provides a convenient date to pinpoint the time of composition of the *Franciscanus*.[5]

Apart from these satirical works, Buchanan began to assume in Scotland some of the functions of a court poet, and his position obviously put him in contact with a number of influential people. For example, he was acquainted with Gavin Dunbar, the Archbishop of Glasgow (*Epigrams* I.43) as well as with Sir Adam Otterburne, who handled certain diplomatic negotiations with England and in his spare time wrote poetry, now no longer extant. *Epigrams* II.16 is addressed to him and was probably written before 1538, since he was arrested at Dumbarton in that year. *Epigrams* II.15 must date from just before that time as II.16 is Buchanan's answer to a charge that he had plagiarised Otterburne in II.15. *Epigrams* II.2, 3 and 4 on the death of James's first wife, Madeleine de Valois, and probably *Epigrams* II.1, an epitaph to James IV, mark Buchanan's other essays at court poetry, and may form only a small part of his output at this time. On reaching England in 1539, the Scottish poet tried to curry favour by his verse with Thomas Cromwell (*Miscellany* 13) in an appeal for patronage:

> Illius haud duro munuscula suscipe vultu
> Mente tuus tota qui cupit esse cliens;
> Qui vagus exul inops terra iactatur et unda
> Per mala quae fallax omnia mundus habet;

but his cry seems to have fallen on deaf ears. A similar response met *Miscellany* 15, addressed to Henry VIII, and the original version of *Fratres fraterrimi* 5 which was at first also intended for the English king.[6]

Buchanan's return to France in 1539 and subsequent rediscovery of many of his friends and colleagues in Bordeaux acted as a considerable stimulus to his poetic output. One of the duties of the teachers at the Collège de Guyenne was the annual composition of a Latin play in which the students of the school acted. Montaigne himself later boasted: 'j'ai soustenu les premiers personnages és tragedies latines de Bucanan, de Guérente et de Muret, qui se représentèrent en notre collège de Guyenne avec dignité.'[7] Buchanan had already made a preliminary sortie into the field of drama in his Latin translation of the *Medea*, which he no doubt revised for performance by the students of the Collège de Guyenne.[8] Vascosan's first edition of 1544 bears at the end the legend 'Acta fuit Burdegalae, Anno M.D.XLIII', and the other tragedies, *Alcestis*, *Baptistes*, and *Jephthes*, were all written at this time with the same intention.

Bordeaux also saw the composition of many of Buchanan's longer non-dramatic works. Shortly after arriving at the Collège de Guyenne, the Scottish poet was entrusted with the task of writing a poem of welcome to the Emperor Charles V, who had made his entry into Bordeaux on 1 December 1539 (*Silvae* 1); and *Silvae* 2, a bucolic lament on the absence of Ptolomée de la Taste, probably dates from a few years later. Of the Elegies, the 'Maiae Calendae', with its reference in line 102 to the 'Vasconis uva', dates from this period, as does the mock encomiastic 'Pro lena', addressed to the Bordeaux *conseiller* Briand de Vallée, who died in 1544. *Elegy 5*, written for François Olivier on behalf of the Collège de Guyenne, and the accompanying *Miscellany* 4 probably date from 1545. Other semi-official poems from the Bordeaux sojourn are *Epigrams* I.7 and 8 on the pine tree planted in the college courtyard, and *Miscellany* 9, to the youth of Bordeaux. Personal poems addressed to people living in Bordeaux and the South-West include *Hendecasyllables* 9, *Epigrams* I.49 (to J. C. Scaliger), *Epigrams* I.11 and 50 (to Marguerite de Navarre), and *Epigrams* II.5, 17 and 19 (all about prominent Bordelais).

Despite a more cautious attitude than in Scotland to the expression of his religious views, Buchanan wrote several satirical compositions on certain aspects of the Church. *Fratres fraterrimi* 22, 'De monachis S. Antonii' refers to a monastery near Bordeaux, while *Fratres fraterrimi* 26 and 27 seem to be about the Dominican Goynelli who was temporarily in charge of the Collège de Guyenne before Buchanan's arrival there. *Fratres fraterrimi* 32, 'In Codrum', probably dates from this time as the last two lines were reported to have been found in a book of Buchanan's verse in about 1548.[9] Other poems likely to have originated during this period are *Fratres fraterrimi* 6 ('Pistoris et pictoris dialogismus'), as well as 3, 7, and 8 against the cult of images; *Fratres* 19, 22, and 25 on the morals of the clergy; and *Fratres* 20, 21, and 24 against one particular Franciscan with the Horatian sobriquet Pantalabus (cf. Horace, *Satires* 1.8.11 and 2.1.22). To the years in Paris, on the other hand, very little in the way of verse composition can be attributed with the exception of *Elegy* 4, on his illness, and possibly *Epigrams* I.2 and 3 addressed to Jean du Bellay and Charles de Marillac, Bishop of Vienne. Marillac was the French ambassador in London from 1538 till 1542, and may have afforded some assistance to Buchanan in 1539 while he was in the English capital. The opening lines of *Silvae* 4, the epithalamium for Mary Stuart, may also have been written at this time, but intended for Henri de Navarre.[10]

Buchanan's shorter poems during this period are altogether typical of the epigrams which flowed from the pens of many contemporary humanists and poets, in both Latin and French. However, in his tragedies and extended satires, Buchanan was well ahead of his times, providing, in the latter case at least, models which were still being followed in the seventeenth century.[11]

Satire

Both France and Scotland enjoyed a flourishing strain of satire in the first half of the sixteenth century, although the position of the satirist could be perilous in either country, as is illustrated by the lives of Clément Marot and of Buchanan himself. In France, the satirical epigram, often with a Martialian sting in the tail, was a very popular verse form, especially amongst the Neo-latin poets, although Marot used the form to good effect in the vernacular.[12] As far as religious satire was concerned, France also witnessed a vigorous popular tradition of anti-Franciscan feeling, which was given literary expression in such works as the *Libellus mercatorum* of 1534, the *Alcoran des cordeliers*, and a number of stories in the *Cent nouvelles nouvelles* and the *Heptaméron*, while in the realm of poetry, Clément Marot, again, produced the occasional indictment of the Greyfriars' conduct. The *livres de colportage* also formed a useful popular means of propaganda for anyone with an axe to grind against the Franciscans, while Erasmus' *Encomium Moriae* of 1511 provided an excellent example of Lucianic prose satire. This work contains a number of criticisms which Buchanan was to level at the members of the mendicant order, such as their abuse of confession and indulgences, and the nature of their sermons. It is, however, noteworthy that these longer works are predominantly prose writings. Buchanan is one of the first poets in France to write extended verse satire whose stylistic roots are firmly set in the poetry of Juvenal.

Nevertheless, the influence of Scottish satirical poets on Buchanan in the 1530s should not be disregarded. The early decades of the sixteenth century were particularly fertile ones for Scottish poetry, thanks to the combination of a strong native tradition with classical and foreign influences, and a helpful amount of royal patronage. This is exemplified in the energetic and varied poetry of William Dunbar, whose outspoken satires obviously impressed the young Buchanan.[13] The tradition was carried on in the vernacular by Sir David Lindsay, whose morality play, *Ane Satyre of the Thrie Estaits*, must have been written during Buchanan's final sojourn in Scotland before his exile. Satire, and particularly religious satire, was very much in the air.

Buchanan had already tried his hand at satire in France in the shape of *Elegy* 1 on the lot of the humanities teacher in Paris, although this is a somewhat gentler composition than the Scottish satires were to be. The poem is an apparently personal account of the hardships which beset the poet/teacher in Paris, and falls easily into three sections. The first of these, lines 1–30, describes in general terms the frustrations, inconveniences, and unhealthiness of the poet's life compared with other professions; section two, lines 31–84, gives an account of the daily routine of the schoolteacher and the problems with which he has to deal; and the final section returns to the subject of the poet, this time dwelling on his traditional poverty and misfortune, before ending as the elegy had begun by bidding the Muses farewell. Unity of theme is only preserved provided that we recognise a total identity between poet and teacher, indicated in line 92, 'sive poema canis, sive poema doces'; and when du Bellay came to translate this poem, he found it necessary to omit the central section and replace it with further details concerning the poet's life. However, Buchanan no doubt revised the poem before it was first printed in 1567, and we cannot be sure of the form of the poem which du Bellay translated. The Bibliothèque Nationale MS latin 8140 in which *Elegy* 1 appears has a large number of variants for the first and third sections, but relatively few for the middle one, possibly indicating different dates of composition.[14] The poem has generally been considered to be an extremely personal statement of disillusionment with both poetry and college teaching, and yet, perhaps more than in Buchanan's later works, it is composed of a number of artfully connected common-places and classical tags.[15] Buchanan's skill in this poem is to blend these elements together to form a harmonious whole, which is marked by its general urbanity of content and expression.

Such is Buchanan in gentle mood. In his Franciscan satires, on the other hand, his attacks became increasingly stinging, culminating in the *Franciscanus*,. where he spares no aspect of the Greyfriars' conduct. Although before the Portuguese Inquisition Buchanan claimed of the 'Somnium' (*Fratres fraterrimi* 34), 'I translated an old epigram written in Scots into Latin verse, in order to avenge myself on the Franciscans', even a superficial comparison between the 'Somnium' and Dunbar's original piece is sufficient to demonstrate that Buchanan's poem is much more than just a translation. A comparison of the two poems will serve to highlight Buchanan's poetic and satirical techniques.[16]

> This hinder nycht befoir the dawing cleir,
> Me thocht Sanct Francis did to me appeir,
>   With ane religiouss abbeit in his hand,
>   And said, 'In this go cleith the my serwand;
> Reffuss the warld, for thow mon be a freir.'   5
>
> With him and with his abbeit bayth I skarrit,
> Lyk to ane man that with a gaist wes marrit:
>   Me thocht on bed he layid it me abone,
>   Bot on the flure delyuerly and sone
> I lap thairfra, and nevir wald cum nar it.   10
>
> Quoth he, 'Quhy skarris thow with this holy weid?
> Cleith the thairin, for weir it thow most neid;
>   Thow, that hes lang done Venus lawis teiche,
>   Sall now be freir, and in this abbeit preiche;
> Delay it nocht, it mon be done but dreid.'   15

Quod I, 'Sanct Francis, loving be the till,
And thankit mot thow be of thy gude will
  To me, that of thy clayis ar so kynd;
  Bot thame to weir it nevir come in my mynd;
Sweit Confessour, thow tak it nocht in ill.   20

In haly legendis haif I hard allevin,
Ma sanctis of bischoppis, nor freiris, be sic sevin;
  Off full few freiris that hes bene sanctis I reid;
  Quhairfoir ga bring to me ane bischopis weid,
Gife evir thow wald my saule zeid vnto Hevin.   25

My brethir oft hes maid the supplicationis,
Be epistillis, sermonis, and relationis,
  To tak this abyte, bot ay thow did postpone;
  But ony process, cum on thairfoir annone,
All sircumstance put by and excusationis.   30

Gif evir my fortoun wes to be a freir,
The dait thairof is past full mony a zeir;
  For into every lusty toun and place
  Off all Yngland, from Berwick to Kalice,
I haif in to thy habeit maid gud cheir.   35

In freiris weid full fairly haif I fleichit,
In it haif I in pulpet gon and preichit
  In Derntoun kirk, and eik in Canterberry;
  In it I past at Dover our the ferry
Throw Piccardy, and thair the peple teichit.   40

Als lang as I did beir the freiris style,
In me, God wait, wes mony wrink and wyle;
  In me wes falset with every wicht to flatter,
  Quhilk mycht be flemit with na haly watter;
I wes ay reddy all men to begyle.'   45

This freir that did Sanct Francis thair appeir,
Ane feind he wes in liknes of ane freir;
  He vaniest away with stynk and fyrie smowk;
  With him me thocht all the housend he towk,
And I awoik as wy that wes in weir.   50

Mane sub auroram nitidae vicinia lucis
  Pallida venturo cum facit astra die,
Arctior irriguos somnus complectitur artus,
  Demulcens placido languida membra sinu,
Cum mihi Franciscus, nodosa cannabe cinctus,   5
  Astitit ante torum, stigmata nota gerens.
In manibus sacra vestis erat, cum fune galerus,
  Palla, fenestratus calceus, hasta, liber;
Et mihi subridens, 'Hanc protinus indue' dixit,
  'Et mea dehinc mundi transfuga castra subi.   10
Linque voluptates cum sollicitudine blandas,
  Vanaque continui gaudia plena metus.
Me duce, spes fragiles et inanes despice curas,
  Et superum recto tramite limen adi.'
Obstupui subita defixus imagine, donec   15
  Vix dedit hos tandem lingua coacta sonos.
'Pace' inquam, 'vestri liceat depromere verum
  Ordinis; haud humeris convenit ista meis.
Qui feret hanc vestem, fiat servire paratus:
  At mihi libertas illa paterna placet.   20
Qui feret hanc, ponat perfricta fronte ruborem:
  At non ingenuus nos sinit ista pudor.
Qui feret hanc, fallat, palpet, pro tempore fingat:
  At me simplicitas nudaque vita iuvat.
Nec me Phthiriasis, nec rancida cantio terret,   25
  Inque diem ignavae vivere more ferae:
Ostia nec circum magno mugire boatu,
  Si tamen his nugis aetheris aula patet.
Pervia sed raris sunt coeli regna cucullis,
  Vix Monachis illic creditur esse locus.   30
Mentior, aut peragra saxo fundata vetusto
  Delubra, et titulos per simulacra lege:
Multus honoratis fulgebit episcopus aris,
  Rara cucullato sternitur ara gregi.
Atque inter Monachos erit haec rarissima vestis.   35
  Induat hanc, si quis gaudeat esse miser.
Quod si tanta meae tangit te cura salutis,
  Vis mihi, vis animae consuluisse meae?
Quilibet hac alius mendicet veste superbus;
  At mihi da mitram, purpureamque togam.'   40

(Early in the morning at dawn when the approach of bright daylight makes the stars pale, on the point of daybreak, a deeper sleep swamped my limbs, caressing my languid body in its peaceful bosom, when Francis stood before my bed, wearing a knotted rope around his waist and bearing his well-known stigmata. There was a religious habit in his hands, a hood with a rope, a mantle, the holed shoe, a staff and a book. Smiling on me, he said: 'Put this on straightaway, come over from here to my camp, deserting the world. Leave behind pleasant delight along with anxiety, and empty joys which are full of constant fear. Under my leadership, despise fragile hopes and empty worries, and approach the gateway of the gods on the straight and narrow path.' I was amazed and astonished by the sudden apparition, until at last I forced my tongue to give forth these sounds: 'By your leave, allow me to bring out the truth about your order. This garment does not suit my shoulders. Whoever wears this, let him be prepared to be a slave; but I like my ancestral freedom. Whoever wears this, let him put on a bold face and cast off modesty; but a noble sense of shame does not allow me to do that. Whoever wears this, let him deceive, flatter, and feign to suit circumstances; but I like simplicity and a life unadorned. I am neither alarmed by the prospect of being lousy, nor the nauseous chanting, and living for the day like an ignoble beast, or groaning in a loud bellow outside doorways, but only if the heavenly courts lie open by such nonsense. But the kingdom of heaven is accessible to few cowls, and there is thought to be scarcely any place for friars. Either I am lying, or if you wander through churches built with ancient stone, and read the inscriptions on the statues, many a bishop will shine out among the honoured monuments, but rare is the monument set up for the hooded flock. And this habit will be very rare among the friars. Let anyone who delights in being wretched wear this. But if you are affected with so much sollicitude for my salvation, do you want to look after me and my soul? Let anyone else proudly beg in this habit; but give me a bishop's mitre and purple cassock.')

In the first place, it will be noted that Buchanan and Dunbar concentrate on very different aspects of the situation. For example, Dunbar sets the scene in one line, 'This hinder nycht befoir the dawing cleir', which Buchanan expands into the first four lines of his poem, managing to include an allusion to Cicero's 'Somnium Scipionis' ('arctior quam solebat somnus complexus est' from *Republic* 6.10), which in turn is extended to produce the sensual image of line 4. Similarly, lines 2–3 of Dunbar's poem are dealt with in four lines of the 'Somnium' (lines 5–8) in which we are regaled with a description of the saint and his 'religiouss abbeit'; and Dunbar, lines 4–5, in which the poet is told to put on the clothes and become a friar, in the 'Somnium' become lines 9–14 (where the metaphor 'mundi transfuga' is taken from Lucan 8.335). Thus, in a forty-line translation, Buchanan has devoted fourteen lines to Dunbar's first stanza, incorporating a few details from stanza three. Lines 15–16 of the 'Somnium' express the surprise of the second and third stanzas of Dunbar's poem and introduce the poet's reply to Saint Francis, in which the satire of the poem is contained, and it is at this point that Buchanan virtually forgets his model. In a series of parallel couplets (lines 19–24) in which the vices of the Franciscans are expressed concisely as general principles followed by an antithetical statement emphatically rejecting them, Buchanan attacks their servility, shamelessness, and deceit. The sense of crescendo is heightened by the anaphora of

'Qui feret hanc' in lines 19, 21, and 23, and the succession of verbs in line 23, 'Qui feret hanc, fallat, palpet, pro tempore fingat'. (In these lines too, Buchanan slips in a phrase in line 20 based on Tibullus 2.4.2, 'iam mihi, libertas illa paterna, vale'.) Buchanan's final criticisms are contained in lines 25–8 where, in a device common to many satirists including Juvenal, he reduces the Franciscans to the level of animals. Line 26 contains the only simile of the poem, 'ignavae vivere more ferae'. Buchanan's final topic, dealt with in twelve lines, is based on the fifth stanza of Dunbar's poem, where the poet points out that there are more saints who were originally bishops than friars (lines 29–40). In an elegant piece of rhetoric, Buchanan makes this the final *pointe* of his poem, building up to it in a series of rhetorical questions (lines 31–2, 37–8), antitheses (lines 33–4), oxymoron ('si quis gaudeat esse miser'), and irony.

Thus, the 'Somnium' is very far from being a mere translation. It uses the ideas of the first and fifth stanzas of Dunbar's poem, one or two details from the remaining eight verses, but for the rest, it is an original piece of work. This comparison serves to illustrate two key concepts of Renaissance poetry: the Erasmian idea of *copia*, and the sixteenth-century attitude towards original-ity.[17] In the *De duplici verborum ac rerum copia*, first printed in Paris in 1512, Erasmus points out that any concept can either be expressed succinctly or at length. Either method is valid, but the second way when used properly has the advantage of avoiding tautology and produces variety in a work. *Copia* can be achieved in two ways: by variety of verbal expression through such devices as synonymy, enallage, metaphor; and variety of thought, by piling up *exempla*, similes, and the like. In order to achieve this in writing, the potential author was to read every kind of literature, notebook in hand, and *exempla*, anecdotes, and other quotations were to be entered under appropriate headings. It was this principle which guided humanist writing for much of the sixteenth century, and which is apparent in the 'Somnium'. As far as orig-inality is concerned, one of the keys seems to lie in eclecticism. Buchanan was not content to produce a straightforward translation of Dunbar's poem. He is extremely careful in the choice of those elements which he uses to avoid any details which would detract from the tightly-knit structure of his poem. The very details which Dunbar lingers over, like the interchange between poet and ghost in the third and fourth stanzas, and which give the Scottish poem much of its vitality, are avoided by Buchanan, whose dialogue is nothing if not rhetorical. At the same time, Buchanan introduces elements from classical writers. We have already noted the Ciceronian tag in line 3, which acts to establish the poem's literary pedigree, as well as other tags in lines 10, 20, and 21, where the expression 'ponat perfricta fronte ruborem' is taken from Martial 11.27.7. This amalgam of so many diverse elements ensures that the result is wholly novel.

One factor which provides the 'Somnium' with much of its interest is the dramatisation of a central event (the encounter with Saint Francis) which serves as a vehicle for satire but which at the same time maintains the reader's attention on its own merits. When Buchanan came to write the 'Palinodiae', he would exploit this and other satirical techniques which he had used in the 'Somnium'.

These two poems are almost certainly intended to form a whole, with *Fratres fraterrimi* 35 acting as an introduction to the recantation proper, *Fratres fraterrimi* 36.[18] In the first poem, Buchanan recounts a dream in which he ascends to heaven to appear before a court composed of Franciscans, with Saint Francis himself acting as judge. His crime— revealing to the public what the Franciscans get up to—is punished by flogging, until the poet promises to recant. There then follows, in the second poem, the palinode in which the poet, after describing the Greyfriars' way of life 'so ambiguously in word and meaning that the reader could easily interpret it in either one of two ways',[19] goes on to relate how, on one occasion, Saint Francis himself assuaged his sexual lusts. The satire ends with the poet's waking up from his sleep.

The narrative framework in the 'Palinodiae' has thus been extended, and much of the effect of the poems is derived from the considerable elements of parody present in them. So, the central incident of the first poem—the dream in which Buchanan is put on trial and punished by the Franciscans—is closely based on Saint Jerome's account in his *Letters* (22.30) of a vision in which he was tried and condemned by God to be flogged for his erudition and scorn for the literary style of the Christian writers. Similarly, the wholly sacrilegious story about Saint Francis in *Fratres fraterrimi* 36 is a parody of an event in the saint's life related in the *Golden Legend*.[20] The vast gap between the aims of the original stories—the self-denigration of Saint Jerome and the glorification of Saint Francis—and the purpose to which Buchanan puts his adaptations makes the satire all the more effective because of its startling irreverence. In recognising the original contexts (as Buchanan must have intended), the reader enters into a kind of complicity with the satirist.[21]

This sense of complicity between poet and reader is further strengthened by the use of stylistic parody, a device common to most satirists including one of Buchanan's principal models, Juvenal. Although the 'Palinodiae' differ greatly from Juvenal in spirit, with their strong ingredients of exuberant fantasy, Buchanan, in common with the Roman poet, achieves comic results by parodying the epic style, with Virgil, of course, providing many of the basic elements. For example, the first four lines of the poem, with their grandiloquent periphrases, lead on in lines 5–6 to an impreca- tion, 'Fas mihi sit mundi reserare arcana latentis,/Fas mihi sit vera pandere visa fide', obviously taken from the *Aeneid* 6.266–7:

> sit mihi fas audita loqui, sit numine vestro
> pandere res alta terra et caligine mersas.

(A similar device had been used by Juvenal in *Satires* 4.34.) Buchanan maintains this process throughout the poem, producing all the characteristics of the epic style. In his early poetry, Buchanan uses the extended simile very rarely, and in most cases where it is found, the intention is ironic. This is certainly true of the 'Palinodiae', in which we have already noted the comparison with Saint Jerome in lines 63–4 of the first poem. This is immediately followed by a mythological comparison concerning Marsyas (probably based on Ovid, *Metamorphoses* 6.387):

> Sic cute direpta Satyrum videre Calaenae,
> Tibia cum blandae est victa canore lyrae.

Comparison with animals is a useful device in the satirist's repertoire, and Buchanan includes a number of implicit examples, such as lines 23–4:

> Omnibus unus erat cinctus, color omnibus unus,
> Qui solet esse asinis anseribusque feris.

Mythological allusions have an important role in the pastiche of the grand style, and Buchanan has no shortage of these, referring to Pegasus (line 2), the battle of the gods and giants (line 7), Prometheus (line 10), Tantalus (lines 11–12), Marsyas (lines 65–6), and many others. In most cases, he does not refer directly to them, but makes frequent use of periphrases, to heighten the recondite nature of the allusions, and hence to increase the comic effect. The word order of the poem also parodies the grand style at times, with lines such as the climactic:

> Sacra fero, miranda cano, memoranda revolvo   (l. 13)

in which the parallelism and gradual lengthening of the predicate of the three verbs produces a resounding effect; the carefully balanced

> Omnibus unus erat cinctus, color omnibus unus   (l. 23)

with its chiasmus; and skilful use of word combinations, assonance, and alliteration, in many cases simply for the sheer joy of the sonorities produced, as in lines 55–6:

> Alternantque vices, et acerbant verbera verbis,
> Verba oculis, oculos nutibus atque minis.

The lessons which Buchanan had learnt in writing the 'Somnium' and the 'Palinodiae' were put to good use in the final extended satire against the Franciscans, the *Franciscanus*.[22] In this work, we are dealing with a satire whose form and style are undoubtedly Juvenalian, even though Buchanan's own poetic individuality shines through distinctly. The *dispositio* of the poem, with its loose connections and transitions, rhetorical content, and dramatic form, is certainly derived from Juvenal, as is the poem's opening. The use of a series of questions addressed to a friend in lines 1–8 is reminiscent of the beginning of Juvenal's ninth satire, lines 1–11. From this starting point, Buchanan goes on to compose a satire which, in its final form, was longer and fuller than any of Juvenal's. Just as Juvenal's style owed a considerable debt to the schools of rhetoric, so indirectly the same can be said of Buchanan's.[23] The *Franciscanus* can be divided up into the traditional *exordium* (lines 1–72) where the subject is introduced, as we have noted, by a series of questions which are later resolved; *narratio* (lines 73–267), a general statement about the degeneracy of the Franciscans along with specific examples of this; *confirmatio* (lines 268–928), provided by the self-condemnation of the opposition, and including a number of historical instances of their deceit; and *peroratio* (lines 929–36), summing up the burden of the poem and returning the reader to the original starting point, the conversation between the poet and his friend.

The poem is very lengthy (half as long again as Juvenal's sixth satire), yet Buchanan manages to maintain our interest by the variety of speakers and styles, the introduction of anecdotal material, and the occasional lyrical passage. In matters of style, he employs a number of rhetorical tropes and figures favoured by Juvenal, whose conversational tone is derived to a large extent from his use of dialogue, interrogation, hyperbole, exclamation, apostrophe, antithesis, anaphora, etc. Juvenal also tends to provide an abundance of illustrative *exampla* and to express the same thought in different ways for the sake of emphasis. In his vocabulary, he includes a large number of Greek words, diminutives, and rather prosaic expressions like 'adde quod', 'quod superest', and 'quod cum ita sit'. Buchanan too makes extensive use of these devices, for example dialogue (the opening of the *Franciscanus*), interrogation (lines 324–5, 595–6), hyperbole (lines 702–3), exclamation (lines 757–8, 902), repetition (lines 197, 247–50, 379–80, 886–7), enumeration (lines 94–101, 213–16, 227, 677–9). In matters of vocabulary, he uses a significantly larger percentage of Greek words in the *Franciscanus* than in any of his other poetry, ranging from Greek expressions (line 324 ἐς κόρακας, line 629 ταῦτ' ἀπαμειβόμενος) and other words not normally found in classical Latin (*empusa* line 115, *soloecus* line 630, *cacodaemon* lines 640, 848, 873, *rhapsodia* line 657) to slightly less unusual borrowings (*danista* line 316, *gnoma* line 619, *sophia* line 273). Diminutives too are common, for example *cerebellum* line 220, *paterculum* line 124, *pinguiculus* lines 136, 485, *rancidulus* line 245, along with prosaic expressions like 'adde quod' (line 455), 'adiice praeterea' (line 157). Thus, there are important affinities between Buchanan's style and vocabulary in the *Franciscanus* and Juvenal's satires.

Despite these points of similarity, the reader does not gain the impression of being presented with a pastiche of Juvenal. In the first place, the difference in tone between the Roman poet and Buchanan is very great. Juvenal's 'saeva indignatio' has little place for true humour; Buchanan, on the other hand, obviously takes pleasure in his writing, and humour is encountered throughout the poem. His style, too, has a personal aspect. For example, the imagery of the poem does much to set its tone and create an atmosphere of cunning deceit. Hunting metaphors abound, almost forming a leit-motif, for example:

Tandem captatum trahat in sua retia piscem	(l. 116)
. . . et in laqueos viduas trahat	(l. 229)
. . . haec fatuo tenduntur retia vulgo;[24]	(l. 648)

and battle metaphors, highlighting the constant opposition between the friars and the laity, occur frequently, for example:

Haec thalami clausas frangebat machina portas	(l. 799)
Interea vacuos valido tu Marte penates Oppugna. . . .[25]	(ll. 544–5)

The light/darkness imagery as applied to human knowledge is also common, and emphasises the obscurantism of the Franciscans, while at the same time evoking a dark, brooding atmosphere, for example, line 230 'involvatque orbem tenebris', and lines 28–9, 74, 81, 189, 416, and 753. Other important images are taken from the animal world (lines 52, 208, 265, 761, 928), nautical terms, medicine, agriculture, and architecture. Similes are not frequent, with only four extended ones, and as in the 'Palinodiae', their intention is ironic rather than serious. One concerns a ship in a storm (lines 12–14) and, placed in the mouth of the would-be Franciscan, is deliberately pretentious; a mythological image about Tages used by Eubulus is heavily ironic (lines 235–7); while the two others are put into the mouth of the old Franciscan, and are intentionally pompous, see lines 301–3 and 284–5:

> Nam, ceu Tiresias Ithacum, Priameius heros
> Magnum Anchisiaden iterumque iterumque monebat. . . .

Periphrasis is also used ironically a number of times, to show the speaker's pompous character, as when the old Franciscan says:

> Iam prope decurso spatio spectare propinquam
> Fata iubent metam, iam quinquagesima messis
> Sub calido semper placide transacta cucullo,
> Liberat officiis vitae.   (ll. 279–82)

As in earlier poems, Buchanan's word order is carefully balanced and he manages to produce some pleasing effects, frequently favouring the tripartite sentence, for example:

> . . . iam de balatrone modestus,
> De lenone pudens, et de latrone severus   (ll. 214–15)

where the parallelism of the three examples emphasises the idea of change. Elsewhere, a kind of double chiasmus is employed:

> Et pede tange pedem, dextram dextra, oribus ora,   (l. 376)

and even in less structurally formal periods, word order and balance are always well handled, so that the verses flow smoothly at all times.[26] The combination of word order and repetition are sufficient to achieve humorous effects at times, for example in lines 247–50:

> Conceptis verbis aperire et claudere portas,
> Conceptis verbis de somno surgere, mensam
> Ponere, adire, referre, iubere, orare, salutem
> Dicere, conceptis urinam reddere verbis.

Similarly, Buchanan takes great care with the sonorities of his poem, creating different effects by alliteration and variations in the rhythm of the hexameters.

On the question of tags, Buchanan borrows expressions from a host of classical authors, although the percentage of Juvenalian echoes in the *Franciscanus* as compared with his other poems is significantly higher. We have already noted the Juvenalian opening of the poem. Other expressions taken from the Roman satirist include 'rauci . . . circi' (line 5, cf. Juvenal 8.59), 'huc omnes tanquam ad vivaria currunt' (line 93, cf. Juvenal 3.308), and 'inermis/Gingivas' (lines 270–1, cf. Juvenal 10.200), while the image concerning 'aconita' in line 183–4 is based on Juvenal 10.25–7. This kind of borrowing, along with the processes we have seen above, helps to establish the Juvenalian diction of the poem. However, Buchanan's delight in parody is seen in his borrowing whole lines from Virgil, compare line 602 with the identical line in *Aeneid* 9.525, 'Vos, o Calliope, precor, aspirate canenti', and lines 704–5:

> Dum Papa omnipotens Capitoli immobile saxum
> Accolet imperiumque Pater coleatus habebit

cleverly modelled on *Aeneid* 9.448–9.[27]

Despite important elements of parody, Buchanan's basic style had already begun to take shape in the early satirical poems, characterised by a reliance on the metaphor as the principal rhetorical trope, with similes tending to be used only for purposes of irony. Epithets play an important part in the overall tone of a poem, while word order is also used skilfully to achieve particular effects.

The last extended satire which Buchanan wrote before departing for Portugal, *Elegy* 3, the 'Pro lena', is very different from the committed anti-Franciscan poems. Addressed to Briand de Vallée, a highly respected *conseiller* in the Bordeaux Parliament from 1527 until 1544, the year of his death, it is the most original in conception of Buchanan's Bordeaux compositions. Briand de Vallée probably had leanings towards the reformed Church, and attempted in 1539 to institute monthly lectures on Saint Paul at the Collège de Guyenne. If he shared Saint Paul's somewhat austere views on sexual morality, Buchanan may well be teasing him for this in the 'Pro lena'.

The poem is, of course, a mock encomium, containing fulsome praise of the procuress and her profession, and is firmly rooted in the Lucianic tradition of satire. Buchanan probably has Lucian's 'De parasitu' in mind, as well as Erasmus' *Encomium Moriae*, but the poem which he produces is very distinctly his own work and, dedicated to a lawyer, it exploits many of the rhetorical devices of the profession. The poem begins on a note of incredulity: surely Vallius is not becoming opposed to bawds. He cannot be so hard-hearted, and besides, he too has made use of their services in the past. Buchanan then sets about proving his case, first by mentioning a number of bawds who were revered as goddesses and heroines (lines 33–44), then by mentioning bawds who have found favour with the gods, including the Muses (lines 57–76). He goes on to attack chastity because it leads to depopulation, and claims that a chaste wife is a dull one. He praises the pleasures of sex and points out that Vallius himself has had occasion to use the services of the *lena*. What will happen to the young men, foreign visitors, friars, and monks if all the brothels are closed? Besides, the forbidden fruit is always the most enjoyable, and conjugal sex becomes boring. The last part of the poem is taken up with *ad hominem* arguments. It is hypocritical to consider a vice something which, when it was of service, was accepted freely. The poem ends with an imaginary plea made by all the *lenae* and prostitutes whose services Vallius has enjoyed. Thus, although the poem is long, Buchanan maintains the reader's attention by the constant shifts in perspective, the alternation between expository argument and *exempla*, and the switch from generalised to personalised *confirmationes*.

As in his other satirical works, the highly rhetorical, parodistic style of the 'Pro lena' presents a considerable contrast with the subject matter, thus providing the poem with much of its humour. However, Buchanan goes even further than in his previous satires in the accumulation of details and extravagant use of rhetoric to produce a mock epic tone. This is illustrated by lines 73–100:

> Respice Pieridas, Valli, tua numina, Musas;
> 　Virgo in virgineo vix erit ulla choro.
> Orphea mulcentem silvas agnoscit et amnes　　　　　　　75
> 　Calliope genetrix, Uranieque Linum.
> Furta tegens uterus reliquas facit esse pudicas.
> 　Quae casta est? sterilis, vel sine teste parens.
> Nec taedis super astra fides servata maritis,
> 　Nec patrem appellas ipse, Gradive, Iovem.　　　　　　80
> Forte pudicitiae seclis fuit ampla vetustis
> 　Gloria; sed titulo gloria sola tenus.
> Quam nunc utilitas, mos, consensusque recusat
> 　Publicus, haud falso si licet ore loqui.
> Cum mare, cum tellus homines populetur et ignis,　　　85
> 　Tot pereant morbo, tot fera bella necent,
> Cumque hominum in peius solertia callida semper
> 　Inveniat caussas in sua fata novas,
> Tun' prohibere potes Veneris commercia? lenas
> 　Si tollis, Veneris commoda quanta vetas?　　　　　　90
> Tun' prohibere audes Veneris commercia, sola
> 　Humanum poterunt quae reparare genus?
> Nam neque Partheniis nunc quercubus editur Arcas,
> 　Curetes pluvio nec geniti imbre cadunt;
> Nec gravida fratres funduntur nube bimembres,　　　　95
> 　Nec vivunt Pyrrhae saxa animata manu;
> Myrmonidas nusquam gignit formica, nec usquam
> 　Ficta Prometheo spirat imago luto.
> Una quidem superest, superest ars unica, Valli,
> 　Quae reparat nostrum continuatque genus.　　　　　100

(Consider the Pierian Muses, your own deities, Vallée. There will hardly be a single maiden in the maidenly band. Calliope acknowledges Orpheus, as he charms the woods and streams, as his mother, and Urania does the same with Linus. A womb hiding secret loves makes the others seem virtuous. Who is chaste? a barren woman or one whose motherhood is unwitnessed. Nor in heaven is Fidelity in marriage preserved by husbands, and Mars, you yourself do not call Jupiter your father. Perhaps there was great glory in chastity in ancient times. Now it is a glory in name only. Expediency, custom, and public opinion refuse it now, if I may be permitted to speak the truth. Since the sea, the land, and fire devastate men, and so many perish from sickness, and fierce wars slaughter so many, and since men's cunning expertise for evil always finds new occasions for their destruction, can you put a stop to Venus's trade? If you remove the procuresses, how many of Venus's services are you forbidding? Do you dare put a stop to Venus's trade, which alone will be able to renew mankind? For nowadays, the Arcadian is not produced from oak-trees on Mount Parthenios, the Curetes do not fall born from rain showers; the twin-shaped brethren are not poured forth from pregnant cloud, and stones do not come to life from Pyrrha's hand; nowhere does an ant bring forth Myrmidons, nor is there anywhere breath in models made from Promethean mud. One art and one alone is left, Vallée, to renew and continue our race.)

Irreverence is again the hallmark of this section, where even the Muses are not immune from ribaldry. The exuberance of these lines is produced to a large extent by enumeration used with an almost Rabelaisian abundance (lines 75–6, 85–6, 93–8); repetition (lines 86, 89–91, 99); apostrophe (lines 33, 99); rhetorical questions (lines 78, 89–92); and peri-phrasis, often found amongst the copious allusions to mythological figures (lines 89–91, 95).

One facet of the poem's playful erudition is seen in the number of allusions to classical authors which it contains. These are either in the form of verbal reminiscences, or are presented as frequently oblique references to mythological and historical legends. The 'querna corona' of line 36 comes from Ovid, *Tristia* 3.1.36, and is a reference to a crown given to Augustus as saviour of his citizens. The ironical 'quod si parva licet magnis componere' (line 57) is used twice by Virgil (*Georgics* 4.176 and *Eclogues* 1.23), while the expression in lines 115–16 is taken from Horace, *Satires* 1.10.7, 'non satis est risu diducere rictum/auditoris'. The two *adynata* at the opening of the poem in lines 3–4,

> Idem posse suos in fontes flumina labi
> Credat, et aversis astra redire rotis

are probably based on Ovid, *Tristia* 1.8.1, but these are quite common themes. The inexpressibility *topos* of lines 163–4,

> Quosque foret longe numerare molestius, undae
> Quam Libycae fluctus si numerare velis,

may be derived from Virgil, *Georgics* 2.104 sqq., although this too is a common concept in classical poetry. Mythological and historical allusions in the 'Pro lena' either refer to general attributes of gods and heroes, or to specific events. Of the first kind are lines 107–8,

> Iuppiter et Bacchus succurret munere lenae,
> Atque geret partes Mars et Apollo viri,

and the list of Roman deities concerned with marriage (lines 59–76), which is taken almost exclusively from Saint Augustine's *Civitas Dei*, 6.9 and 4.8. Of the second kind are the examples of spontaneous generation no longer to be encountered, lines 93–8, or the instances of divine infidelity in lines

157–62. Historical allusions are found in lines 109–12 which are derived, in the case of the Alexander *exemplum*, from Plutarch, *Alexander* 2.4, and in the case of Scipio from Livy 26.19 (who also mentions Alexander), and Aulus Gellius 6.1.

Buchanan successfully combines all these ingredients of erudition, hyperbolic style, and rhetoric to form a poem whose principal aim is entertainment. Of all the extended poems written in the 1540s, this is certainly the most original in its spirit and conception, if one of the most derivative in terms of its constituent elements. It helps to underline one of the basic principles of Neo-latin poetry, that it is not novelty of verbal expression or choice of imagery that is important, but the skilful combination of these elements, which are all subservient to the idea inspiring the poem.

Buchanan was virtually the only writer in France in the first half of the sixteenth century to approach the genre of extended verse satire, either in the Juvenalian or the Lucianic mould. Even the Pléiade failed to produce any formal satires, and it was not until the end of the century and the advent of Vauquelin de la Fresnaye and, more importantly, of Mathurin Régnier that the genre really began to develop; and even then, much of the fiery commitment of the young Buchanan is missing. But for many decades, Buchanan's example stood out as one of the only contemporary models in this field.

Occasional Verse and Epigrams

If Buchanan's satirical verse was to be an enduring model for later generations of poets, this is less true of his other early works, despite the fact that they are all competent and include some very beautiful poems. The Scottish humanist's associations with the Collège de Guyenne meant that a number of official compositions were required of him (for example *Silvae* 1, *Elegy* 5, *Miscellany* 4), while *Elegy* 2 is an altogether more lighthearted piece on the advent of spring in Aquitaine. Friendship played a vital part in Buchanan's life, and is the inspiration behind *Silvae* 2 and *Elegy* 4.

With the exception of *Miscellany* 4, these poems are all in dactylic metres. However, relatively early in the history of Neo-latin poetry in France, Buchanan also produced some compositions in lyric metres: *Fratres fraterrimi* 5, an alcaic poem originally addressed, as we have seen, to Henry VIII; *Miscellany* 9, a sapphic ode to the youth of Bordeaux; and the iambic poem *Epigrams* I.49 to J. C. Scaliger. The majority of the other poems dating from this period are epigrams, ranging from satires to epitaphs.

Although these poems are largely conventional in nature, they are marked by a certain wit which enables even the official verse to rise above the merely banal. *Silvae* 1, the address to the Holy Roman Emperor in the name of the Collège de Guyenne, is one of the most formal of all Buchanan's official and occasional pieces. Charles V entered Bordeaux on 1 December 1539, having requested and obtained permission from François Ier to pass through France on his way to Ghent, and he was received with due pomp in a number of French cities. Clément Marot, amongst others, would celebrate his arrival in Paris in his *Cantique* VIII 'sur la venue de l'Empereur en France', in which he principally stresses the peaceful concord between the Emperor and the French King. Buchanan's poem is part of the tradition of the panegyric, of which there are a number of examples in later Roman poetry, starting with the pseudo-Tibullan 'Panegyricus Messalae' (*Corpus tibullianum* 3.7), and including contributions by Statius (*Silvae* 5.2), Claudian, Apollinaris Sidonis, and the anonymous writer of the 'Laus Pisonis'. Unlike most of the ancient examples, Buchanan's panegyric at least has the virtue of brevity, although the themes with which it deals derive largely from ancient sources. Because of the formal nature of the panegyric, its *inventio* and *dispositio* tended to be very stylised. The subject's ancestors are usually praised, but naturally, he outshines them all in virtue (cf. *Silvae* 1, lines 46–7); his fame is universal, usually underlined at great length by mention, in geographical periphrases, of the four points of the compass (cf. lines 37–8); he is compared, always to his advantage, with other gods and heroes (see the opening of the poem, and the mythological allusions throughout to Theseus in line 24, Hercules in lines 24–5, Jupiter in line 27); and even Nature, both animate and inanimate, is keen to honour him (cf. in Buchanan the references to the various rivers which rush to see Charles, lines 12–20). The metre chosen for such panegyrics is invariably the hexameter, the metre of heroic verse, and therefore virtually a compliment in itself, while the style and tone of the poem are of course those of the *sermo grandis*.

Even with such an unpromising subject, Buchanan manages to ring some changes to produce a poem which, if it does indulge in conventional flattery, at least includes the occasional novel touch to arouse the reader's interest. At the same time, it is a good illustration of the Erasmian principle of *copia*, showing how one idea, the honour which Bordeaux is receiving at the visit of the Emperor, can be expanded into seventy lines of verse.

By contrast, the fifth elegy, addressed to the French Chancellor, François Olivier, although another official poem written on behalf of the Collège de Guyenne is far from being merely traditional and functional. Olivier had been attached to the court of Marguerite de Navarre at Nérac before becoming chancellor of France in May 1545. He seems to have been an austere, intransigent man, set on curbing the excessive spending of the Court, and, while being a Catholic, not fanatically opposed to the Protestant cause. Buchanan's appeal to him is in fact put into the mouth of one of the Muses who, laying aside her maidenly reserve, presents the Chancellor with nothing short of an ultimatum: he owes his position to the Muses (cf. line 33, 'Cum tamen ad summos per nos sis vectus honores'), and if they receive no aid from him, there are plenty of other places where they will be welcome:

> Quaelibet excipient Musas loca, nam neque deerit
> Inter inhumanos hospita terra Getas.

(ll. 59–60)

The style of the poem is familiar but dignified. The somewhat conversational tone is ensured by direct addresses to Olivier (e.g. lines 61–4), by the use of interrogation (lines 23–4, 25, 35–6), and the Catullan device of repeating whole lines of the poem, for example lines 48 and 50, and lines 43–5;

> Aut si per steriles comites frustremur arenas,
> Non habeat faciles nostra querela Deos.
> Sed neque per steriles comites frustramur arenas. . . .

Repetition of shorter elements in the poem is also common, similarly reinforcing this familiar tone, as in the anaphora on 'quid modo' in lines 23 and 25:

> Quid modo squalentes turpi rubigine mores
> Profuerit studiis excoluisse bonis?
> Quid modo barbariem iuvet expugnasse rebellem. . . .

However, the dignity of the piece is achieved by the use of distinctive metaphors such as the agricultural image in line 30, 'Nec sinit Aoniis credere semen agris'; the sailing image of line 41, 'Non petimus velum deprensae obtendere culpae'; and the medical metaphor of line 54, 'Vulnera nec lenta nostra fovere mora'. Periphrases also help in this as in lines 9–10:

> Pene suum rediit circumfluus annus ad ortum,
> Et prope defessis Phoebus anhelat equis.

Other elements from the epic style include the use of geographical allusions (e.g. lines 55–60):

> Haec ubi spes aberit, vicinos altera Iberos,
> Aut petet aurifero littora flava Tago;
> Aut modo pacatos trans aequora lata Britannos,
> Aut iuga Sithonia semper operta nive;

(ll. 55–8)

and the inclusion of a number of classical *topoi*, for example lines 17–20 on the effects of the return of Peace:

> Nunc mala tempestas belli desaevitt, urbes
> Pax fovet, et pleno copia larga sinu.
> Rura quies secura colit, mercator inermis
> Impavido tutas remige sulcat aquas.

These two contrasting tonal elements, the familiar and the elevated, produce a certain amount of tension in the poem, investing it with an added interest, and reflecting the ambiguous attitude towards the figure of the Chancellor himself. It inevitably creates some degree of humour in the poem, and results in a successful piece of badinage whose purpose, the winning over of the Chancellor, is achieved wittily and neatly.

Such is Buchanan in official mood. *Elegy* 2, the 'Maiae Calendae' is also closely associated with the Collège de Guyenne, but shows Buchanan in a highly informal light, addressing the school concerning the holidays which Mayday heralded each year. The mythological scenario of the opening of the poem, giving the impression of a Renaissance *primavera*, peopled with deities and allegorical figures (Cupid, Venus, Genius, Voluptas), gradually melts into a more realistic setting to describe the effects of Spring on animate and inanimate Nature. The second half of the poem (line 83 to the end) is devoted to the 'carpe diem' motif, exhorting the young to make the most of their short lives and, somewhat less traditionally, bidding the old to lay aside their cares and become rejuvenated:

> Carpite, dum fas est, fugitivae gaudia vitae,
> Credite vos iuvenes esse, fuisse senes.   (ll. 93–4)

While Horace and Virgil provide much of the inspiration for this poem,[28] Ausonius' poem 'De rosis nascentibus' has also influenced Buchanan, which is interesting in view of the ancient poet's close connections with Bordeaux. Ausonius' description of spring with its conclusion:

> collige, virgo, rosas, dum flos novus et nova pubes,
> et memor esto aevum sic properare tuum

reminds us of Buchanan's lines 133–4:

> Carpe rosas, et, ni carpas, peritura ligustra,
> Et vitae credas haec simulachra tuae.

Through the combination of a number of traditional common-places, along with carefully selected descriptive detail, Buchanan succeeds here in producing a poem of universal application, yet at the same time one that is rooted in personal experience.

Silvae 2 represents one of Buchanan's early essays at pastoral verse. This

was a particularly popular genre in sixteenth-century France, whose introduction may be traced via such Italian humanists as Balbo and Fausto
Andrelini through Clément Marot, who translated Virgil's first Eclogue in
the *Adolescence clémentine* of 1532.[29] The eclogue enjoyed considerable
popularity in France, not least in the Poitiers of the 1540s where Ptolomée
de la Taste is represented as living in *Silvae* 2 (see lines 2 and 42–3), which
may explain the choice of this poetic form in which to address him.
Buchanan would obviously turn to Virgil for inspiration in the bucolic field,
although he would not have been ignorant of Theocritus, the later pastoral
writers like Calpurnius Siculus and Nemesianus who were quite popular in
the schools, and the influential Neo-latin poets Mantuan and Sannazzaro.
He incorporates into his verse many of the traditional elements of the
pastoral: themes of thwarted love and desertion, a stylised view of bucolic
reality, rural comparisons, vows, prayers, and recantations, elements of
magic, and certain stylistic devices. However, far from being a mere trans-
position or adaptation of Virgilian themes, *Silvae* 2 is a true expression of
personal feelings, gaining in wit and urbanity from being composed in the
bucolic genre.

Ptolomée has deserted his homeland around Bordeaux, a region which is
far more beautiful than the sterile land of Poitou, his new home. The whole
of Gascony is in silent grief at his absence, punctuated only by the shrieks
of birds of ill omen, and even the poet can no longer play his pipes. Agrius is
particularly grief-stricken at the loss of his friend and, after wondering
how he can bear to live in Poitiers, wishes dire things on the region, but
recants and finally hopes that Ptolomée will be moved by his song. The
poem ends with the setting of the sun.

The themes, diction, and style of the poem are distinctly Virgilian. As in
the *Eclogues*, Nature is often seen as being in sympathy with the poet; the
countryside, although real, is peopled with idealised nymphs and
shepherds; love is bisexual; and elements of reality are carefully allegorised
to avoid any discordance. The ending of the poem with the setting of the
sun is suggested by *Eclogues* 1, 6, and 10. As far as vocabulary is concerned,
Buchanan uses a large number of typically Virgilian words and expressions
(e.g. *fistula*, line 14; *dumus*, line 23; *consortia tecta*, line 38. cf. *Georgics* 4,
153; *Oceantides*, line 31). Naturally, this bucolic diction is reinforced by the
inclusion of textual allusions to Virgil, compare:

> Pallida cum niveis vaccinia ferre ligustris   (l. 6)

and

> alba ligustra cadunt, vaccinia nigra leguntur;   (*Eclogues* 2.18)
> Ipsi etiam montes, ipsae etiam convalles   (l. 33)

and

ipsi te fontes, ipsa haec arbusta vocabunt;   *(Eclogues* 1.38)
Sub quibus arguta carmen modulentur avena   (l. 85)

and

carmen pastoris Siculi modulabor avena;   *(Eclogues* 10.51)
Et quacunque feres gressus,' tibi balsama sudet
Quercus. . .   (ll. 91–2)

and

quid tibi odorato referam sudantia ligno   *(Georgics*
balsama. . . ;   2.118–19)
. . . mella rubis, tribulisque legatur amomum   (l. 92)

and

mella fluant illi, ferat et rubus asper amomum.   *(Eclogues* 3.89)

In most of these cases, the references are quite vague, and unlike some other uses of the tag which we have already noted, Buchanan has no intention here of recalling the original context. He is simply interested in establishing a Virgilian feel to his poem. Other reminiscences do occur (cf. 'nulla redimitus arundine frontem', line 67, and Velleius Paterculus 2.83.2, 'caput harundine redimitus'; and the various names and details of birds such as *noctua, acanthis, bubo, cornix,* and *strix,* taken largely from Pliny),[30] but they avoid imposing a different style on the poem. This is confirmed in the bucolic tradition by a number of rhetorical devices such as the dramatic monologue of Agrius, the use of enumeration and exclamation, and the inclusion of parenthetical comments. Repetition, as usual in Buchanan quite frequent, is employed in a manner typical of Virgil, cf. lines 3–5:

. . . nec te socium pecorisque larisque
Cura tenet, nec quam sociis pecorique larique
Praetuleras;

and lines 31–3:

Ipsae etiam in tumidis Nymphae Oceantides undis,
Ipsae etiam in placidis Nymphae Dordonides antris,
Ipsi etiam montes, ipsae etiam convalles. . . .

Although the reader may consider *Silvae* 2 to be an artfully conceived piece of verse, he is not aware of any insincerity on the part of the poet, nor indeed is there any. Possibly, one of the reasons for the popularity of the pastoral genre in the Renaissance is the allegorical and artificial nature of that genre in ancient times. It was no more a natural means of expression in

Virgil's day than it was in later years. What is needed to make it a success is quite simply that the poet should have something to say. All too many subsequent attempts sacrificed content to form, and therefore failed. This is not, however, the case with Buchanan who, whatever else he may have scorned, placed a high value on friendship, just as the Ancients had done. It is for this reason that at times he can so successfully take over their verse forms and adapt them to reflect his own emotions.

These longer compositions fit in quite well with trends in vernacular poetry (especially as represented by Marot) and Neo-latin poetry written in the first half of the century. Buchanan also made a sortie into the field of lyric verse at this time, notably *Fratres fraterrimi* 5, and *Miscellany* 4 and 9, written in the alcaic and sapphic metres. It is interesting that, along with these Horatian metres, Buchanan also takes up the Horatian themes of the important role of the poet and his unique ability to confer immortality. So, in *Miscellany* 4, where Buchanan is thanking François Olivier for saving the Muses in Bordeaux, the Neo-platonic idea of divine inspiration is introduced:

> Quod si ad Garumnae littora Vasconis
> Abs te impetrato perfruar otio,
> Liberque curis entheoque
> Pieridum furiatus oestro.   (ll. 29–32)

The theme of *Miscellany* 9, a poem addressed to the youth of Bordeaux, is that poetry alone can last for ever, and incidentally immortalise those whom it celebrates:

> Sola doctorum monumenta vatum
> Nesciunt fati imperium severi,
> Sola contemnunt Phlegethonta et Orci
> Iura superbi.   (ll. 29–32)

Both these themes would later play an important part in Pléiade thinking, and particularly in the works of Ronsard, although they were not new to the Renaissance. Marullus in Italy had written of Jupiter 'Enthea divino praecordia concutis oestro/Ignotasque vias aperis' (*Hymni naturales* 1.1.11–12), while more recently in France (c.1530), Salmon Macrin had written:

> Oestro nusquam animos valdius entheo
> Nyaeusque bicorniger   ·
> Insignisque chelys Delius incitant.   (*Carmina* I.20.28–30)

So, by the time the Pléiade came to adopt these themes, they were quite well established amongst the Neo-latin writers.

Epigrams formed the staple crop of the Neo-latin poet in the first half of the sixteenth century. While a number of these were no doubt occasioned by public events or written for the purposes of winning patronage, many others were simply a reaction to incidents in the poet's own life, or summed up his feelings about current affairs, often for the purposes of satire. This last group proved to be very popular, with the religious satires in particular finding their way into many manuscript collections, especially later on in the century.

Buchanan used the epigram for all these purposes. The wit and, often, the obscenity of the Martialian epigram were a continuing source of inspiration, but the Greek Anthology also provided subjects and conceits in addition to the poems which Buchanan translated.[31] Amongst other genres, Buchanan wrote many epitaphs in the course of his life, and although some were no doubt simply commissioned, many were written out of a sincere regard for the deceased.[32] *Epigrams* II.5 is in honour of Briand de Vallée, whom we have met as the dedicatee of the 'Pro lena':

> Dignus erat Pylio canescere Vallius aevo,
>   Hospite si tanto digna fuisset humus.
> Ergo seni, quo nil melius nec doctius orbe
>   Permenso vidit sol, Deus astra dedit.

(Vallée would have deserved to grow old and grey, living as long as Nestor, if the ground had been worthy of such a great guest. Therefore, God has given the stars to an old man who is unsurpassed in worth and learning beneath the immense orbit of the sun.)

Buchanan's sincerity is evident here, despite the hyperbole. Nevertheless, he could at times use the genre for satirical purposes, as in the two poems written on the death in 1544 of Robert Cairncross, *Epigrams* II.13 and 14. The text of the second of these is:

> Corpore cum foedo species sit foedior oris,
>   Foedum pectus habet, foedius ingenium.
> A cruce Parca dedit nomen praesaga futuri;
>   Haud alia hoc dignum morte cadaver erat.

(Although the sight of his face is more foul than his foul body, he has a foul heart, and a fouler mind. Fate, foretelling his future, named him after the cross; this corpse deserved no other kind of death.)

Renaissance poets did not believe in understatement.

Buchanan also seems to have been quite outspoken in his religious satires during this period, attacking the corruption of the religious orders and the worship of images and relics. His eclecticism is often apparent here, as in *Fratres fraterrimi* 8, where the central conceit is based on Psalms 115.8, compare:

Oscula, serta, rosas das et libamina saxo?
Teque pium dici, cum facis ista, cupis.
Quid tibi pro tanta maius pietate precemur,
Quam ut fias numen tu quoque, quale colis?

(Do you give kisses, garlands, roses, and libations to a stone? And you want to be
called pious when you do this! What greater reward should we pray for you in
recompense for such piety than that you too should become like the god whom you
worship?)

with the Psalmist's words: 'Similes illis fiant qui faciunt ea: et omnes qui
confidunt in eis' (see also Psalms 135.18). Another epigram, omitted from
the published collection of the *Fratres fraterrimi* no doubt because of its
obscenity, was very popular in manuscript collections of an anti-Catholic
nature, and seems likely to date from this period. The text is as follows:

Cum monachus monacham premeret gemibunda, 'Mihi' inquit
'Vae miserae haec inter ludicra perdo animam.'
Quam pius antistes verbis solatur amicis,
Inguinaque inguinibus, osculaque ore tegens.
'Hos aditus ego praecludam, tu, ne exeat' inquit,
'Quicquam animae porta posteriore, cave.'[33]

(As a monk was lying on top of a nun, she groaned out: 'Alas I'm losing my soul in
this sporting!' The pious priest consoles her with loving words, covering her loins
with his loins, her mouth with his lips. 'I'll close off these exits,' he said, 'you make
sure that no part of your soul gets out by the back door.')

The influence of Martial in such pieces is evident, although it would not be
for a few years that Buchanan turned to Catullus as a source of inspiration
for the genre.

Drama

While Buchanan was keeping his friends and colleagues amused in
Bordeaux with his epigrams and other occasional poetry, he was also
engaged in an activity in which he led the field in France for a number of
years, the composition of tragedy.

We have seen that Buchanan had already produced his translation of the
Medea before starting to teach in Bordeaux.[34] In a letter to Daniel Rogers
(*O.O.*II.755) dated 9 November 1579, he speaks of the composition of the
tragedies:

My four tragedies have been published, of which two were translated from the
Greek. The *Medea* had not been written for the purposes of publication but, when

I was studying Greek literature without a teacher, in order to give more careful consideration to individual words as I was writing. I published it at the pressing entreaties of my friends when I was teaching Latin literature in Bordeaux, and was compelled to come up with a play each year to be performed by the boys. Since the play contained a lot of rather negligent slips, I revised it after a number of years and patched up some of its wounds in such a way that the scars are still apparent in places. I devoted more work to the composition of the other three plays in Bordeaux.

Buchanan was conscious of following in Erasmus' footsteps by translating the *Medea* into Latin verse, as he indicates in his preface to the play (*O.O.* II.536), although he has less to say about the composition of the two original plays. It is clear, however, that he saw tragedy as serving a moral purpose. In the preface to the *Alcestis*, he writes:

> For once the action is brought to life with speech and breath, it makes a stronger impression on the senses than bare moral lessons, and influences the mind more easily. And where it has penetrated, it clings more firmly, and virtually takes root.

And in a prophetic preface addressed to James VI, Buchanan writes that he hopes that his *Baptistes* will show posterity that if the King turns into a tyrant, it will be James's fault and not that of his tutors (*O.O.*II.217).

Translating the *Medea* and the *Alcestis* would certainly have been a good method for Buchanan not only of improving his Greek, but also of fixing the overall pattern of a Greek tragedy in his mind. And it is that pattern which he followed when he came to write the *Baptistes* and the *Jephthes*, with some help from Seneca, especially in metrical matters.[35] As one would expect, his Latin versions are both accurate and elegant, endeavouring to capture the tone as well as the meaning of the original. Vocabulary is occasionally obscure, perhaps in an attempt to find the *mot juste*, and the use of diminutives detracts at times from the serious tone, see, for example, *Medea* 1184–5 where the queen wishes to hear the report of the death of Jason's bride:

> Sed ne gravere *tantulum* nobis morae
> Dare, pereundi donec explices modum.

In general, however, Buchanan produces sensitive translations of the plays.

What lessons would he have drawn from these two plays? Certainly, they are very different in nature, and anyone searching for the essence of tragedy in these plays alone would be hard put to it to come to any firm conclusions. Medea's flaw goes beyond what most people would find acceptable in a tragic hero or heroine, while the *Alcestis* is also not typical of the tragic theatre, with its apparently happy ending and elements of humour in the character of Heracles. We are a long way here from Aristotle's description of tragedy in the *Poetics*.

Yet as in all fields of poetry, Buchanan seems to have learnt as much from example as from precept, and it is interesting to consider what he took over from Greek tragedy and the way in which he adapted it. In the first place, he seems to have considered biblical stories as being most analogous to the mythological subjects of the Ancients, although he seized upon resemblances between plots, for example the Jephtha story and the events of the *Iphigenia in Aulis*, so that allusions to the ancient texts might give greater depth to his own plays. In this, he is obeying Horace's teaching in the *Ars poetica*, both to follow the example of the Greeks (lines 268–9), but also to choose subjects nearer to home:

> nec minimum meruere decus vestigia graeca
> ausi deserere et celebrare domestica facta.   (ll. 286–7)

Despite the example of the happy ending in the *Alcestis*, Buchanan chooses plots for his two sacred dramas whose dénouements result in death. He also follows closely the *dispositio* of the Euripidean tragedy, dividing the various episodes by choruses, but ignoring the Horatian precept to split the play into five acts (*Ars poetica* 189–90). Like many Euripidean tragedies, both his plays begin with prologues, one human and one supernatural. He follows Horace's advice to keep horrific or improbable events off-stage (*Ars poetica* 182–8), to use the chorus as an integral part of the plot rather than just commenting on the action (lines 193–201), and to have no more than three speaking actors on stage in any one scene (line 192). Apart from the occasional lapse, his style is altogether suitable for the subjects with which he is dealing, and he may even be indebted here to Euripides for some rhetorical devices like *traductio* (the juxtaposition of the same word in different cases).

The *Baptistes* and the *Jephthes* have earned their place in French theatrical history as being the first recognisably neo-classical dramas to be written in France, appearing a good decade before the first vernacular attempt at the genre, Jodelle's *Cléopâtre captive*.[36] Apart from their novelty, however, how good are they as sacred tragedies?

It seems unlikely that Buchanan was influenced by Aristotle's *Poetics* in his conception of tragedy and the tragic hero: it was not until somewhat later in the century that the Greek philosopher's views began to exercise any influence in this field in France. Certainly, according to Aristotelian principles, John the Baptist is far from being a tragic hero since he is tainted by no *hamartia*, although a century later, Pierre Corneille would still be writing tragedies with saintly heroes (for example *Polyeucte*), justifying his choice of subject by the doctrine of *admiration*. As we have seen, Buchanan, like Seneca and Corneille, saw the purpose of tragedy as being an essentially didactic one, and the figure of the Baptist clearly represents the heroic struggle of the individual against a corrupt system (however one likes to interpret this in sixteenth-century terms).[37] Herod, although not totally wicked, is led astray by evil counsel to act in a tyrannical fashion against John, a theme that would preoccupy Buchanan increasingly over the next few decades. The hero of the *Jephthes* is guilty of making an ill-advised vow, which he himself comes to regret:

> . . . quod utinam prudentior
> Voto fuissem nuncupando et cautior.   (ll. 722–3)

Jephtha comes far closer to the concept of the tragic hero, therefore, than John the Baptist. His essential goodness is marred only by his one rash action, the making of a vow whose consequences he has failed to consider in advance. He is caught in a true dilemma, and it is his intransigent piety which brings about the tragic dénouement. Perhaps instinctively, Buchanan has approached the Aristotelian definition of the tragic hero of one 'who is not pre-eminent in moral virtue, who passes to bad fortune not through vice or wickedness, but because of some piece of ignorance (*hamartia*), and who is of high repute and great good fortune' (*Poetics* 1453a, translated by M. E. Hubbard).

Tragedy, then, for Buchanan serves the basic purpose of educating, and this is hardly surprising given the circumstances of the plays' composition for performance by the pupils of the Collège de Guyenne. Apart from the central message of the two plays, *sententiae* abound, generally of a reformist nature, condemning the worship of graven images and statues, or reflecting on the duties of the prince. The linguistic and rhetorical features of the plays would also have been considered just as important as the moral teaching they embodied. In all this, Buchanan showed the way ahead for the Jesuit theatre, which would flourish well into the seventeenth century throughout Europe.

While the plays are competent and important for the development of neo-classical drama in France, they are not great successes from the theatrical point of view. The first original play, the *Baptistes*, suffers from a lack of action and suspense. The main body of the play is devoted to set-piece debates between the various characters, which Buchanan, as a teacher of the art of *disputatio*, a school exercise which he favoured all his life, would have been in an excellent position to compose. However, they do little to advance the action, and the events leading to the death of the Baptist are dealt with relatively hastily. True, the various confrontations between the characters, especially between John and Herod, provide some interest, but the length of the speeches even here would tend to detract from any dramatic interest. The didactic aims of the author gain the upper hand, a feature owing more to Seneca (whose plays were never intended for performance) than to Euripides, who even in his longer speeches maintains the audience's attention.

The *Jephthes*, on the other hand, is more successful, and even the angelic Prologue, announcing the dénouement of the play, helps to enhance the dramatic irony which is a feature of much of the first half of the drama. An atmosphere of foreboding is created by Storge's description of her premonitory dream (an essentially Senecan device), while after the arrival of Jephtha himself, there is genuine suspense as to whether the king will carry out his vow, so monstrous does the proposed action appear. There is a better balance in the length of speeches and the variation with stichomythia than in the *Baptistes*, although even in this play, there is a tendency towards the end to indulge too much in lengthy discussions, which is harmful to the dramatic interest of the play. Despite this, the end of the play, with the account of the death of Iphis, is full of pathos, and comes as a fitting climax.

The style of the two plays is, naturally, guided by *decorum*. Particularly noteworthy is the inclusion of a large number of extended similes, which had made only rare appearances in Buchanan's poetry hitherto, and even then had often been used for humorous or ironic purposes. Here, however, they lend *gravitas* to the plays, as, for example, in the Angel's opening speech in the *Jephthes*:

> . . . Qualis in dominum furit
> Equi ferocis contumax protervitas,
> Imperia paullum si remissa sentiat,
> Ac vix lupatis domitus, et calcaribus
> Duris cruentus, redit ad officium, et suo
> Obtemperat hero. . .   (ll. 20–5)

Although Lebègue complains of the absence of biblical feeling in the style, the Bible has left its mark, particularly in the choruses, but in a humanised form,[38] similar to Buchanan's treatment of the Psalms.

We have already noted Buchanan's contact in the early 1550s with future French dramatists, and no doubt his experience would have been of considerable use to them.[39] Apart from the general structure of neo-classical tragedy, the Scottish humanist demonstrated the way in which the Judeo-Christian heritage could be exploited just as the Greeks had made use of their own cultural background, while at the same time situating this heritage in an essentially classical framework. The underlying allusions to Greek plays, especially in the *Jephthes*, add a richer dimension to the Old Testament story. Certainly, the religious tragedy became a well established genre in the course of the sixteenth and seventeenth centuries, culminating in Racine's two contributions, *Esther* and *Athalie*, which interestingly were also written for performance by schoolchildren. The wheel had come full circle.

Buchanan's plays helped to establish the diction and style appropriate to tragedy: the *gravitas* produced by the Homeric simile or the striking metaphor, the occasionally hyperbolic use of repetition, exclamation, and apostrophe, the vivid descriptions in messenger speeches, and, very importantly, the lyricism of the choruses. It was a tradition which had its faults, as Buchanan's own plays did, but it was one that lasted into the seventeenth century where its last significant exponent was Alexandre Hardy.

CHAPTER 5

Buchanan, Horace and Catullus

Although Buchanan's reputation was well established in Neo-latin circles by the time of his departure for Coimbra in 1547, his impact on vernacular poetry had not so far been very great. However, as we have seen, he had become acquainted with a number of those poets who were later to form the Pléiade, and he was welcomed by them as an ally on his return to France in 1552.[1] While in Portugal, his poetry underwent a distinct change, following a course which the Pléiade was soon to pursue, with the result that, throughout the 1550s, Buchanan's poetry and the writings of the Pléiade were in perfect harmony.

While he did not altogether abandon previous genres of poetry, Buchanan turned for inspiration in the closing years of the 1540s to two Roman poets in particular: Horace and Catullus. Although the Scotsman had produced some Horatian odes before this time, it was his project to paraphrase the Psalter which provided him with the impetus to master the various lyric metres, and to produce poetry very much in the grand style. This would also have been good preparation for many of the Court poems which he composed in the 1550s. However, Horace, like Buchanan, was not an unrelievedly serious poet, and his vituperative iambic poems were the starting point for the series of poems addressed to Leonora.

Buchanan also looked to Catullus at this time for many of his epigrams. Marullus and Joannes Secundus had already helped to establish the Neo-catullan style outside France, and Buchanan turned his attention in this direction for the rather scurrilous poems aimed at his Coimbra colleague, Beleago, as well as for the amatory verse addressed to Neaera. Naturally, the Scotsman continued to compose in forms of poetry which he had practised previously: satirical verse, epigrams, and longer compositions. But the largest project which he undertook would ultimately prove to be too ambitious: the *De sphaera, a poem in five books on the nature of the universe*.

In order for French Renaissance poetry to be taken seriously, two things were necessary: a style sufficiently grand to stand comparison with the best poets of the ancient world and the Italian Renaissance; and subjects of great enough importance to convince an audience of the prestige to which poverty lay claim. The writings of Buchanan and his fellow Neo-latinists had certainly succeeded on the first count, but many of their compositions had dealt with subjects that may have had a serious intent (for example, the satirical verse), but which nevertheless lacked the *gravitas* which would enhance the poet's status in the world. Guided in the first place, perhaps, by previous Neo-latin achievements, the Pléiade would be working towards these two goals in the 1550s. But it was in the closing years of the 1540s that Buchanan began to fulfil the second of these two requirements.

Buchanan and Horace

As Dorothy Coleman demonstrates in *The Gallo-Roman Muse*, Horace could provide the Pléiade poets with the key to successful poetic composition in his theoretical works, his attitude to poetry, as well as in his poetic writings.[2] And it was to Horace that Buchanan looked for inspiration while in Portugal, although his views on 'serious' poetry differed in some respects from those of the Pléiade. Whereas Ronsard and his colleagues would seek prestige by evoking a mystical, Neo-platonic world vision, Buchanan turned to the Bible for his serious poetry, just as he had done for his tragedies.

Buchanan's interest in the Psalms had been awakened during his time in Paris in the 1540s under the influence of Jean de Gagnay, the early French paraphrast, at whose house the Scottish humanist had stayed.[3] Even before his incarceration by the Inquisition in the monastery of San Bento, Buchanan had worked on some paraphrases, but once there, he devoted himself wholly to the task in accordance with the orders of his captors. No doubt the project seemed a particularly apt one for a number of reasons. Because of the psalmist's preoccupations with exile, oppression, hope and despair, the project enabled Buchanan to give vent to his own feelings, as in the impassioned Psalm 137, 'Super flumina Babylonis'.[4] It also allowed him to gain expertise in a number of metres with which he was not very familiar, and to write poetry in the grand style, but in a Christian context. Moreover, as a genre, the Psalm paraphrase was closely associated with the Protestant cause, especially in its early days.[5]

It is not known how many of the paraphrases were completed while Buchanan was in Portugal, and the first complete edition of the work from the Estienne presses did not appear until around 1565.[6] Before this, however, Henri Estienne had printed a selection of the Psalms in 1556 along with some translations by four other poets of whom, with the exception of M. A. Flaminio, Estienne has a low opinion.[7] In addition to the verse translations, this work also contains the Latin prose translation by Sanctes Pagninus. In all, nineteen of Buchanan's versions are included, Psalms 1–15, 114, 128, 137, and at the end of the collection 104. From Estienne's prefatory letter to Buchanan (page 3 sqq.), it would seem that certain of the paraphrases at least had been circulating in manuscript form for some time:

> You have been too long in hiding, my dear Buchanan. Now, as you see, you must come out into the open. Whether you like it or not, I shall bring you out of your hiding-place.

The task facing any would-be paraphrast of the Psalms was quite a formidable one. The Hebrew text that had been handed down was relatively corrupt, and, because of the nature of the Hebrew language which originally recorded only the consonants of each word, open to all kinds of ambiguity. Moreover, the tense system of the Hebrew verb, with only the present and past in the indicative mood and a single-tense imperative, did not translate readily into the far more precise Greek and Latin systems, and it was left largely to the translator to decide whether the past, present, or future was being referred to. The Septuagint translation tended to be totally mechanical in its choice of tense to represent the Hebrew verb, and generally speaking, it is very literal, making little attempt to explain the meaning of the original text. It is upon this version, and not the Hebrew text, that the normal Vulgate translation is based, although Saint Jerome did produce a Latin text, the 'Hebrew' Psalter, which was based upon the original. The way still lay open for a good, intelligent translation in accordance with the developing sciences of scriptural exegesis and textual criticism, and various attempts at both commentaries and translations were made, notably by Vatable, Sanctes Pagninus, and Bucer. However, as the writer of the Preface to the New Testament of the New English Bible remarks, 'if the best commentary is a good translation, it is also true that every intelligent translation is in a sense a paraphrase'. Thus, the best of the Renaissance Psalm paraphrases fulfilled the dual functions of accuracy and elegance, and required a considerable amount of scholarly effort in order to be successful.

In his approach to the Psalms, Buchanan seems to steer an independent course. His versions are in sympathy with the context of the poems, especially in the choice of tenses, and while he occasionally insists on interpretations which receive little support from modern translators, it is apparent that he was anxious to find the correct reading. At the same time, since he was producing a paraphrase and not a translation, he felt at liberty to add epithets and phrases for which there is no equivalent in the original text. In accommodating a poetic language as remote from Latin as Hebrew, Buchanan evidently felt that some licence was necessary in order to present the full impact of the original, albeit in a different manner. He was not attempting to represent the particular characteristics of Hebrew poetry in his Latin verse paraphrases. The very different nature of Hebrew and

Latin poetics makes this an impossible task. He was, however, trying to convey the feeling and tone of the original in the different cloak of Latin verse forms, and the success of the project must be judged according to this brief. While others might try to represent such Hebrew poetical devices as the superlative genitive which are not native to Latin, Buchanan on the whole avoids this, while preserving the carefully balanced parallelism and antithesis native to both Hebrew and Latin poetry. Choice of metre, for which there is no Hebrew equivalent, was also an important factor for Buchanan. To some extent, he is keen to demonstrate his virtuosity in the lyric metres, using as many different kinds as possible in the opening Psalms, much as Horace had done in book I of the *Odes*. On the other hand, he is not a slave to this scheme, being more concerned to fit the sentiments expressed in the Psalms to a suitable metre, although he does demonstrate a much greater metrical variety than in his secular poetry.

To illustrate the differing aims of the Hebrew psalmist and of Buchanan, it will be useful to compare two versions of Psalm 114. For an idea of the Hebrew version, I use the translation and commentary of A. Cohen.[8]

Quum domus Isacidum patrias remearet ad oras,	1
Barbaraque invisae linqueret arva Phari,	
Ipse Deus Iudam coelesti numine tutum	2
Fecit, erat populi signifer ipse sui.	
Vidit, et attonitas trepidum mare diffidit undas;	3
Iordanis refugas in caput egit aquas;	
Dura per intonsos salierunt culmina montes,	4
Ut saturas gestit dux gregis inter oves;	
Celsaque frondentes movere cacumina colles,	
Agnus ut in pratis luxuriare solet.	
Quid, mare, vidisti solito cur cesseris alveo?	5
Cur fugis in fontes, fluminis unda, tuos?	
Cur ita concusso saliistis vertice montes,	6
Ut satur exsultat dux gregis inter oves?	
Cur ita frondenti saliistis vertice, colles,	
Agnus ut in pratis luxuriare solet?	
Nempe Dei trepidum praesentia terruit orbem,	7
Cui cadit in Solymos victima multa focos,	
Qui lapidum venas laticum laxavit in usum,	8
Cui fluxit largo flumine dura silex.	

(When the house of the descendants of Isaac were returning to their ancestral shores, and leaving the alien fields of hated Egypt, God Himself made Judah safe through His heavenly power, He Himself was the standard-bearer of His people. The sea saw it and in fear divided its terrified waves; He drove the fleeing waters of the Jordan to its source. The hard summits leapt throughout the well-wooded

mountains, just as the leader of the flock gambols amongst the well-fed sheep; and
the leafy hills moved their lofty heights, just as the lamb is wont to frolic in the
meadows. What have you seen, oh sea, to stop you following your usual channel?
river waves, why do you flee to your source? Why, you mountains, did you leap
with shaking summit, just as the well-fed leader of the flock gambols amongst the
sheep? why, you hills, did you leap with your leafy summit, just as the lamb is wont
to frolic in the meadows? Surely, the presence of God has terrified the frightened
world, for Whom many a victim falls on the altar-fires of Jerusalem, Who loosened
the veins of rock to be used as liquid, and for Whom the hard flint flowed in a wide
stream.)

When Israel came forth out of Egypt,	1
The house of Jacob from a people of strange language;	
Judah became His sanctuary,	2
Israel His dominion.	
The sea saw it, and fled;	3
The Jordan turned backward.	
The mountains skipped like rams,	4
The hills like young sheep.	
What aileth thee O thou sea, that thou fleest?	5
Thou Jordon, that thou turnest backward?	
Ye mountains, that ye skip like rams;	6
Ye hills, like young sheep?	
Tremble, thou earth, at the presence of the Lord,	7
At the presence of the God of Jacob;	
Who turned the rock into a pool of water,	8
The flint into a fountain of waters.	

The poetic qualities of the original depend upon a limited number of
devices. In the first place, the reader is struck by the parallelism used in
every verse of the Psalm, whereby a statement is made, and repeated in
different terms, reflecting, no doubt, the antiphonal nature of the chanting
or singing of the poems. Repetition also plays an important part, with
elements from verses 3 and 4 occurring in verses 5 and 6; while the overall
structure of the poem, with its three sections of two, four, and two verses,
further underlines the crucial role of symmetry and balance for the
psalmist's effect. In addition, personification and apostrophe, coupled with
simile, play an overriding and almost startling part in the imagery. The
images in verse 3 of the sea fleeing and the Jordan turning backwards are
relatively unexceptional. Such terms are used, especially in *adynata*, in
Greek and Latin poetry, and would be familiar to sixteenth-century
readers. On the other hand, the idea of the mountains skipping like rams
and of the hills like young sheep is an altogether different matter, and the
reader cannot help being struck by the image, underlining the miraculous
nature of Israel's exodus from Egypt. The poem closes, seemingly abruptly,

with reference to two miracles involving God's absolute control over Nature, and at the same time his care for the unfortunate (cf. Exodus 17.6 and Numbers 20.11), thus, in fact, reflecting the opening of the Psalm. The contrast between 'rock' and 'pool of water', 'flint' and 'fountain of waters', underlined by the juxtaposition of these terms in the Hebrew text, forms a forceful and telling conclusion.

In adapting this Psalm to the particular genius of Latin poetry, Buchanan was faced with a number of difficulties which had to be resolved. His choice of metre, the elegiac couplet, cannot in this case have been a difficult one to make. The parallelism in each of the Hebrew verses and the way that each verse forms a self-contained unit strongly indicate the use of this metrical form. Having made this choice, however, Buchanan tries to mitigate to some extent the parallelism of the Hebrew, compare:

> Judah became His sanctuary,
> Israel His dominion

with:

> Ipse Deus Iudam coelesti numine tutum
> Fecit, erat populi signifer ipse sui.

In later versions, Buchanan is less concerned with preserving the parallelism of the original than in his first attempts. Thus, the line of verse 4 which in the 1556 version is repeated in verse 6, 'Ut saturas gestit dux gregis inter oves', is changed in the *O.O.* to 'Ut satur exsultat dux gregis inter oves', presumably for purposes of variety. The imagery of verses 4 and 6 obviously presents Buchanan with problems of interpretation. At first (1556) he saw the *culmina* and *cacumina* as leaping with delight (*laeta*), but later reviewed this, replacing *laeta* with the emotionally neutral adjectives *dura* and *celsa*. Moreover, as if to excuse such a bold image in Latin, he has taken refuge in a Virgilian allusion, which is more explicit in the 1556 version, cf. *Eclogues* 5.62–4;

> ipsi laetitia voces ad sidera iactant
> intonsi montes; ipsae iam carmina rupes,
> ipsa sonant arbusta . . .

where, if the mountains and crags are not exactly leaping around, they are at least given human attributes.

Generally speaking, Buchanan's version is both more explicit (as one would expect in a paraphrase) and more descriptive than the original text. Hebrew makes very little use of adjectives, which in Latin represent one of the keystones of poetic style. Therefore, Buchanan makes up for this deficiency so that Egypt (verse 1) becomes *invisae,* the waters of verse 3 are *attonitas, trepidum,* the mountains of verse 4 *intonsos* or *frondentes,* and so forth. Other rhetorical devices (the interrogation of verses 5 and 6, the similes of 4 and 6, and the personification and apostrophe) are retained from the original.

At first sight, it is perhaps a little surprising that Buchanan includes a number of textual allusions to classical writers, especially to poets like Propertius. Thus, for example, 'patrias remearet ad oras' seems to derive from Tacitus, *Annals* 14.25 'patrias in sedes remeavere'. We have already noted the Virgilian associations in verses 4 and 6. Verse 6 also appears to contain some Propertian reminiscences, compare Propertius 3.13.53–4:

> at mons laurigero concussus vertice diras
> Gallica Parnasus sparsit in arma nives,

and also line 40 of the same poem, 'dux aries saturas ipse reduxit ovis'. (The expression 'dux gregis' for *ram* is also used by Ovid, *Metamorphoses* 5.327 and 7.311.) Moreover, the position in the line of *alveō* with its synizesis (the only way it can be accommodated in a hexameter) in verse 5 is attested by Virgil, *Aeneid* 7.33, where it also has the meaning of receptacle for a body of water ('adsuetae ripis volucres et fluminis alveo'). 'Dura silex' (verse 8) also has Virgilian associations (*Aeneid* 6.471). Buchanan is obviously at very great pains, therefore, to establish the classical diction of the poem and, far from endeavouring to convey the tone of the original, he sets out to remove it from its ancient Hebrew setting. Even the proper names and adjectives—*Isacides, Pharus, Iuda, Solyma*—are expressed in typically classical moulds. However, there is evidence to suggest that Buchanan had second thoughts about the inclusion of tags, since one of the criteria in his revision of the Psalms seems to have been to change words in order to make allusions more obscure and unrecognisable.

Buchanan's treatment of the Psalms seems to depend to some extent on the nature of the poem in question. There are broadly three kinds of psalm in the collection: those praising God, those outlining the righteous life, and those expressing the particular feelings of the psalmist. Accordingly, Buchanan's aims are somewhat different in each type. A comparison of Psalms 104, 1, and 6 may serve to illustrate this.

Psalm 104 is a hymn of praise to God, the creator of the universe, and Buchanan's paraphrase was considered one of his finest compositions. For such a lofty theme, he chooses the only possible metre, the dactylic hexameter, and is at pains throughout the poem to endue his verse with a Virgilian grandeur worthy of its subject. The resounding opening lines set the tone of the piece, while recalling the beginning of the *Te Deum*:

> Te rerum, Deus alme, canam Dominumque patremque,
> Magne parens, sancta quam maiestate verendus,
> Aetheris aeternas rector moliris habenas!
> Te decor, auratis ambit te gloria pennis,
> Et circumfusum vestit pro tegmine lumen.

The addition of such elements as the 'auratis ... pennis' seems to be to produce greater vividness and elevation. This tendency towards more decoration is present throughout the Psalm. Buchanan can be as concise as the original, compare verse 4:

> Who makest winds Thy messengers,
> The flaming fire Thy ministers

and:

> Apparent accinctae aurae flammaeque ministrae,
> Ut iussa accipiant,

but he seldom chooses this course. In verse 17, the statement 'As for the stork, the fir-trees are her house' becomes:

> ... abies tibi consita surgit,
> Nutrit ubi implumes peregrina ciconia foetus.

Here, the apparently gratuitous inclusion of 'nutrit ... implumes ... foetus' might seem unjustified, but is totally vindicated by Cohen's note:

> the stork. Hebrew *chasidah*, from *chesed* 'lovingkindness'. It is said to receive this name because of its great affection for its young.[9]

Elsewhere, in verse 19, compare:

> Who appointeth the moon for seasons:
> The sun knoweth his going down

and:

> Tu lunae incertos vultus per tempora certa
> Circumagis; puroque accensum lumine solem
> Ducis ad occiduas constanti tramite metas,

where Buchanan's version is more intelligible and at the same time in keeping with the character of Latin poetry. He may not always be correct, but this principle of exegetical accuracy coupled with elegance was certainly at work in his paraphrases. The tone of the poem is distinctly Virgilian and derives from the choice of vocabulary, the imagery, and a number of textual allusions, including one whole line in verse 23, 'Donec sera rubens accendat lumina vesper', taken from *Georgics* 1.251. Thus, the rendering of the Psalm into an equivalent diction and tone, while preserving the meaning and the implications of the original, seems to be Buchanan's chief concern here.

In Psalm 1, a poem outlining the righteous life, the style is far more straightforward and expository, as we might expect, although even here Buchanan does not abandon *copia* of expression altogether.

Felix ille animi, quem non de tramite recto	1
Impia sacrilegae flexit contagio turbae;	
Non iter erroris tenuit, sessorque cathedrae	
Pestiferae facilem dedit irrisoribus aurem;	
Sed vitae rimatur iter melioris, et alta	2
Mente Dei leges noctesque diesque revolvit.	
Ille, velut riguae quae margine consita ripae est	3
Arbor, erit, quam non violento Sirius aestu	
Exurit, non torret hiems; sed prodiga laeto	
Proventu beat agricolam, nec flore caduco	4
Arridens, blanda dominum spe lactat inanem.	
Non ita divini gens nescia foederis, exlex,	
Contemtrixque poli; subito sed turbine rapti	5
Pulveris instar erunt, volucri quem concita gyro	
Aura levis torquet, vacuo ludibria coelo.	
Ergo ubi veridicus iudex in nube serena	6
Dicere ius veniet, scelerisque coarguet orbem,	
Non coram impietas moestos attollere vultus,	
Nec misera audebit iustae se adiungere turbae.	
Nam pater aetherius iustorum et fraude carentum	7
Novit iter, sensumque tenet; curvosque secuta	
Impietas fraudum anfractus scelerata peribit.	

(Happy in mind is he whom the sinful contact of the sacrilegious mob has not turned from the straight path. He has not kept to a course of error nor, sitting on the seat of destruction, has he given easy ear to the scornful. But he searches for the course of a better way of life, and in his innermost mind ponders God's laws day and night. He will be like the tree which has been planted on the edge of the well-watered river bank, which is unscorched by the violent heat of the Dog star, unseared by winter; but it blesses the farmer lavishly with luxuriant crops, nor smiling on him with fleeting flower does it deceive its hungry master with alluring hope. The nation which does not know God's covenant is not like this, being lawless and scorning heaven. But they will be like dust carried away by a sudden whirlwind, which a light breeze, roused into swift eddies, swirls around, a plaything for the empty sky. Therefore, when the truth-speaking judge comes in a serene cloud to pronounce judgement, and convicts a world of sin, the ungodly will not dare to raise their sad faces in His presence or miserably join the crowd of the righteous. For the heavenly father knows the path of the just and those who lack deceit, and understands their thoughts; and the ungodly who have followed the winding path of sins will perish in their guilt.)

Thus, verse 6 is based on the two lines:

> Therefore the wicked shall not stand in the judgement,
> Nor sinners in the congregation of the righteous,

obviously an important section whose implications Buchanan wishes to emphasise fully. The diction of the poem is quite Virgilian, compare 'alta mente' in verse 2 and *Aeneid* 1.26: the reference to Sirius in verse 3 and *Aeneid* 3.141 'tum sterilis exurere Sirius agros'; and the choice of 'gyro' in verse 5 and *Aeneid* 7.379. There may also be a reference in the same verse to Horace, *Odes* 1.14.15 'nisi ventis/debes ludibrium'. The 'beatus vir' theme, of course, is an excellent one to link the biblical and the classical worlds, and although the psalmist and poets like Virgil and Horace might well envisage happiness in different ways (cf. *Georgics* 2.458 sqq. and *Epodes* 2), the pastoral imagery is, at least in this Psalm, common to both. *Gravitas* in Buchanan's version is ensured by the hieratic authority of the content, the strength of the imagery (cf. verses 3 to 5), and the use of compound adjectives (*pestifer, veridicus*) and unusual substantival expressions ('sessorve cathedrae', 'contemtrix poli' etc.). Buchanan would exploit these devices in his Court poetry of the 1550s.

Psalm 6 represents the third category of Psalm, in which the poet is giving vent to very personal feelings, in this case, as frequently, an expression of the agony caused by both physical and mental troubles, but ending in an expression of confidence in God.

> Dum fervet ira, Domine, dum mens aestuat,   2
>   Ne me merentem corripe;
> Dum saevientis flagrat in cursu furor,
>   Exigere poenas abstine.
> O parce, parce; languor aegrum conficit.   3
>   Manum salutarem admove.
> Corpus, solutis ossium compagibus,
>   Enerve vires deserunt,
> Mentemque graviter moeror angit turbidam.   4
>   Quo me usque miserum negliges?
> Quo me usque linques? iam reverte, ac libera   5
>   Aegrum inferum de faucibus.
> Ubi saeva duram mors manum iniecit semel,   6
>   Quis amplius meminit tui?
> Quis mortis alta subrutus caligine
>   Nomen celebrit tuum?
> De nocte pectus anxium suspiriis   7
>   Pulsans, gemensque lacrymis

Lavo cubile: strata fletuum madent
  Rorata largis imbribus.
Caligat acies luminum, doloribus
  Hebetata longis; hostium
Interque risus et dolos emarcuit
  Color vigorque corporis.
At tu sceleribus turba gaudens impiis   9
  Facesse, spem pone irritam.
Lamenta Dominus et meorum fletuum
  Placatus audiit sonum.
Dominus benignus supplicem me exaudiit,   10
  Orationique annuit.
Subitus ut hostes obruat pudor meos,   11
  Vultusque confundat rubor;
Tristi repente ut palleant infamia,
  Fugamque turpem moereant.

(Lord, as Your wrath rages, as Your mind seethes, do not snatch me up as I deserve.
As your fury blazes on the headlong path of one who raves, keep from punishing
me. Oh spare, oh spare me. Weakness consumes me in my sickness. Bring to me a
healing hand. Strength has deserted my feeble body, my joints are weakened.
Dismay sorely troubles my disordered mind; how long will You neglect me in my
misery? how long will you abandon me? Return now, and free me in my sickness
from the jaws of hell. When once cruel death has cast a harsh hand on me, who
further is there to remember You? Who is there to sing of Your name when I am
overwhelmed in the deep darkness of death? At night, as my anxious heart heaves
with sighs and I groan, I soak my bed with tears; my couch grows wet, drenched
with the copious showers of my weeping. My eye-sight grows dim, weakened
through long periods of grief. And amidst the scorn and deceit of my enemies, the
colour and strength of my body have dwindled. But you, mob who delight in evil
sins, be off; put off a vain hope. The Lord has been placated and has heard my
lamentation and the sound of my weeping. A kindly Lord has listened to me in
supplication, and granted my prayer. May sudden shame overwhelm my enemies,
and blushing confound their faces; may they suddenly grow pale at their sorry
disgrace, and grieve at their shameful flight.)

Buchanan's choice of alternating iambic trimeters and dimeters, giving an
impression of unstudied urgency, is very apt, and unlike some of his other
paraphrases, he adds very little to the original text. Any adornment would
be superfluous and tend to detract from the naked force and vigour of the
psalmist's words. Buchanan preserves a simple style, with the occasional
rhetorical device like the pathetic repetition of 'parce' in verse 3 and of 'Quo
me usque' in verses 4 and 5. The use in the 1556 version of the present
tense ('neglegis' and 'linquis') in these verses seems to add a greater sense of
urgency to the poem, as does the original 'Quis *noctis* altae subrutus
caligine' of verse 6 instead of the later (and more correct) 'Quis mortis alta

subrutus caligine'. Buchanan, who suffered from ill health (cf. *Elegy* 4) as well as the mental anguish of his situation in Portugal, could identify completely with the psalmist's feelings, and no doubt gained some solace from this empathy.

Thus, Buchanan does vary his approach to each Psalm according to its subject, with poetic beauty, precision, or sincerity of feeling as the over-riding factors in different paraphrases. Obviously, the choice of metre will be quite important in defining the tone of the poems, and Buchanan is careful to avoid inappropriate rhythms, with solemn metres like the alcaic stanza playing an important part. Within this metrical scheme, he largely follows the rhetorical devices of the original texts, with the exception that *copia*, especially in the use of epithets, leads to greater expansion of the Hebrew version. This enables Buchanan both to make his Psalms sound like good Latin poetry, and to make the meaning, implications, and subtleties of the original clearer.

Buchanan is essentially successful in the Psalm paraphrases. It is clear that he took considerable pains to unravel and clarify the often obscure meaning of the original, and equally clear that he did not simply rely upon translations for this, whether it be the Vulgate or the Pagninus version. What at first may appear to be mere decoration in the paraphrases often turns out to be based upon hidden implications in the Hebrew text. At the same time, the paraphrases are frequently good poems in their own right, especially where Buchanan identifies closely with the psalmist's situation (although inevitably in a collection of 150 poems, there will be some which did not inspire him). It is therefore not without justification that Buchanan's reputation was enhanced by this work, and in his aims of accuracy and elegance, he seems to have been more successful than later critics have given him credit for. Moreover, the search for a suitable mode of expression for the Psalms seems to have had an important impact on Buchanan's own poetic style.

Buchanan was a writer of many contrasts, and the cycle of poems addressed to Leonora, which seems to date from the years in Portugal, could not be further removed in tone from the Psalm paraphrases.[10] Whether or not Leonora did actually exist is not known, but her characterisation is on the whole well-rounded and she is given a clear biographical past. She and her mother are seen as corrupting the youth of Coimbra:

> . . . vos Conimbricae scholae
> Scopuli, iuventutis lues
>
> (*Iambi* 2.29–30)

and indeed, there seem to have been many such ladies of easy virtue who
haunted university centres in the sixteenth century. Leonora, it seems, is
the daughter of a prostitute turned bawd (Peiris) and was married until
her insatiable greed drove her husband to the Portuguese colonies in
India (see *Iambi* 2, *Miscellany* 7). She has a daughter whom she claims is
the child of a Franciscan (*Epigrams* I.47) and who is carrying on the family
business (*Epigrams* I.41). Leonora at one time had a close association with
the Franciscans but has since developed a distinct penchant for cooks
(*Elegy* 7, *Iambi* 2); she wears an excess of make-up which reflects her
duplicity and falsehood (*Elegy* 8, *Epigrams* I.16, 17, 22, 28, 52, *Miscellany*
6); she is described as being old and unattractive (*Iambi* 2 and 4); and this
will soon deprive her of young men willing to slake her unquenchable
sexual thirst (*Iambi* 5, *Epigrams* I.25, *Miscellany* 19). Many of these themes
are common in Greek and Roman poetry, but in spite of the conventional
aspects of Leonora's character, she is nevertheless convincing, especially
in the iambic poems where, thanks to the vigour of the description and
the close linking of Leonora to the Coimbra background, she really comes
to life.

Although, therefore, many of these themes are not new, the figure of
the prostitute is seldom a target in the ancient world. She is accepted as
part of everyday life by the Greek Anthology poets, and while she may
occasionally be quite acquisitive, her character is rarely described in
sufficient detail for the purposes of satire. Amongst the Roman writers,
the poet's mistress is generally a courtesan of some kind (with the notable
exception of Catullus' Lesbia) and it is the *lena* who bears the brunt of the
poet's wrath for corrupting his mistress with ideas of gaining money (for
example, Ovid, *Amores* 1.8; Propertius 4.5; Tibullus 1.5). Even Juvenal in
his sixth satire is not so much interested in prostitutes as he is in the
behaviour of Patrician women. The Roman comic writers, especially
Plautus, are the authors mainly responsible for portraying the *meretrix*
and *lena*, but in the case of the former at least, she is normally seen as an
amiable character, with the exception of the calculating Phronesium in the
Truculentus. Even here, it is unusual for the prostitute to be portrayed in
such detail as Leonora is.

Something of the direct, hyperbolic and vituperative tone of the iambic
poems is conveyed in *Iambi* 4:

> Miniata labra, sordidae creta genae,
>   Hiatus oris indecens
> Rictu canino, putridi dentes, pares
>   Mammae caprinis utribus,
> Laciniosi gutturis deformitas,   5
>   Sulcique laterum pinguium,

Crassoque venter extumens abdomine,
  Ego vos amavi? brachiis
Fovi, refovique, et fatigavi meis
  Viscata labra basiis?   10
Plebi lupanar prostitutum sordidae
  Vocare amores pertuli?
O fraus, amorque, et mentis emotae furor,
  Et impotens impetus,
Quo me abstulistis? vindices Erinnyes,   15
  Quo vapulavi crimine
Vestrum ad tribunal? non enim Cupidinis
  Dolui sagitta saucius,
Sed vestra adustus, vestra adustus lampade,
  Furore vestro insanii.   20
Ergo pudendis liberatus vinculis,
  Meique iuris redditus,
Sanctae Saluti sospitatrici meae
  Et has catellas ferreas,
Monumenta duri servitî, et tabellulam   25
  Hanc sanitatis indicem
Per eam receptae, et memoris animi pignora
  Dono, libensque dedico.

(Lips covered with red paint, cheeks filthy with chalk, the shameless cleft of your mouth with its dog-like grin, rotting teeth, breasts like a she-goat's udders, the ugliness of your double chins, and the wrinkles in your fat flanks, and your belly swelling in a fat paunch, did I love you? did I caress and caress you again in my arms, and tire your alluring lips with my kisses? could I bear to call you 'my love', you bordello prostituted to the dirty rabble. Oh deceit and love, insanity of a disturbed mind, and raging impulse, where did you take me? Avenging Furies, for what crime was I flogged before your judgement seat? For I did not smart from the wound of Cupid's arrow, but I was burnt with your torch, burnt with your frenzy I was mad. So, freed from my shameful bonds and restored as my own master, I give and gladly dedicate to sacred Health, my saviour, these iron chains, the monuments of my harsh slavery, and this plaque which indicates the return of my sanity thanks to her, and the pledges of my grateful heart.)

The poem, consisting of a description of Leonora past her prime and an expression of surprise by the poet that he ever loved her, ends with a dedication of the symbols of his bondage to the gods of reason, to thank them for the return of his sanity (for the general idea of which, see Horace, *Odes* 1.5). The description in the first seven lines is particularly bitter and violent, and has much in common with Horace, *Epodes* 8, compare lines 7–10 of that poem:

> sed incitat me pectus et mammae putres,
>   equina quales ubera,
> venterque mollis et femur tumentibus
>   exile suris additum.

There is no attempt at wit here. Rather, the poet is demonstrating his abilities as a virtuoso of denigration, constantly searching for lurid images which sufficiently sum up his antipathy, his physical revulsion for Leonora. We are presented with the vision of an ageing and naked Leonora, the most intimate parts of her anatomy exposed to our critical gaze. Yet the description is crueller than this, for the poet is addressing Leonora directly, destroying any illusions she may still have about herself. The incredulous rhetorical questions (lines 8–17), reflecting the poet's sudden return to sanity and the realisation of what he has escaped, are reminiscent of Catullus, as is the use of repetition and diminutives; but Buchanan does not yet exhibit all the characteristics of the Neo-catullan style which he would exploit in the Neaera cycle. As the poem progresses, it is as if Leonora is forgotten, so final is the break. The Furies become the subject of the second half of the poem until finally, the poet makes his thank offering. Even his rage has now abated and he can contemplate his former errors with equanimity.

Miscellany 6, typical of the elegiac poems addressed to Leonora, deals like *Elegy 8 and Epigrams* I.22 and 28 with the parallel between her artful beauty preparations and her inherent falsehood. There is a marked difference of tone between the iambic compositions and these poems, characterised by a greater impression of balance, a less spontaneous-sounding style, and a more studied wit in the elegiac verse. *Miscellany* 6 is a carefully argued piece in which the poet, as in *Iambi* 4, is addressing Leonora directly. He presents his evidence against her using a diction which owes much to Martial,[11] but there is none of the hyperbole which characterises the iambic poems. The *pointe* in the final distich relies on the reader's acquaintance with the ancient painter and sculptor, Apelles and Myron, and may have been suggested by Propertius 1.2, where the poet also criticises his mistress's use of cosmetics, cf. lines 21–2:

> sed facies aderat nullis obnoxia gemmis,
>   qualis Apelleis est color in tabulis.

Buchanan is highly conscious in the Leonora poems of the concept of *decorum*, in which the original choice of metre is of paramount importance. From this follows the style of the poem, the diction, and to a large extent even the subject matter. The occasional obscenity of the iambic poems has shocked Buchanan's critics in the past, and they have sought to excuse him by pointing to the educative nature of the poems. Certainly, they contain some elements of satire, but these tend to be in the form of oblique attacks against the Franciscans. The obscenity here is much more akin to that of the 'In Scaraboeum' where the author, in the manner of Catullus or Martial, simply revels in the virtuosity of his powers of abuse, so that it is much more simply a function of the genre of verse that Buchanan is following.[12] He seems to have enjoyed this hyperbolic use of language in the Leonora poems, and composing them as he did in the late 1540s, he is anticipating the mainstream of anti-bawd/prostitute poetry, which was to be a popular subject with a number of the Pléiade poets, although Marot too had indulged in this theme in several of his *Epigrammes*. Du Bellay and Ronsard both have verses against bawds, for example, the former's 'L'Antérotique de la vieille et de la jeune amie' (1549), and the later compositions 'Contre une vieille' and 'La Courtisane repentie'; and Ronsard's 'Contre Denise sorcière' (1550) and the third *Folastrie* (1553).[13] But these poems are much more in the tradition of Ovid, *Amores* 1.8 and Propertius 4.5. More similar in tone to Buchanan is Etienne Forcadel's poem 'A Ysabeau':

> Avecques je ne sçay quel fard
> Plus que toymesmes tu es belle.
> La nuict ta face couche à part
> Et dans cent boetes on la cele.[14]

Jacques Tahureau, whose *Premières poésies* first appeared in 1554, also has a number of poems which are similar in tone to Buchanan's, for example 'A Nérée':

> Ne t'ebahis plus si Nérée
> Vend si cher maintenant l'amour.
> Elle veut avoyr, la rusée,
> Dequoy l'achepter à son tour;

and 'De Denise':

> Qu'il y vienne un vieillard baveux,
> Palle, ridé, tousseux, morveux,
> Mais qu'il soit quelque peu paillard,
> Mon Dieu, quel brusque et beau vieillard.[15]

It is not only in the area of erotic poetry that the literary tastes of Buchanan and his vernacular colleagues coincided. Throughout the 1550s, after his return to France, there is a considerable degree of fellow-feeling, if not collaboration, between Buchanan and the Pléiade with respect to Court poetry, where Horace, once again, provides much of the inspiration.[16] As we have already seen, Buchanan soon became accepted by the French

Establishment, and *Miscellany* 8 on the relief of the siege of Metz, written at the encouragement of the Pléiade in rivalry with Mellin de Saint-Gelais, marks the beginning of a series of poems concerning national affairs.[17] *Miscellany* 3 and 23 are both devoted to Charles de Brissac, Buchanan's future patron and employer, the first poem being a general eulogy, while the second celebrates his capture of Vercelli in 1553. However, this association with Brissac did not prevent Buchanan from celebrating the Guises, and in *Miscellany* 1, their fame and French nationalism are notable in a poem marking the recapture of Calais by François de Guise.

These four poems represent Buchanan's most sustained effort in Horatian lyric poetry in the secular realm, and they exhibit some characteristics of style which are relatively new to the Scottish poet. *Miscellany* 23, addressed to Cossé after the capture of Vercelli, is written in couplets composed of iambic trimeters and dimeters, like several of the Leonora poems. Lines 1–28 announce the subject of the poem, first by two questions which set the scene in Italy, then after dismissing a number of possible attractions across the Alps, by concentrating on Cossé himself. Vercelli and the events concerning its capture form the central section of the poem (lines 29–82) with particular emphasis throughout on the peaceful way in which the campaign was conducted. The poem ends with Buchanan's praise of Cossé, both for his *robur* and his *clementia*.

The tone of the poem is grand in style, owing a great deal to the Horatian ode. This is apparent to a certain extent in the vocabulary which includes a number of expressions borrowed from the Roman poet, for example line 2 'curru volucri', cf. *Odes* 1.34.8; line 19 'columbas . . . imbelles', cf. *Odes* 4.4.31; line 20 'ales minister fulminis', cf. *Odes* 4.4.1; line 21 'decoro squallidum pulvere', cf. *Odes* 2.1.22. Buchanan's use of geographical names, especially in Greek forms, is also typical of Horace (for example, Oenotria for Italy, line 4; Pelasgi, line 11). Unlike some of Buchanan's other poems at this time, but in common with Horace, there are no compound adjectives to be found. However, elevation of tone is assured by a number of similes and comparisons, such as the anatomical comparison of lines 73–4, the astronomical simile of lines 14–15, the bird imagery of lines 19–20, and the reference to Orpheus in lines 77–82, where Nature is surprised to see her laws being reversed no less spectacularly

> Quam vatis olim Thracii
> Ad carmen manes stare, silvas currere,
> Cervo leonem, ovi lupum
> Mitem accubare, et acribus lepusculum
> Latus Molossis iungere.

Buchanan also develops a theatrical metaphor at some length in lines 35–7, speaking of Vercelli:

> Inusitato quam theatrum coelites
>   Elegerint spectaculo;
> Cum, te chorago, pace cum placida feram
>   Mars copulavit dexteram.

Throughout the poem, considerable emphasis is laid on themes of peace and discord, on the benefits conferred by Orpheus, on Nature, and on nostalgia for the Golden Age, themes which were also important in Ronsard's poetry around this time.

Another aspect of *Miscellany* 23 is the care which Buchanan has taken over pattern rhetoric and the sonorities of the verse. Repetition, as we have observed in Buchanan, is used to good effect, as in lines 29–31:

> Vercella pectus una sollicitat meum,
>   Vercella sola macerat,
> Vercella victa, Galliis, dum vincitur

where alliteration on the letters *v*, *c*, and *t* also adds to the insistent tone. Later on, the repetition of *non* in lines 49–52 hammers home the point which the poet is making, and this is taken up once more in lines 55–61. Further down, in lines 61–4, the alliteration and assonance help to conjure up the sounds of battle:

> . . . Subitus oppressae sonus
>   Urbis, tubarum et cornuum
> Clangor, virorum clamor, armorum fragor,
>   Vulgi insidebant auribus[18]

(cf. Virgil's expression in *Aeneid* 2.313 and 11.192, 'clamorque virum clangorque tubarum'). Moreover, the poem is generally smooth-flowing, with few elisions and hiatuses.

Buchanan's style here is a good demonstration of what the Pléiade was aiming at in the 1550s: erudite, elevated, but nevertheless managing to avoid arid obscurity. Vocabulary, with the use of periphrasis (e.g. 'ales minister fulminis', 'plumbeaeque grandinis procella', 'vatis Thracii'), carefully chosen, apt epithets, and noble terms, has an important role in this, along with the use of metaphors and extended similes, and grand-sounding proper nouns. Horace's influence, as we have seen, is important here, but other non-Horatian elements help to establish the style and diction. As usual, Buchanan is being quite eclectic.

Another important political ode, this time written in the alcaic metre, was *Miscellany* 1, on the capture of Calais.[19] The grand opening (lines 1–12) asserts God's control over the world (and incidentally, Buchanan's faith in the Ptolomaic system) in a manner reminiscent of some of his own Psalm paraphrases. Confirmation of this is provided in the central section of the ode, describing the duc de Guise's victory over the English, which is explained by the conduct of the English queen (lines 89 to the end).

The poem is largely descriptive and expository, and does not make extensive use of imagery. Epithets, on the other hand, do have a significant role in setting the tone of the poem. There are three compound adjectives (*imbrifer*, line 20; *horrifer*, *line 60; and terrificus*, line 104) which are relatively uncommon in classical Latin, as is *ninguidus* (line 73). However, it is the combinations of epithets which do so much to produce graphic images throughout the poem, compare lines 41–4:

> Hiems retuso languida spiculo
> Vim mitigavit frigoris asperi;
> Siccis per hibernum serenum
> Nube cava stetit imber arvis.

In fact, adjectives describing meteorological phenomena play a central part in the ode, and strongly influence the overall impression created, cf. *algidus*, line 31; *nivalis*, line 33; *acutus*, line 34; *algens*, line 35; *canus* line 58, etc. Moreover, a number of these expressions are probably modelled on classical poets, compare line 34 and Horace, *Odes* 1.9.3–4 'geluque/flumina constiterint acuto'; line 44 'nube cava', a common expression in classical Latin, cf. Virgil, *Aeneid* 1.516 and 5.810; cf. also 'canis . . . nivibus' and Horace, *Satires* 2.5.41. Lines 45–7 probably have *Aeneid* 1.52–4 in mind:

> . . . hic vasto rex Aeolus antro
> luctantis ventos tempestatesque sonoras
> imperio premit ac vinclis et carcere frenat.

So, to a large extent, it is the choice of adjectives, and in some cases their allusive qualities, which help to set the elevated tone of *Miscellany* 1.

Other forms of imagery are not completely absent, of course. For example, winter is described in military terms in lines 54–5, virtue is spoken of as following a path (lines 85–6), and in a particularly vivid metaphor, Mary Tudor is described as

> et civium et hostium
> Hirudo communis, cruorem
> Aeque avide sitiens utrumque.

Mythology plays some part, although not an obtrusive one in a poem about God's control over world events. However, we have seen allusions to Neptune and Aeolus (line 46), Naples is referred to as Parthenope (line 78), an allusion to one of the Sirens after whom the city was named, and Nemesis occupies a significant position at the end of the poem. The effect of these and other mythological references is to heighten the tone of the poem, but without recalling their contexts too closely. Word order and pattern rhetoric are as important as ever in Buchanan (see, for example, lines 11–12 and 65–6), while throughout the poem, he fully exploits the different rhythms within the alcaic metre, assisted by alliteration and assonance.

Buchanan and Catullus

Horace, then, provided Buchanan with an important model during his period in Coimbra and Paris. But at the same time, he drew on a very different source of inspiration, Catullus, for two contrasting groups of poems. The Beleago poems constitute a sustained attack on the Scotsman's colleague at the Colégio das Artes, while the Neaera poems, probably written in the early 1550s, form a short cycle of amatory verse in honour of an almost certainly imaginary beloved.

Outside France, Michael Marullus and Joannes Secundus had already written poetry inspired by Catullus, and a recognisable Neo-catullan style had evolved, which exaggerated many of the tendencies to be found in the Roman poet. The poetry is characterised by a limited number of recurring themes, like the 'odi et amo', the 'basium', and the 'vivamus atque amemus' motifs, while the style owes its individuality to a number of points, which may be illustrated from the epigrams of Marullus.

(a) Diminutives

These occur very frequently, seldom with any important shade of meaning. Occasionally, double diminutives are used (*misellulus, ocellulus*). They tend to set the tone of the poems, however, and in the vernacular poetry of the Pléiade, they are an important component of the *style mignard*. See Marullus, *Epigrams* 4.2:

> Tota es candida, tota munda, tota
> Succi plenula, tota mollicella.

(b) Indefinite constructions

These usually involve a comparative of some kind, and are often repeated a number of times in the course of the poem, for example Marullus, *Epigrams* 1.28.4, 'Aut si triste magis potest quid esse', which is repeated at line 9.

(c) Repetition

This also occurs frequently, and ranges from the repetition of single words to whole line and sentences, cf. Marullus 1.13:

> Ut, ni me lacrimae rigent perennes,
> Totus in tenues eam favillas.
> Sic rursum lacrimae rigant perennes. . . .

(d)   Abstract nouns

These are often used in the plural to refer to the poet's mistress, for example 'nequitiae meae', 'mei lepores', 'vita', 'lux mea'.

(e)   Familiarity of Tone

This is exhibited in the frequent use of questions, parenthetical remarks, exclamations, etc., for example:

> Ne time: ah miser, ah miser peribo!   (Marullus, 1.18)
>
> Te ne vivere ego queam relicta?   (Marullus, 1.2)
>
> Vixi carior omnibus medullis—
> Nisi iam hoc quoque denegas—tuisque
> Qui nunc sic miserum necant, ocellis.   (Marullus, 2.12)

(f)   Adverbs

Finally, the use of adverbs ending in *-im* is quite widespread among the Neo-catullan poets, for example *paullatim, conchatim, ubertim,* while the *huc . . . illuc* and *modo . . . modo . . .* constructions are also common.

The metre most commonly used for Neo-catullan poems is the hendeca-syllable.

The series of poems addressed to Beleago is something of an enigma.[20] Belchior Beliagoa is an odd figure, whose relations with Buchanan and his Bordeaux friends are difficult to fathom. As the butt of Buchanan's satire, it would seem that he was an incorrigible liar and a profiteer. He certainly seems to have started unfounded rumours that three of Buchanan's colleagues who left the Colégio das Artes in 1549 went straight to Geneva, and it is perhaps in direct retaliation for this that the Scotsman accuses him of being a Jew. However, he seems to have spent a certain amount of time in the company and as a guest of the Bordeaux teachers, and when called upon by the Inquisition to give evidence, he did not incriminate any of the three defendants, Buchanan, Teive, and Costa.

The poems directed against him are written in iambic metres with the exception of *Hendecasyllables* 7 and *Epigrams* I.18. *Fratres fraterrimi* 2 is perhaps the most typically Catullan in tone:

> Beleago fomes et parens mendacii
> Ab ore cuius pavida veritas fugit,
> Mali sussurat nescio quid clanculum;
> At fama de illo non sussurat, sed palam
> Hoc universus populus affirmat, quod est   5

'Beleago fomes et parens mendacii,
Ab ore cuius pavida veritas fugit.'
Hoc igitur aequus aestimator iudicet,
An mentiatur populus universus, an
Beleago fomes et parens mendacii,   10
Ab ore cuius pavida veritas fugit.

(Beleago, the source and father of deceit, from whose lips truth flees in terror, is whispering something evil on the quiet. But about him Rumour does not whisper, and the whole nation affirms publicly as follows: 'Beleago is the source and father of deceit, from whose lips truth flees in terror.' So, let a fair arbiter judge whether the whole nation is lying or whether Beleago is the source and father of deceit, from whose lips truth flees in terror.)

The refrain-like repetition of lines 1–2 in lines 6–7 and 10–11 is reminiscent of Catullus' use of repetition in, for example, *Carmina* 29, 57, 112 etc., and the diminutive 'clanculum', although a pre-classical word, is true to the spirit of Neo-catullan diction. The direct tone and absence of any witty conclusion is also typical of the Roman poet, as compared with the more consciously humorous epigrams of Martial. It is the pure insistence of the poem that produces its effect.

In contrast, the Neaera poems form a far gentler cycle in praise of the poet's beloved.[21] The majority (with the exception of *Elegy* 9, and *Epigrams* I.26, 27, and 31) are in hendecasyllables, and are very clearly Neo-catullan in style. Diminutives are scattered throughout (see, for example, *Hendecasyllables* 1.3 'ocelluli miselli'; 4.38 'turgidulas papillas'); the indefinite construction appears a number of times, e.g. *Hendecasyllables* 4:

Et quicquid malesana corda amantum
Blanda ebria fascinat venenis

and *Hendecasyllables* 6:

. . . Deisve
Si quid altius est beatiusve.

Both these lines are repeated in the course of the poem, and this use of repetition is employed frequently by Buchanan in the Neaera poems, ranging from anaphora involving a single word (e.g. 'frustra' in lines 16–19 of *Hendecasyllables* 4) to the repetition of several lines such as:

Risus, blanditiae, procacitates,
Lusus, nequitiae, facetiaeque,
Ioci, deliciaeque, et illecebrae,
Et suspiria, et oscula, et susurri   (*Hendecasyllables* 4.1–4)

which are repeated in the middle of the poem and at the end. The tone of the *Hendecasyllables* too is direct and conversational, as was the case with Marullus. Questions are common:

Quid me mollibus implicas lacertis?
Quid procacibus intuere ocellis?
Quid fallacibus osculis inescas?   (*Hendecasyllables* 4.24–6)

and exclamations are also present, for example 'O saevissime numinum Cupido' (*Hendecasyllables* 2.14).

Despite mastering with little difficulty the idiom of Neo-catullan amatory verse, it is a genre which Buchanan obviously did not feel altogether at home with, rather like du Bellay in *L'Olive* (1549). He seems to find it hard to take either himself or his poetry seriously, as is illustrated in *Hendeca-syllables* 1:

Cum primum mihi candidae Neaerae
Illos sideribus pares ocellos
Ostendistis, ocelluli miselli,
Illa principium fuit malorum,
Illa lux animi ruina nostri.   5
Sic primis radiis repente tactus
Totus intremui cohorruique,
Ut leves nemorum comae virentum
Primis flatibus intremunt Favoni.
Et cor iam meditans ad illam abire   10
Per pectus trepidansque palpitansque
Iamque evadere iamque gestiebat:
Ceu solet puer artubus tenellis,
Quem nutrix gremio fovet, parentem
Affectare oculis et ore, parva   15
Iactans brachia: ceu solent volucres
Adhuc involucres volandi inani
Infirmas studio movere pennas.
Tum mens provida, virium suarum
Quippe conscia, ne locus dolosis   20
Esset insidiis, miselli ocelli,
Vos ad pectoris excubare portas
Insomni statione iussit. At vos,
Sive blanditiis dolisve capti,
Seu somno superante, sive sponte   25
Consensistis, herumque prodidistis,
Fugit corque animusque, me relicto
Excorde, exanimo. Quod ergo fletu
Nunc satisfacere arbitremini vos,
Nil est; quem lacrymis movere vultis   30
Non adest animusve corve. Ad illam
Ite: orateque et impetrate ab illa.
Ni exoraritis, impetraritisque,
Faxo illam aspiciatis usque et usque,
Donec vos ita luce reddat orbos,   35
Ut me corde animoque fecit orbum.

(When first, wretched little eyes, you showed me those eyes of fair Neaera which are like the stars, that light was the beginning of our woes, that was the downfall of our soul. Suddenly touched by the first rays of that light, I trembled and shuddered all over, as the light leaves of the verdant woods tremble at the first breath of the West Wind. And my heart, which was now thinking of going over to her, beating fast and pounding in my breast, now desired to escape, just as a child of tender little limbs, caressed in the nurse's bosom, is accustomed to try to get his parent's attention with his eyes and face, throwing about his little arms, or as birds still unable to fly are accustomed to move their feeble wings in a vain desire to fly. Then my prudent mind, knowing its own strength, to prevent any opportunity of a treacherous ambush, oh wretched little eyes, ordered you to keep watch by the doors of my heart in a sleepless sentry-duty. But whether you were overcome by allurements or deceit, or over-powering sleep, or whether you agreed of your own free will, you betrayed your master, and my heart and soul fled, leaving me heartless and soulless. So it is of no avail that you think you are now making amends with weeping. The soul and heart which you wish to move with tears are not here. Go to her, beg and implore her. Unless you beg and implore, I shall make you gaze upon her constantly until she deprives you of your sight as she has deprived me of my heart and soul.)

We are presented here with a description of the *innamoramento* with Neaera, a topic dealt with time and again by Renaissance writers. As is often the case, it is the eyes that have played a dominant role, 'illos sideribus pares ocellos' (cf. Ovid, *Metamorphoses* 1.498–9, 'videt igne micantes/sideri-bus similes oculos'). In many ways, Buchanan seems to follow Plato's des-cription of falling in love in *Phaedrus* 251 sqq. much more closely than is usual:

> But he who is newly initiated, who beheld many of those realities, when he sees a godlike face or form which is a good image of beauty, shudders at first, and something of the old awe comes over him.[22]

Compare this with lines 6–7. Buchanan's heart 'per pectus trepidansque palpitansque' is mirrored in Plato's soul which 'is all in a state of ferment and throbbing' (ζεῖ οὖν ἐν τούτῳ ὅλη καὶ ἀνακηκίει). The simile of lines 16–18 may be suggested by Plato's description of the soul sprouting wings (*Phaedrus* 251 b and c), and the loss of the poet's heart and soul to the beloved is certainly part of the Neo-platonic tradition. However, although much of the imagery and detail of this poem is Platonic, (and Buchanan seems much closer to the *Phaedrus* than to later vulgarisations), the tone of the second half is less serious. The military imagery of the mind putting the eyes on sentry duty to guard the heart, their betrayal 'sive blanditiis dolisve capti', and the flight of the heart and soul can only raise a smile. Buchanan is indulging himself in a game which he can play as well as the next man, but which he cannot take too seriously. Instead of finally coming round to glory in the pain of his love, as one would expect as the conclusion of a

Renaissance *innamoramento* poem, the poet ends with a threat to his eyes (lines 34–6). The Platonic opening, suggestive of the search for Beauty, is shattered by a distinctly down-to-earth conclusion.

Buchanan introduces a reasonable amount of variety into the Neaera cycle. *Hendecasyllables* 2, for example, is firmly rooted in the Petrarchan tradition as far as imagery is concerned, although the slightly more sensual tone of the poem has more in common with Ronsard's *Amours* 12 and 44 (Laumonier IV.16 and 44); while *Hendecasyllables* 3 is based on the 'odi et amo' theme popularised by Catullus 85, and later taken over and elaborated by Marullus (Epigrams 4.29), who in turn was paraphrased by Ronsard in the *Nouvelle continuation des Amours* (as 'Je te hay bien . . . '). Elsewhere, Buchanan takes his inspiration from the Greek Anthology (compare *Epigrams* I.44 and *Elegy* 9 with Anthologia Palatina 5.230), or, turning to more contemporary sources, produces *Epigrams* I.31, a description of Neaera's cruelty.

> Illa mihi semper praesenti dura Neaera,
>   Me, quoties absum, semper abesse dolet.
> Non desiderio nostri, non moeret amore,
>   Sed se non nostro posse dolore frui.

She only regrets the poet's absence because she is unable to enjoy the spectacle of his torment. This little epigram expresses the same sentiments as a *dizain* by Mellin de Saint-Gelais,[23] and the textual similarities indicate that one of the two poems is based closely on the other, compare Mellin's lines:

> . . . je croy certainement
> Que ce n'est point pour me voir lointain d'elle,
> Mais pour me voir esloigné de torment

with the final two lines of Buchanan's poem.

Like the Leonora cycle, with which they were often circulated, the Neaera poems proved to be very successful, and attest Buchanan's sympathy for the vernacular poetry of his contemporaries. Although it is perhaps dangerous to make too much out of a small number of poems, there is evidence to suggest that his tastes continued to be in step with the fashions of the Pléiade throughout the 1550s. For example, Ronsard's gradual move away from the ode to alexandrine verse is paralleled by Buchanan's favouring hexameter compositions once again towards the end of the decade. Thus, it is the hexameter which he chooses for the long epithalamium on the marriage of Mary Stuart to the dauphin François in 1558 (*Silvae* 4); and the same metre is used to mark the latter's death in 1560 (*Silvae* 5).[24]

The 'De Sphaera'

Buchanan's most ambitious project at this time, the *De sphaera*, also reflects the interest of Ronsard and other members of the Pléiade in cosmographical poetry.[25] It must, however, be admitted that Buchanan's attempt at presenting this subject is less successful from the poetic viewpoint than, for example, Ronsard's *Hymnes*; for despite a careful, often Lucretian, style (*decorum* continues to determine Buchanan's *elocutio*), the occasional purple patch (for example, the description of Avarice, 1. 181–211), and, following the *Georgics*, the obligatory myth in the last book (the story of Endymion, 5.116–96), the poem does have its *longueurs*, and the information it contains is anything but novel. Upholding the Ptolemaic system, Buchanan sets out to refute modern ideas on astronomy, stoutly maintaining the traditional view of things.

Book I, dealing with the sublunar (mortal) and supralunar (immortal) division of the universe, a frequent theme in Ronsard, argues forcefully for the roundness and immobility of the Earth. Dealing as it does with general concepts in a lively and rhetorical manner, this section proves to be an entertaining one. Book II propounds a geocentric view of the universe, covers the motion of the planets, refutes Epicurean ideas on astronomy, and speaks of the quintessence.[26] Book III deals with the stars, the Zodiac, the zones of the Earth, ending with an expression of admiration for the theories of Posidonius. Most of the fourth book, on the courses of the stars and planets, remains incomplete, while the fifth book is concerned to a large extent with eclipses. Much of the information in this section is put into the mouth of Sulpicius Gallus, which at least has the effect of injecting variety into the material. It is a device Buchanan had previously used in the *Franciscanus*.

Although the *De sphaera* was started in the 1550s (in 2.136 Buchanan refers to himself sitting by the river Po with his pupil, the poem's dedicatee Timoléon de Cossé), it took many years before the Scotsman brought the poem to its present unfinished state, despite considerable encouragement from his friends.[27] One reason may be his involvement, on his return to Scotland, in other projects of greater import: the history of Scotland, affairs of state, and the education of James VI. But there may be other reasons too. In spite of his undoubted interest in astronomy (attested in later life by his friendship with Tycho Brahé),[28] the subject may not have proved so tractable to being versified as he might have wished. It is certainly the polemical passages, along with the digressions, which contain most interest, at least for the modern reader, and it is no doubt significant that it was the most technical of the five books which Buchanan left largely unfinished.

From this consideration of the works which Buchanan composed between his departure for Portugal in 1547 and his final return to Scotland, it is clear that his poetic style and tone underwent a number of changes, following as well as setting literary fashions. At the same time, it is probably incorrect to speak of these changes in terms of a radical shift of direction, since to a large extent it is as always the principle of *decorum* which is at work, shaping Buchanan's style.

Judging by the serious nature of many of his projects (the Psalm paraphrases, the *De sphaera*, the Court poetry), Buchanan would seem to be moving towards a somewhat loftier view of poetry than hitherto, and he invokes the names of Apollo and the Muses more frequently than in his earlier compositions. Mythological allusions increase in number, while his imagery now embraces the extended simile (previously reserved mainly for ironic contexts), more elaborate metaphors, antonomasia, and a generally more elevated diction. Careful choice of epithet had always been an important consideration, but he now becomes bolder in his selection of adjectives, using compounds, at times, perhaps, of his own formation. Horace is probably the single most influential poet on Buchanan throughout this period.

All these tendencies kept Buchanan very much in contact with vernacular writers. Independently of the Pléiade, his verse had been moving in the same direction as theirs; indeed, it had contained at the outset many of the principles which they were later to espouse. Neo-latin poetry had for years shown the path which the Pléiade eventually established in the vernacular by its inherent demands to be taken seriously. It was by definition erudite, was firmly rooted in classical antiquity, while at the same time being innovatory. Buchanan's poetry must certainly have guided the future members of the Pléiade in the 1540s when he was involved in so many of the pursuits which du Bellay was to recommend in the *Deffense et illustration*. He would therefore quite naturally have been turned to as an ally on returning from Portugal, and whilst he needed to modify his poetic style to accommodate the new tastes which were developing in encomiastic and Court poetry, this by no means necessitated any great upheaval on his part. Buchanan's renewed association in the 1550s with the Pléiade thus proved to be mutually beneficial, and marks the apogee of his poetic powers.

CHAPTER 6

The Final Years

Buchanan's final years in Scotland, from 1561 until his death in 1582, were not to be very fruitful ones as far as poetry was concerned, although we have seen that the Scottish humanist was far from idle in other fields of activity.[1] As regards poetry, the final two decades of his life were devoted largely to completing old projects (the Psalm paraphrases, the *De sphaera*), revising earlier works, and composing epigrams, mostly of a personal or occasional nature. The only substantial pieces written at this time are *Silvae* 7, a poem celebrating the birth of James VI in 1566, and the 'Satyra in Carolum Lotharingum Cardinalem', written in the aftermath of the Saint Bartholomew Day massacre of 1572. Buchanan's close association with the Scottish royal family also led him into the field of Court entertainment in the composition of *Pompae* for Mary Stuart's marriage to Darnley, and on the birth of their son.

In a poem to Walter Haddon (*Iambi* 1), presumably written around 1565 (see line 13), Buchanan sets out his reasons for not writing as much poetry as hitherto. It seems that Haddon, a product of Eton and King's College, Cambridge, and since the accession of Elizabeth I a master of the court of requests, had asked Buchanan for some poetic compositions. Haddon himself had something of a reputation as a Latin poet, and when Queen Elizabeth was asked which of the two she preferred, Haddon or Buchanan, she is reported to have produced the tactful reply: 'Buchananum omnibus antepono, Haddonem nemini postpono.' Moreover, the temperaments of the two men seem to have had much in common, including their sometimes off-hand way of dealing with royalty. When Elizabeth complained of the smell of Haddon's boots, he replied: 'I believe, madam, it is not my new boots which stink, but the old petitions which have been so long in my bag unopened.'[2]

In response to Haddon's request, Buchanan claims, in terms reminiscent of Horace, that he is no longer capable of producing the juvenilia of former years.

> Nunc, cum capillis sparserit canentibus
> Declivis aetas tempora,
> Cum pulset annus pene sexagesimus
> Animique langueat vigor,

Surdus roganti Phoebus aurem denegat,
  Musae vocantem negligunt.
Nec Phyllidis me nunc iuvat flavam comam
  Praeferre Bacchi crinibus,
Nec in Neaerae perfidam superbiam
  Saevos Iambos stringere.   (ll. 11–20)

(Now that declining years have sprinkled my temples with white hair, now that almost my sixtieth year is knocking at the door, and my mental acuity is weakening, Apollo turns a deaf ear to my requests, the Muses neglect me when I call. I no longer delight in preferring Phyllis's golden hair to the locks of Bacchus, or in launching my cruel iambic verse on Neaera's treacherous pride.)

His thoughts are now turned, he says, to political issues, and the future of his country whose well-being he sees in an alliance with England, all the more enduring for being strengthened by a common religion:

Dicam Gradivum vinculis coërcitum,
  Legum coactam iniuriam
Parere frenis, vim repressam et aurei
  Beati secli commoda.
Et nostra si quid audiendum vox dabit,
  Laudi Dearum serviet
Virtute quarum pax agros Britanniae,
  Urbes fides, fora aequitas,
Et templa pietas, impiis erroribus
  Procul relegatis, colet.   (ll. 53–62)

(I shall sing of Mars enclosed in bonds, of injustice forced to obey the reins of law, of the suppression of force and the benefits of a blessed Golden Age. And if our voice produces anything to be heard, it will serve to praise the divinities thanks to whom peace dwells in the countryside of Britain, faith in the cities, justice in the market-places, and piety in the churches, with ungodly error banished far away.)

This elegant reply to Haddon, which demonstrates that despite his modest disclaimers, Buchanan has lost none of his poetic skill, reflects very accurately the Scotsman's new preoccupations. Poetry was now a secondary concern to statesmanship, although it could where necessary be put at the service of the state.

Although Buchanan did not break off all connections with French friends and colleagues after his return to Scotland, he did, almost for the first time, establish literary contacts with English writers, which were perhaps due to a large extent to his political activities at Court.[3] Walter Haddon, for example, was a friend of Roger Ascham, who had been tutor to Elizabeth from 1548 to 1550. Buchanan and he must have shared views on a variety of subjects, and the Scotsman speaks of their friendship very warmly in

Epigrams 1.39. They also shared the friendship of Elizabeth's influential minister, William Cecil, who like Ascham had been educated in Cambridge at Saint John's College. Cecil's second wife, Mildred, was the daughter of Sir Anthony Cooke, and Buchanan appears to have been on excellent terms with the rest of this erudite family. Ann Cooke was married to Sir Nicholas Bacon, who was another of Elizabeth's ministers and father of the more famous essayist, Francis; and Catherine Cooke married Sir Henry Killigrew, one of Elizabeth's diplomats, who had been in Paris in 1556 and 1559. Buchanan may have met him at this time, as well as Thomas Randolph, a Marian exile, who later acted on behalf of Elizabeth's government in Scotland. All these people had much in common: most were ardent Protestants, highly educated, and were concerned with affairs in Scotland, which partly explains their connections with Buchanan; and he seems to have enjoyed close literary relations with them, exchanging Latin poems or writing verse on their behalf.[4]

But Buchanan's poems were also destined for a Scottish audience, and *Silvae* 7, on the birth of James VI, contains a clear statement of his political and religious hopes for Scotland. In the ancient world, the *genethliacon* was generally a poem written to celebrate someone's birthday, rather than the actual event of their birth, and there are examples of this in Tibullus (1.7 and 2.2), Ovid (*Tristia* 3.13), and Statius (*Silvae* 2.7). However, Virgil's fourth *Eclogue*, written in advance of the birth of the child concerned (whoever he may have been), provides a model for sixteenth-century writers. Du Bellay, amongst others, produced such a poem in his 'Ode sur la naissance du petit duc de Beaumont' (Chamard V.282–99) which opens with conventional predictions of the return of the Golden Age.

Buchanan too starts off his *genethliacon* with predictions of a future Golden Age resulting from James's birth, but it is a political paradise which he is foretelling, in which the only beasts that will lie down together in peace are the lion and the unicorn of England and Scotland.

> Cresce, puer, patriae auspiciis felicibus orte,
> Exspectate puer, cui vatum oracla priorum
> Aurea compositis promittunt secula bellis.
> Tuque peregrinis toties pulsata procellis,
> Pene tuo toties excisa Britannia ferro,   5
> Exsere laeta caput, cohibe pacalis olivae
> Fronde comam, repara flammis foedata, ruinis
> Convulsa, et pulso cole squalida tecta colono.
> Pone metum, aeternam spondent tibi sidera pacem.
> Iam neque Saxonidae Scotos, nec Saxona Scotus   10
> Infestus premet, et cognato sanguine ferrum
> Polluet, et miseras praedando exhauriet urbes.
> Sed quibus ante feri tractabant arma Gradivi,
> Iam dehinc pacatis coniungent foedera dextris.

(Oh child who have been born with glad omens for your country, grow quickly, long-awaited child, for whom the oracles of former prophets promise a Golden Age, with wars put to rest. And you, Britain, who have so often been buffeted by foreign storms and so often almost been destroyed by your own sword, gladly lift up your head, bind your hair with the peaceful olive's leaves, and repair dwellings disfigured with flames, and fallen into ruin, and tend those places which are neglected after the farmer's expulsion. Lay aside fear, the stars promise you everlasting peace. Now the Saxon race will not oppress the Scots nor the Scot in enmity oppress the Saxon, and stain their swords with a kinsman's blood, and lay waste wretched cities with plundering. But they who previously wielded the arms of fierce Mars will be joined henceforth by treaties, their hands joined in peace.)

The opening words, 'Cresce puer', are taken from Ovid, *Metamorphoses* 2.643, a passage where Ocyrhoë foretells the future of the infant Aesculapius, described as 'toto. . . salutifer orbi'. This context, in addition to Buchanan's reference to the 'vatum oracla priorum', helps establish the hieratic tone of the opening of the poem. However, this is not to be a vague catalogue of future triumphs, but very soon turns into a set of instructions on the upbringing and role of the Protestant prince (lines 15–95), an exposition of Buchanan's ideas on popular monarchy. The conduct of a nation, he argues, is entirely dependent on the behaviour of its ruler, who must constantly strive to outdo his subjects in piety, morality, and subservience to the laws of the land. Moderation must be his guide in all things, and a needlessly bellicose foreign policy or a repressive internal regime are doomed to failure. A moderate prince is the true image of God on earth ('vera Dei vivensque . . . imago', line 77), but if he acts despotically, the people are justified in deposing and even killing him. (This is one lesson which, as history shows, James did not take to heart, but which might have benefited his successor, Charles I.) The final lines of the poem (95–114), which had not been included in editions before that of Hart in 1615, contain more general advice about the Prince's academic education.

The style of the poem is in the grand, didactic manner, with similes playing an important part, as they had in the court poetry of the 1550s. Particularly noteworthy is the extended simile concerning the phoenix (lines 27–35) which is based on Claudian, *De consulatu Stilichonis* 2.414–21:

> Sic ubi de patrio redivivus funere phoenix
> Aurorae ad populos redit, et cunabula secum
> Ipse sua, et cineres patris inferiasque decoris
> Fert humeris, quacunque citis adremigat alis,
> Indigenae comitantur aves, celebrantque canoro
> Agmine; non illas species incognita tantum,
> Aut picturatae capiunt spectacula pennae,
> Quam pietas, pietas etiam intellecta volucrum
> Sensibus: . . .

(So, when the phoenix, risen from a father's corpse, returns to the peoples of the East, and brings with him on fair back his own cradle and a father's ashes and funeral offerings, wherever he flies on swift wings he is accompanied by the native birds, and his praises are sung in a tuneful flock. It is not so much his unknown appearance or the sight of his many-coloured feathers which captivate them as piety, piety which is even understood by the intellect of birds.)

Other shorter similes set the tone of the poem (lines 20–1, 39, 53) which is further reinforced by the use of quite striking metaphors as in lines 17–18 'sanctumque bibat virtutibus amorem/Cum lacte', and line 63 'Et nimium laetam vitiorum comprimit herbam'.

Such a poem may not have been calculated to endear Buchanan to his royal patrons, although in many other respects, he did fulfil the role of the court poet, producing more conventional celebrations when necessary. Masques formed an important part of court entertainment in the 1560s, and Buchanan was called upon a number of times to provide Latin verses. *Miscellany* 2, 'In Castitatem', and 16, 'Mutuus Amor', were both written for the Shrovetide festivities held in Holyrood Palace in February 1564. After an Italian poem by Mary Stuart's secretary, David Rizzio:

> The second course was ushered in by a fair young maid representing Chastity, and Latin verses by Buchanan were sung in her praise. A child, in the character of Time, accompanied the third course, and again the servants sang Latin verses by Buchanan, foretelling that, so long as heaven and earth should endure, the mutual faith and affection of Mary of Scotland and Elizabeth of England should flourish green in remembrance.[5]

The Court also witnessed celebrations in July of the following year on the occasion of Mary's marriage to Darnley. This time, the festivities lasted three days, and a masque, with words by Buchanan, was presented on each day. Day 1 was marked by the 'Pompa Deorum in nuptiis Mariae' (*O.O.* II.400–2); day 2 by the 'Pompae equestres' (*O.O.* II.402–3); and day 3 by the four Maries' address to the goddess of Health (*Miscellany* 35). On the birth of James VI, a masque involving rustic gods was composed by Buchanan and produced by one of Mary's *valets de chambre*, Bastien Pages.

> When the dishes were to be brought in, they were placed upon a table so constructed, that it seemed to move through the great hall of its own accord, accompanied by musicians in female attire, singing songs, and playing upon instruments. A procession of Rural Gods marched before, each group as it passed the dais reciting a few lines of Latin.[6]

The Englishmen present were apparently offended when the satyrs wagged their tails at the audience, 'fancying that it was done in their derision'. After the masque, there came 'a discharge of fireworks from a mimic fortress, the possession of which was contested by motely bands of Moors, Highlanders, Centaurs, Lanzknechts, and Fiends'.

Buchanan's connections with both the Scottish and the English courts were also responsible for the majority of the epigrams composed during his final years in Britain. From the poetical point of view, there is not a great deal to be said about these pieces. They are competent, well written, elegant, as one would expect, but their interest lies mainly in their content. Piercing through the conventional flattery, we have glimpses of Buchanan's relationships with the leading figures of his day, with some of whom he was evidently on close terms. The *Strenae*, or New Year's poems, of *Epigrams* III attest the Scotsman's links with the Cecil family (12–16) and Sir Anthony Cooke (17), whose erudite daughters, as we have seen, were married to some of the principal personages of the Elizabethan court. The fairly easy familiarity of these compositions contrasts strongly with the more conventional flattery of the verses addressed to Elizabeth, for example *Miscellany* 34 or *Epigrams* II, 'Icones' 25:

> Cuius imago Deae, facie cui lucet in una,
> Temperie mixta, Iuno, Minerva, Venus?
> Est Dea, quid dubitem? cui sic conspirat amice
> Mascula vis, hilaris gratia, celsus honos.
> Aut Dea si non est, Diva est quae praesidet Anglis,
> Ingenio, vultu, moribus aequa Deis.

(Of which goddess is this a picture, when on a single face there shines in due proportion Juno, Minerva, and Venus? She is a goddess—why should I doubt it?—when manly strength, delightful grace, and high honour unite so harmoniously. Or if she is not a goddess, she is a saint who presides over England, equal to the gods in intellect, beauty, and character.)

Many years before, Buchanan had spoken in just such terms of Marguerite de Navarre (*Epigrams* I.11 and 50).

Annual celebrations at court also seem to have demanded a poetic response from Buchanan. In addition to the New Year *étrennes* (*Epigrams* III), there were the feast of the Epiphany and Saint Valentine's day (*Epigrams* III, 'Valentiniana'). Moreover, the deaths of friends, colleagues, and court figures kept Buchanan busy with the composition of epitaphs. All in all, his role was that of poet laureate, first for Mary Stuart, then, after her overthrow, for the ruling Protestant faction.

But one event did reawaken the full force of Buchanan's *saeva indignatio*: the Saint Bartholomew Day massacre of 24 August 1572. In the wake of this slaughter, which provoked horror throughout the Protestant world, Buchanan composed not only the 'Satyra in Carolum Lotharingum Cardinalem', but also several unpublished works, including the 'De Casparo

Colignio Franc. Admirallio' on Coligny's death in the massacre, and a
number of epigrams addressed to the Cardinal of Lorraine and Catherine
de Médicis.[7]

The 'Satyra' clearly demonstrates that Buchanan had lost none of his
poetic vigour. The poem starts in a solemn tone, reflecting on God's punishment of the Guise family as a whole:

> Esse Deum tandem, qui iustis temperet orbem,
> Legibus, oppressos vi qui respectet egenos,
> Et premat elatos, poena didicere magistra
> Guisiadae; numerosa cohors, quae brachia coelo
> Intentare ausa est, pietatem expellere mundo   5
> Conata est, scelerique suas permittere habenas;
> Ad paucos contracta fugam, latebrasque saluti
> Respicit, et damnat sumta infeliciter arma.
> Proque tot insana quos credulitate triumphis
> Sperarat, numerat clades. Hunc dira phrenesis   10
> Abstulit, hunc moeror; fugiendo dimicat ille,
> Et vicisse putat, si visum evaserit hostem.

(The Guise family has at last learnt, taught by their punishment, that there is a God
to control the world with just laws, to respect the needy who are oppressed by
violence, and to crush the proud. Their large throng, which dared to raise their
arms against heaven, tried to drive true religion from the world, and give free rein
to crime. Reduced to a few, they look for flight and hiding-places to save themselves,
and curse the arms they unhappily took up. Instead of all the victories which they
had hoped for in their mad credulity, they count their disasters. One was destroyed
by dreadful madness, another by grief; another fights by fleeing, and thinks he is
victorious if he escapes from the enemy he has sighted.)

The opening lines seem to allude to the words of the *Magnificat*, 'Deposuit
potentes de sede, et exaltavit humiles. Esurientes implevit bonis: et divites
dimisit inanes' (Luke 1.52–3). From line 22 to the end of the poem,
Buchanan concentrates his attention, however, on the Cardinal of Lorraine
himself, in an outraged, hyperbolic style. The instigator of the massacre
survives, Buchanan asserts, to contemplate the crimes that he has
committed and to live in dread of the punishment that awaits him. He
should look at the results of his actions:

> Aspice vexatas, qua Gallia panditur, urbes,
> Aut flammis foedata aut deformata ruinis
> Oppida, disiectis tot rura inculta colonis;
> Aspice tot viduas, puerosque parentibus orbos,
> Sedibus eiectae tot mendicabula plebis,   75

> Inter fumantes villas, taboque natantes
> Sanguinis innocui campos, inhumataque passim
> Ossa virûm, laceros artus, deformiaque ora,
> Perfidiae monumenta tuae, convivia corvis
> Exposita, et canibus coenam, te dante, cruentam.   80

(See throughout France the devastated cities, the towns blackened by flames or disfigured by ruins, and all the fields which lie fallow, the farmers scattered. See all the widows, and orphaned children, all the beggars from the people who have been driven from their homes, amongst the smoking farms and fields swimming in the gore of innocent blood, men's bones everywhere lying unburied, torn limbs, hideous faces, all monuments to your treachery, feasts exposed to the crows, a bloody meal for the dogs, and all given by you.)

Further on, Buchanan adds even more revolting details, in a style similar to that adopted in later years by d'Aubigné in *Les Tragiques*.

> . . . At tu si caede cruentum
> Non poteris satiare animum, tua lumina pascant   105
> Viventum sordes, lacrymae, suspiria, luctus,
> Passim exstinctorum laceri crudeliter artus.
> Aut si carnifices oculos lassare tuendo
> Non poteris, pars ulla tui ne sit scelerum expers,
> Semianimes artus et adhuc spirantia membra   110
> Ore vora, crepitentque avidis sub dentibus ossa:
> Atque epulis tandem satur immoriare petitis.
> Aut explere tibi si nulla cadavera possunt
> Sanguinis ingluviem insanam, tua dente cruento
> Ipse tibi lania membra, in tua viscera conde   115
> Viscera: sic digno vita potiere sepulchro,
> Exitio factis, dape conveniente palato.

(But if you cannot sate your bloody mind with carnage, let your eyes be fed on the squalor of the living, their tears, groans, grief, and the cruelly torn limbs of the dead all around. Or if you cannot tire your butcher's eyes in gazing on this, let no part of you be exempt from crime. Devour in your mouth half-living limbs and still breathing members, and let bones crunch between your greedy teeth. And replete, finally die on the feasts you sought. Or if no corpses can satisfy your mad thirst for blood, you yourself tear apart your own limbs with bloody tooth, bury your inwards in your inwards. Thus you will gain a tomb worthy of your life, a fate worthy of your deeds, and a meal to suit your palate.)

As is obvious from these quotations, the style of the 'Satyra' is a muscular one, relying on hyperbolic rhetorical devices like enumeration, apostrophe, vivid use of epithets, repetition etc. Graphic compound adjectives are used (*flexanimus*, line 84, *colubrifer*, line 92, etc.) and, apart from the Christian opening of the poem, there are frequent appeals to classical mythology, especially in the various evocations of Hell. Buchanan had lost none of his satyrical bite.

However, in spite of stylistic similarities with his 1550s compositions, the 'Satyra' does represent yet another shift of direction. For the satirical content of this composition is far more committed and vitriolic than earlier, more urbane works like the 'Palinodes', the 'Pro lena', and even the *Franciscanus*. Agrippa d'Aubigné has already been mentioned, and the comparison with Buchanan is not an inappropriate one, especially if we consider Buchanan's position in the Protestant world after his return to Scotland. As a friend of leading Protestants like Théodore de Bèze and John Knox, as a propagandist for the Protestant cause in Scotland, and as a Protestant political theorist, Buchanan's influence was spreading throughout Europe. It is not therefore surprising that his satirical verse should also have been well received in Protestant circles, and indeed, much of it would find its way into the collection of the Huguenot doctor, Rasse des Noeux.[8] Moreover, Buchanan's connections with other French Protestants like Pierre Daniel, Jérome Groslot, Hubert Languet, and Philippe du Plessis-Mornay ensured that his reputation, and his writings, continued to flourish in France long after he left the country.[9] Translations, paraphrases, and imitations of his poetry and plays were produced in France right into the seventeenth century.[10]

So, even if Buchanan devoted less time to important new poetic projects during the last years of his life, paradoxically, his poetic renown began to spread more extensively and rapidly after his return to Scotland, thanks largely, no doubt, to the publication of his poetic works, which he seems to have resisted while he was still in France. From 1566, the year of publication of the *Franciscanus* and *Fratres fraterrimi*, editions of Buchanan were coming off the press almost annually, and his reputation as the grand old man of Latin literature was firmly established.

Conclusion

How are we to evaluate Buchanan's contribution to world literature? Were his contemporaries and Dr Johnson wrong in praising his abilities to the extent they did, or does his poetry stand the test of time?

In the first place, as far as his technical skill is concerned, there is no doubt that he was an accomplished versifier. We have seen that his understanding of the more usual Latin metres went beyond the information contained in sixteenth-century manuals, and that he possessed a facility in handling Latin to which few of his contemporaries could lay claim. But this is not altogether surprising. Living on the Continent for a major part of his creative life, how much opportunity would he have had for speaking his 'mother tongue', Scots? The occasional *lapsus calami* of which he has been accused (especially as regards prosody) derive perhaps not from an insufficient knowledge of a dead language, but from the creative use of a living one. Is Shakespeare ever taxed with having an inadequate grasp of English because of his grammatical inaccuracies? Buchanan was no purist when it came to vocabulary, for purism leads to sterility. But he did have an intricate, instinctive knowledge of the Latin language derived from a lifelong use of it. And we do not dismiss the works of Conrad, Ionesco, Beckett, Koestler, Nabokov, and others because they are written in a language other than their authors' native tongue. In Buchanan's hands, with the guiding principle of poetic *decorum* to control it, Latin was a living, dynamic language, malleable, and well suited to express his thoughts and feelings.

However, it is not enough for a poet to have a good knowledge of the language and a full understanding of the technicalities of versification. As Quintilian remarked, the greatest qualities, 'talent, facility of discovery, force, fluency, everything that art cannot supply' are not imitable,[1] and it is these indefinable qualities that determine who is the good poet. Buchanan wrote Latin poetry not as a sterile school exercise, but because he had something to say and Latin was the only practical means of expression for much of his life. Not everything he wrote was successful. But in his most committed works, he still speaks to us across the years as powerfully and directly as a Montaigne or a du Bellay, and his use of Latin lends a timeless quality to his writings. Form and content are fused together in absolute harmony in a poetry which is rich in the allusiveness and resonances derived from his intimate acquaintance with the classical and the biblical traditions.

Yet despite the universal quality of much of his poetry, it also has an individuality which has appealed to people of all countries and generations, and since his death, Buchanan has been translated into many languages, and continues to arouse the interest of poets as a worthy source of inspiration. It is his Scottish qualities which were admired by the late Robert Garioch, who not only translated the two sacred tragedies into Scots (because 'the unco-dowie logic o the Hebrew Jephthah juist doesna maik wi English conventions, and the Baptist's thrawn Jewish threipin o ill-faur'd sooth seems mair naiteral when he flytes in Scots'), but was also inspired to translate and reply to Buchanan's first *Elegy*.[2] However, Buchanan's appeal is not a narrowly insular one, and his poetry and drama have found admirers in such unlikely places as Poland and Hungary, as well as France, Holland, England, and Germany.[3]

Buchanan's life contained a mixture of many diverse currents, and in his time he played many parts. Few people who have encountered him, either in his lifetime or since, have felt indifferent towards him, and his role in the history of Scotland in particular has not always won him many friends. But as a poet, he has generally earned the admiration of all his readers, and perhaps he was not so far from the truth when he wrote in *Miscellany* 9:

> Sola doctorum monumenta vatum
> Nesciunt fati imperium severi,
> Sola contemnunt Phlegethonta et Orci
>   Iura superbi.

Notes

NOTES TO PREFACE

1 *Boswell's Life of Johnson*, edited by George Birkbeck Hill, 6 vols (Oxford, 1934–50), IV.185–6.

2 The Scottish Academic Press will be publishing editions of the *Jephthes* and the *Baptistes* edited by Peter Sharratt and Peter Walsh, and the secular poetry, edited by I. D. McFarlane and J. IJsewijn.

3 See in particular *An Anthology of Neo-Latin Poetry*, edited and translated by Fred J. Nichols (New Haven and London, 1979), which includes *Elegy* 2 and *Silvae* 3 amongst other poems, and I. D. McFarlane, *Renaissance Latin Poetry* (Manchester, 1980), which includes the texts of *Silvae* 2 and 4 along with some shorter pieces.

4 Despite its title, Robert Monteith's *The Very Learned Scotsman Mr George Buchanan's Fratres Fraterrimi, Three Books of Epigrams, and Book of Miscellanies, in English Verse* (Edinburgh, 1708) only offers verse paraphrases of a few of the Miscellaneous poems.

NOTES TO CHAPTER 1

1 For an account of the work undertaken on French Neo-latin writers, see J. IJsewijn, *Companion to Neo-Latin Studies* (Amsterdam, New York, Oxford, 1977), pp. 34–7 and 89–100. Recent studies on individual authors include Jean Salmon Macrin, *Le Livre des épithalames (1528–1531); Les Odes de 1530 (Livres I & II)*, edited by Georges Soubeille (Toulouse, 1978), and Jean Dorat, *Les Odes latines*, edited by Geneviève Demerson (Clermont-Ferrand, 1979).

2 See V.-L. Saulnier, *Maurice Scève*, 2 vols (Paris, 1948), II.60, n.2.

3 *La Deffence et illustration de la langue francoyse*, edited by Henri Chamard (Paris, 1904), p. 189.

4 Despite Malherbe's prosodic and poetic reforms, there were still writers in the early decades of the seventeenth century, such as Mathurin Régnier, Alexandre Hardy, and Théophile de Viau, who continued to favour the style developed by the Pléiade.

5   I. D. McFarlane, *Buchanan* (London, 1981).

6   Buchanan was re-elected to this post four times in succession. The German Nation, which included scholars from Britain, was one of the four Nations into which the University of Paris was divided (the other three being France, Normandy, and Picardy).

7   The *Doctrinale* was edited aş late as 1522 by John Vaus of King's College, Aberdeen, who also wrote a *Rudimenta puerorum in artem grammaticalem*.

8   J. Quicherat, *Histoire de Sainte-Barbe*, 3 vols (Paris, 1860), I.160, referring to Archives de l'Université, reg. 16, fo. 184.

9   The poems concerned are *Fratres fraterrimi* 34, the 'Somnium', 35 and 36, the 'Palinodes', and the *Franciscanus*.

10   See, for example, Montaigne, *Essais* I.26 and II.17 (*Oeuvres complètes*, edited by A. Thibaudet and M. Rat, Bibliothèque de la Pléiade (Paris, 1962), pp. 173, 176, and 645).

11   Du Bellay, *Oeuvres poétiques*, edited by Henri Chamard, 7 vols (Paris, 1908–31), IV.190–200.

12   Joaquim de Carvalho, *Notícias chronológicas da Universidade de Coimbra escriptas pelo beneficiado Francisco Leitão Ferreira* (Coimbra, 1937–44), III i.439.

13   These lectures were later published as the *Catullus et in eum commentarius* (Venice, 1554). On Muret's influence on the Pléiade, see Mary Morrison, 'Ronsard and Catullus: the Influence of the Teaching of Marc-Antoine de Muret', *BHR*, XVIII (1956), 240–74, and 'Catullus and the Poetry of the Renaissance in France', *BHR*, XXV (1963), 25–56. See also Isidore Silver, *The Intellectual Evolution of Ronsard*, vol. I, *The Formative Influences* (St Louis, 1969).

14   For Montaigne's meeting with Buchanan see *Essais* I.26 (ed. cit., p. 173) where the Frenchman speaks of Buchanan 'que je vis depuis à la suite de feu Monsieur le Mareschal de Brissac'.

15   *Georgii Buchanani Scoti poetae eximii Franciscanus et Fratres, quibus accessere varia eiusdem et aliorum poemata* (Bâle, [1568]).

16   For further details, see James E. Phillips, 'George Buchanan and the Sidney Circle', *The Huntington Library Quarterly*, XII (1948–9), 23–55.

17   This was not published, however, until some time in the 1590s. For a discussion of this work, see below pp. 30–2.

NOTES TO CHAPTER 2

1 The debate began in the fifteenth century in Italy, with people like Poliziano and Pico della Mirandola opposing Ciceronianism, and Cortesi and Bembo supporting it. Later on Erasmus, Muret, Ramus, and others joined battle against Ciceronians like J. C. Scaliger and Etienne Dolet. For a general view of the subject, see Hermann Gmelin, 'Das Prinzip der Imitatio in den romanischen Literaturen der Renaissance', *Romanische Forschungen*, XLVI (1932), 83–360.

2 The first edition of Joannes Despauterius' *Ars versificatoria* (Paris, n.d.) must have been printed in 1511 or 1512 according to the dates of the prefaces to each of the five books, the last of which is dated May 1511. My references will be to the 1520 Paris edition, virtually identical with the earlier one, but paginated where the ?1511 edition is not.

3 Rodolphus Gualtherus in his *De syllabarum et carminum ratione* (Zürich, 1542) speaking of diphthongs writes that 'reliquae [i.e. *ae, oe, ei*] enim pronunciatione nihil a simplicibus differunt' (fo. 7^v), and Jacobus Micyllus also points out in his *De re metrica* (Frankfurt, 1539) that distinctions between long and short vowels are no longer made in pronunciation (fo. 148^r). National differences certainly existed, cf. Erasmus, *De recta latini graecique sermonis pronuntiatione dialogus* (Bâle, 1528), but these seem largely to have concerned consonants, and in any case, nobody seems to have pronounced long and short vowels with different values at the beginning of the century.

4 These works may be conveniently consulted in Thomas Gaisford, *Scriptores latini rei metricae* (Oxford, 1837), and any references will be to this edition.

5 J. E. Sandys, *A History of Classical Scholarship*, 3 vols (Cambridge, 1931), I.218.

6 The *editiones principes* of these works appeared in *c.*1476, 1504, and 1497 respectively, but may be consulted in Putschius' edition of *Grammaticae latinae auctores antiqui* (Hanover, 1605).

7 Apart from numerous incunabula and sixteenth-century editions, there is a relatively modern one edited by Dietrich Reichling, *Das Doctrinale des Alexander de Villa-Dei* (Berlin, 1893).

8 'An *a* in verb-endings must always be long; in the verb *do*, *a* is short, along with its first conjugation compounds. You must always make *e* long unless it is followed by *r*; when an *r* follows, many examples give a short syllable, and many others a long one.'

9 See *Bibliotheca belgica*, series II, vol. 14, for available editions.

10   There were of course other verse manuals printed between Gaguin's and Despauterius' works on the subject, including one by Petrus Schottus dedicated entirely to prosody, and printed in 1500 in Strasbourg as the *Epitome de syllabarum mensura*. It was reprinted in the same city in 1525.

11   Ulrich von Hutten, *Rudimenta poetices: carmen her[oicum] ab adulescente quondam ipso compositum* (Strasbourg, 1523).

12   The edition which I have consulted is Joannes Murmellius, *Tabulae in artis componendorum versuum rudimenta* (Paris, 1539), which is unpaginated. Before 1560, there were at least 11 editions printed in Paris, and two in Lyons.

13   For other works, see F. Buisson, *Répertoire des ouvrages pédagogiques du seizième siècle* (Paris, 1886).

14   For Plato's theory of imitation, see *Republic* 10.597 sqq.

15   Aristotle's views, expressed in the *Poetics*, were slower than Plato's to gain currency in literary circles, however.

16   Quintilian's theories on literary imitation are to be found in the *Institutio oratoria* 10.2 sqq.

17   For this distinction in Horace, see the *Ars poetica* 408–9.

18   Vida's *Ars poetica* was first printed in 1527. See *The 'De arte poetica' of Marco Girolamo Vida*, ed. R. G. Williams (New York, 1976).

19   See, for example, Despauterius fo. I^v and Hutten fo. Biv^v.

20   On the very important subject of *decorum* and metre, see Horace, *Ars poetica* 73–92.

21   On the use of notebooks in the Renaissance, see R. R. Bolgar, *The Classical Heritage and its Beneficiaries* (Cambridge, 1954), pp. 274 sqq.

22   The full title of the work is *Dictionarium propriorum nominum virorum, mulierum, populorum, idolorum, urbium, fluviorum, montium, caeterorumque locorum quae passim in libris prophanis leguntur* (Paris, 1512).

23   My reference will be to the *Specimen epithetorum* (Paris, 1518).

24   Examples may be found in I. D. McFarlane, 'Reflections on Ravisius Textor's *Specimen epithetorum*', in *Classical Influences on European Culture: AD 1500–1700*, edited by R. R. Bolgar (Cambridge, 1976), pp. 81–90.

25 James Hutton, *The Greek Anthology in France and in the Latin Writers of the Netherlands to the Year 1800* (Ithaca, 1946), p. 5.

26 *Sententiae ex thesauris Graecorum delictae* (Bâle, 1549), fo. 26^r.

NOTES TO CHAPTER 3

1 *Terentiani Mauri venustissimus de literis, syllabis et metris Horati liber* and *Probi Grammatici artium instituta ad Caelestinum* (Paris, 1510). The copy presented by Buchanan to St Leonard's College is now in St Andrews University Library (Typ. FP B10PT).

2 See Thomas Craufurd, *History of the University of Edinburgh from 1580 to 1646* (Edinburgh, 1808), where James claimed in an address to the University of Edinburgh, delivered at Stirling: 'I follow his [George Buchanan's] pronunciation, both of his Latin and Greek, and am sorry that my people of England do not the like; for certainly their pronunciation utterly fails the grace of these two learned languages' (p. 86).

3 J. P. Postgate, *Prosodia Latina: an Introduction to Classical Latin Verse* (Oxford, 1923), § 260.

4 See, for example, W. M. Lindsay, 'Buchanan as a Latin Scholar', in *George Buchanan: a Memorial*, edited by D. A. Millar (St Andrews and London, 1907), pp. 204–11. Further details concerning Buchanan's metrical and prosodic anomalies may be found in the *Opera omnia* II.607–45.

5 For an excellent study of elision in classical poetry, see Jean Soubiran, *L'Elision dans la poésie latine* (Paris, 1966)

6 Soubiran makes a distinction in classical usage between 'grands genres' and 'petits genres', op. cit., pp. 597–611.

7 Of the 15 examples, 7 concern *me, te, se*, the most commonly elided monosyllables in classical dactylic verse, with a further 4 involving *cum, si, iam*, the next most common group (cf. Soubiran, p. 405).

8 See D. S. Raven, *Latin Metre* (London, 1965), §§ 84–7.

9 Endings of three-syllable words are found in *Fratres fraterrimi* 24.12; 26.10; 32.2; 36.26; *Epigrams* I.26.6; 38.4; 43.12; 44.4, 8; 53.2 etc. For four-syllable words see *Fratres fraterrimi* 16.4; 22.6; 36.12, 24; *Epigrams* I.1.2; 41.6 etc. And for five-syllable words, cf. *Fratres fraterrimi* 26.2; 35.22; *Epigrams* I.52.2.

10 See Raven, op. cit., § 41A.

11   See Raven, op. cit., § 34A.

12   Raven, op. cit., § 136.

13   Compare this with the figures given for Horace in Soubiran, op. cit., p. 85.

14   The translations and sources are listed below. Although reference is made for
      the sake of convenience to the modern *Anthologia Palatina* (A.P.) arrangement,
      Buchanan would have known the Anthology in a version based on the Aldine
      edition, *Florilegium diversorum epigrammatum in septem libros* (Venice, 1521).
      In most cases, any textual variants are far from significant.

	Epigrams	I.10	A.P.	9.291
		I.21		9.74
		I.30		5.93/4
		I.36		5.112/13
		I.37		9.359
		I.38		9.360
		I.44		5.229/30
		I.60		9.138
		I.61 & 62		10.73
		I.63		10.26
		I.64		11.435
		I.66		9.110

      Epigrams I.34 is very similar in sentiment to A.P. 11.8, but if it is based on this
      Greek epigram, the translation is extremely free.

15   The Semonides poems, which Buchanan would have found in the Stobaeus
      Anthology, are listed below. The Greek versions may be found in the Teubner
      edition of the Anthology (Leipzig, 1855).

Iambi 10	Teubner III, p. 46
Iambi 11	III, p. 224
Epigrams I.68	IV, p. 19
Miscellany 32	IV, p. 129

      The Simonides poems are:

Miscellany 30	Teubner IV, p. 19
Miscellany 31	IV, p. 95
Miscellany 37	III, p. 227

      There is also a version of a distich attributed to Simonides and cited by
      Clement of Alexandria in his *Stromatum liber* VI:

γυναικὸς οὐδὲν χρῆμ' ἀνὴρ ληΐζεται
ἐσθλῆς ἄμεινον, οὐδὲ ῥίγιον κακῆς.

Finally, Buchanan has two other translations of Greek poems, *Epigrams* I.65 taken from Anacreon 21, and *Epigrams* I.45, a version of an epigram which appears in Plutarch's *Vita Demosthenis* 30.

16 See *Oeuvres complètes de Melin de Sainct-Gelays*, edited by Prosper Blanchemain, 3 vols (Paris, 1873), II.129, for the *dizain* 'Si celle-là qui ne fut oncques mienne'.

17 I. D. McFarlane, 'George Buchanan's *Franciscanus*: the History of a Poem', *Journal of European Studies*, IV (1974), 126–39 (pp. 126–7).

18 Lucretius too, who seldom figures elsewhere in Buchanan's writings, supplies a number of tags in the *De sphaera*, see James R. Naiden, 'The *Sphera* of George Buchanan (1506–1582)' (Ph.D. dissertation, Columbia State University, 1948), pp. 36–7.

19 The allusions and their original contexts are as follows:

'Curetes pluvio . . . geniti imbre'   Ovid, *Metamorphoses* 4.282
'fratres . . . bimembres'   Virgil, *Aeneid* 8.293
'Pyrrhae saxa'   Statius, *Thebaid* 8.305
'Myrmidonas . . . gignit formica'   Ovid, *Metamorphoses* 7.654
'Prometheus'   Ovid, *Metamorphoses* 1.82

20 'Lupercal, derived from *lupa*, is the name given to the place at the bottom of the Palatine hill dedicated by Evander to the Arcadian god Pan, who is called Lycean Pan. Some people would have it so called, however, because the she-wolf fed Remus and Romulus there, cf. Ovid, *Fasti* (2.421–2): "She gave the place her name; this place is the Lupercal. Great is the reward which the nurse receives for the milk she gave."'

21 '*Cucullus* is also a kind of garment, cf. Juvenal (6.118), "the prostitute-empress dared to put on her hooded night cloak". It is generally agreed that our monks use this word wrongly as *cuculla* in the feminine.' The other Juvenal reference is to *Satire* 3.170.

22 See note 19 for the origin of these myths.

NOTES TO CHAPTER 4

1 On the development of Neo-latin poetry in France, see I. D. McFarlane, 'Poésie néo-latine et poésie de langue vulgaire à l'époque de la Pléiade', in *Acta Conventus Neo-Latini Lovaniensis: Proceedings of the First International Congress of Neo-Latin Studies*, edited by J. IJsewijn and E. Kessler (Louvain and Munich,

1973), pp. 389–403, and id., *A Literary History of France: Renaissance France 1470–1589* (London and Tonbridge, 1974), pp. 29–31, 103–4, 262–3, and 370–3.

2   See McFarlane, 'Poésie néo-latine et poésie de langue vulgaire', pp. 391–2.

3   On Salmon Macrin's literary connections, see Soubeille, ed. cit., especially pp. 112–19.

4   There is a certain amount of internal evidence to support this contention. In line 72, the poet speaks of 'neglectumque . . . vile Guidonis opus', which must be a reference to Guy de Fontenay's book of Latin synonyms, an edition of which was printed c.1510 in Paris. Fontenay had been a teacher at Sainte-Barbe, and no doubt some students expected his rather medieval schoolbook to continue to be used there. Lines 73–4 also tend to indicate Sainte-Barbe as the school which Buchanan is leaving: 'Curritur ad Montem magno cum murmure Acutum,/Aut alias aedes, sicubi Beta sapit.' The lightly-veiled reference to the Collège de Montaigu, the neighbouring and rival school of Sainte-Barbe, is telling, as is also the punning allusion to Beta, which must refer to the reactionary theologian Noël Béda, principal of Montaigu from 1502. Any reference to him after 1536, the year of his disgrace and death, would scarcely be relevant.

5   For details concerning the various scandals described in the *Franciscanus*, see George Neilson, 'The *Franciscan*: some Footnotes', in *George Buchanan: Glasgow Quatercentenary Studies, 1906* (Glasgow, 1907), pp. 297–332.

6   See BN MS lat. 8140, fo. 4ᵛ, where the poem is addressed 'Ad Henricū oct. Angliae regẽ'.

7   *Essais* I.26, ed. cit., p. 176.

8   In a letter written in 1579 to Daniel Rogers, he refers to his translation of Euripides' *Medea* as having been undertaken in order to improve his knowledge of the language, see below pp. 70–1.

9   See Carvalho, op. cit., III i.415.

10   See McFarlane, 'George Buchanan's Latin Poems from Script to Print', *The Library*, XXIV (1969), 277–332 (p. 282), and BN MS lat. 8141, fo. 24ʳ, where the poem is addressed 'In laudem Regis Navarrae'.

11   For example, the 'Louange du Maquerellage' attributed to Théophile de Viau is a paraphrase of *Elegy* 3, the 'Pro lena', see *Le Parnasse satyrique du sieur Théophile avec le recueil des plus excellens vers satyriques de ce temps*, 2 vols (Paris, 1861), II.85–91.

12   António de Gouveia, Nicolas de Bourbon, and Théodore de Bèze, for example, produced a number of satirical epigrams, many of an anti-monastic nature.

13   See above p. 45 and below pp. 49–53.

14   See McFarlane, 'George Buchanan's Latin Poems from Script to Print', p. 289.

15   For example, the simile in l. 68 is based on Statius, *Thebais* 1.709; l. 73 is a parody of the *Aeneid* 1.55; l. 77 is taken from Juvenal 7.159–60; l. 93 is a virtual translation of the opening line of *Anthologia Palatina* 16.297; l. 95 refers to Virgil, *Eclogues* 1; ll. 97–8 probably have in mind Ovid, *Tristia* 2.207; and ll. 99–100 are taken from Ovid, *Heroides* 5.151.

16   See *The Poems of William Dunbar*, edited by W. MacKay MacKenzie (London, 1960), pp. 116–17.

17   For further details on *copia*, see R. R. Bolgar, *The Classical Heritage and its Beneficiaries*, pp. 274 sqq., and Terence Cave, *The Cornucopian Text: Problems of Writing in the French Renaissance* (Oxford, 1979).

18   Indeed, they appear so in one manuscript, BN MS lat. 8140, fo. 11^r-13^v, cf. also McFarlane, 'George Buchanan's Latin Poetry from Script to Print', p. 279.

19   *O.O.* II.256.

20   Jacobus de Voragine, *Legenda aurea*, edited by T. Graesse (Leipzig, 1850), p. 666.

21   Buchanan provides the reader with a clue concerning the source of the poem's framework in *Fratres fraterrimi* 35.63–4: 'Talis erat, si vera fides, Hieronymus olim,/Dum studium ob Tulli vapulat ante Deum.'

22   The poem has attracted much scholarly attention. On the sources of the incidents described, see Neilson, art. cit. The literary merits of the work are discussed by McFarlane in 'George Buchanan's *Franciscanus*: the History of a Poem', while the question of vocabulary is the subject of E. W. Bögl's *George Buchanans Satire Franciscanus und Fratres in philologischer Betrachtung* (Innsbruck, 1954). See also J. R. C. Martyn, 'George Buchanan's Franciscanus', in *Acta Conventus Neo-Latini Amstelodamensis*, edited by P. Tuynman, G. C. Kuiper, and E. Kessler (Munich, 1979), pp. 721–46.

23   For details concerning Juvenal's style, see I. G. Scott, *The Grand Style in the Satires of Juvenal* (Northampton, Mass., 1927); Josué de Decker, *Juvenalis declamans: étude sur la rhétorique déclamatoire dans les satires de Juvenal* (Ghent, 1913); and August Thiel, *Juvenalis graecissans; sive, de vocibus graecis apud Juvenalem* (Wroclaw, 1901).

24   See ll. 56, 136, 254, 258, 349, 397, 399, 435, 481, 750, and 829.

25   For other examples see ll. 118, 270, 305, 471, 492 and 680.

26   For further examples of Buchanan's use of word order see ll. 10, 213–14, 385–6, 833–4, 844, 866, and 907.

27   For further tags, see McFarlane, 'George Buchanan's *Franciscanus*', pp. 130–1.

28   cf. Horace, *Odes* 1.4 'Solvitur acris hiems'; 4.7 'Diffugere nives'; and 4.12 'Iam veris comites'. See also Virgil, *Georgics* 2.315–42.

29   On the rise of the eclogue in France, see Alice Hulubei, *L'Eglogue en France au XVIe siècle: époque des Valois (1515–1589)* (Paris, 1938).

30   On the *noctua*, see Pliny, *Historia naturalis* 10.17.19 and 18.35.87; *acanthis*, see 10.63.83 and 10.74.95; *bubo*, see 10.12.16 'bubo funebris et maxime abominatus, publicis praecipue auspiciis'; *cornix*, see 10.12.14 'ipsa ales est inauspicatae garrulitatis'; *strix*, see 11.39.95 and Ovid, *Fasti* 6.145 'pectoraque exsorbent avidis infantia linguis'.

31   See above, p. 37.

32   For example, on 1 March 1570, Thomas Randolph wrote to William Cecil: 'I send you his [i.e. of James Stewart, the regent Moray] epitaph made by Mr. George Buchanan, who never rejoiced since the Regent's death' (*Calendar of Scottish Papers*, III (1569–1571), p.93).

33   This epigram is found in BN MS lat. 8140 (three times, fo. 8ᵛ, 23ᵛ, and 87ʳ); BN MS lat. 8141, fo. 40ʳ (where it is entitled 'De quodam monacho ex Gallico'); MS Dupuy 810, fo. 15ᵛ; and MS Dupuy 951, fo. 54ʳ.

34   See above, p. 46.

35   On the metres used by Buchanan in the tragedies and any anomalies, see Ruddiman's *De metris Buchananaeis libellus* in *O.O.* II.624–30.

36   On Buchanan's place in the history of the French theatre, see Raymond Lebègue, *La Tragédie religieuse en France: les débuts (1514–1573)* (Paris, 1929), pp. 195–254.

37   Many scholars, viewing the play as a *pièce à clé*, have attempted to identify the various characters with contemporary figures (see Lebègue, pp. 210–12), no doubt encouraged in this by Buchanan's own words in his defence before the Inquisition, in which he identifies the Baptist and Sir Thomas More (J. M. Aitken, *The Trial of George Buchanan before the Inquisition* (London and

Edinburgh, 1939), p. 24). This, like all such identifications, must be viewed with a great deal of circumspection, since Buchanan is trying here to make himself appear in as good a light as possible.

38   Lebègue, op. cit., pp. 217 and 244.

39   See above, chapter 1, pp. 7–8.

NOTES TO CHAPTER 5

1   See Introduction, pp. 7–9.

2   Dorothy Coleman, *The Gallo-Roman Muse: Aspects of Roman Literary Tradition in Sixteenth-Century France* (Cambridge, 1979).

3   On the Psalm paraphrases, see I. D. McFarlane, 'Notes on the Composition and Reception of George Buchanan's Psalm Paraphrases', in *Renaissance Studies*, edited by I. D. McFarlane, A. H. Ashe, and D. D. R. Owen (Edinburgh and London, 1972), pp. 21–62. See also Buchanan's words to the Inquisition in Aitken, p. 28, cited in my article, 'George Buchanan et ses paraphrases des Psaumes', in *Acta conventus neo-latini turonensis*, edited by J.-C. Margolin, 2 vols (Paris, 1980), pp. 947–57.

4   For a sensitive appreciation of three of Buchanan's paraphrases along these lines, see John Wall, 'The Latin Elegiacs of George Buchanan (1506–1582)', in *Bards and Makars*, edited by A. A. Aitken, M. P. McDiarmid, and D. S. Thomson (Glasgow, 1977), pp. 184–93.

5   For further details on the Psalm paraphrase in France, see Michel Jeanneret, *Poésie et tradition biblique au XVIe siècle* (Paris, 1969), and Johannes A. Gaertner, 'Latin Verse Translations of the Psalms 1500–1620', *Harvard Theological Review*, XLIX (1956), 271–305.

6   *Psalmorum Dauidis paraphrasis poetica, nunc primum edita* (n.p., n.d.). For further details, see McFarlane, art. cit., pp. 28–9.

7   *Dauidis Psalmi aliquot, latino carmine a quatuor* [sic] *poetis quos quatuor regiones Gallia, Italia, Germania, Scotia genuerunt* (Paris, 1556).

8   *The Psalms: Hebrew Text, English Translation and Commentary*, edited by Abraham Cohen (Hindhead, Surrey, 1945).

9   Cohen, ed. cit., p. 340.

10   The poems concerned are *Elegies* 7 and 8; *Iambi* 2–5; *Epigrams* I.15–17, 22–3, 28–9, 41–2, 47 and 52; *Miscellany* 6–7, 17–19. For further details, see my article, 'Leonora and Neaera: a Consideration of George Buchanan's Erotic Poetry', *Bibliothèque d'Humanisme et Renaissance*, XL (1978), 513–24.

11   cf. the use of *nimbus* (= a cloud of perfume) and *cerrusatus*, both used in similar contexts by Martial.

12   For the text of the 'In Scaraboeum', see Léon Dorez, 'Le MS original des Elégies, Sylves, et Hendécasyllabes de George Buchanan (1566)', *Revue des bibliothèques* (1903), pp. 262 sqq.

13   See du Bellay, ed. cit., I.127–36; V.128–33; V.136–41; and Ronsard, *Oeuvres complètes*, ed. Laumonier (Paris, 1914–75), I.238–43; V.21–9.

14   This poem, dating from 1548, may be found in *Recréation et passetemps des Tristes* (Paris, 1573).

15   See *Poésies de Jacques Tahureau*, edited by Prosper Blanchemain, 2 vols (Paris, 1870), I.161.

16   See my article, 'George Buchanan's Court Poetry and the Pléiade', *French Studies*, XXXIV (1980), 137–52. On the influence of Horace on the Pléiade, see Coleman, *The Gallo-Roman Muse*, especially chapters 4 and 5.

17   See Introduction, pp. 7–8, and for a more detailed study of *Miscellany* 8, see my article, pp. 143–6.

18   The 1725 *O.O.* edition has 'turbarum' in this stanza, but 'tubarum' makes far better sense, and is confirmed by the 1615 Hart edition, the 1621 Elzevir, and the 1715 Ruddiman. Compare too the allusion to the *Aeneid*.

19   This poem was published on its own in 1558 by both Robert and Charles Estienne, and is one of a number of compositions on this subject, see V.-L. Saulnier, 'Les Poètes de la prise de Calais (1558)', in 'Deux œuvres inconnues de Jean Sève et une édition inconnue de Baïf', *Bulletin du bibliophile* (June 1949), 265–79, pp. 270–4.

20   The poems concerned are *Fratres fraterrimi* 2; *Hendecasyllables* 6–9; and *Epigrams* I.18. There is also an unpublished Beleago poem in BN MS latin 8140, fo. 105ᵛ, which seems to be unfinished.

21   The Neaera poems are *Elegy* 9; *Hendecasyllables* 1–4, 6; *Epigrams* I.26–7, 31; and *Miscellany* 20.

22   Quotations from the *Phaedrus* are taken from *Plato in Twelve Volumes*, translated by Harold North Fowler, Loeb Classical Library, vol. I (London and Cambridge, Mass., 1971).

23 See *Oeuvres complètes de Melin de Sainct-Gelays*, edited by Prosper Blanchemain, 3 vols (Paris, 1873), II.129.

24 See 'George Buchanan's Court Poetry and the Pléiade', pp. 147–9.

25 For further details concerning this work, see James R. Naiden, 'The *Sphera* of George Buchanan (1506–1582)' (Ph.D. thesis, Columbia University, 1948), and I. D. McFarlane, 'The History of George Buchanan's *Sphaera*', in *French Renaissance Studies 1540–70: Humanism and the Encyclopedia*, edited by Peter Sharratt (Edinburgh, 1976), pp. 194–212.

26 This 'fifth element' of ancient philosophy (the ether) was considered to be the substance from which the heavenly bodies were made.

27 See McFarlane, art. cit., pp. 196–8.

28 Buchanan was in correspondence with Brahé, cf. *Epistola* 15, *O.O.* II.738.

NOTES TO CHAPTER 6

1 See above, chapter 1, pp. 9–11.

2 See the *Dictionary of National Biography* (London, 1908–9).

3 Apart from travelling to France in the winter of 1565–6 to oversee the publication of an edition of his *Poemata*, Buchanan maintained epistolary contact with Pierre Daniel, Christophe Plantin, Théodore de Bèze, Philippe du Plessis-Mornay, and Elie Vinet, amongst others.

4 See particularly the second and third books of *Epigrams* for Buchanan's English connections.

5 See *Inuentaires de la Royne Descosse Douairiere de France: Catalogues of the Jewels, Dresses, Furniture, Books, and Paintings of Mary Queen of Scots, 1556–1569*, edited by Joseph Robertson (Edinburgh, 1863), p. lxxxiii.

6 See *O.O.* II.404–5, 'Pompae Deorum Rusticorum', and Robertson, ed. cit., p. lxxxvi.

7 See BN MS français 22561, fo. 79^r–80^r, and BN Nouvelles acquisitions latines 106, p. 91.

8 BN MSS français 22560–5. On this collection, see McFarlane 'George Buchanan's Latin Poems from Script to Print', pp. 292–4.

9   On his relations with these men, see *Epistolae* 3, 11, 17, 36, and 39. Many of
    them had connections with the largely Protestant city of Orléans, and in July
    1566, Buchanan instructed Pierre Daniel: 'Saluta Aurelianenses omnes meo
    nomine, dein caeteros, ut erit commodum' (*Epistola* 3).

10 For example, Florent Chrestien translated the *Franciscanus* and the *Jephthes*,
    and Théophile de Viau paraphrased the 'Pro lena' in *Le Parnasse satyrique* as
    'Louange du maquerellage'.

NOTES TO CONCLUSION

1   Quintilian, 10.2.12: 'ingenium, inventio, vis, facilitas, et quicquid arte non
    traditur.'

2   See *Jephthah and The Baptist: Translatit frae Latin in Scots* (Edinburgh and
    London, 1959), p. 6, and *Collected Poems* (Loanhead, Midlothian, 1977),
    p. 34–42.

3   cf. McFarlane, pp. 201–5, 308–19, and 477–84.

GEORGE BUCHANAN'S

Miscellaneorum Liber

Text, Translation, Commentary

Philip J Ford
W S Watt

Foreword

The text of the *Miscellaneorum liber* is that of the 1725 edition of the *Opera omnia*, edited by Ruddiman and Burman, although at a few points, indicated in the commentary, a different text has been either printed or preferred. Orthography, punctuation, and capitalisation have been modernised throughout. The translation, which has no literary pretensions, is intended merely to make clear what we take to be the meaning of the Latin.

P.J.F.
W.S.W.

GEORGII BUCHANANI SCOTI

Miscellaneorum Liber

1 *Ad invictissimum Franciae Regem Henricum II post victos Caletes*

Non Parca fati conscia, lubricae
non sortis axis sistere nescius,
   non siderum lapsus, sed unus
      rerum opifex moderatur orbem,   **4**
qui terram inertem stare loco iubet,
aequor perennes volvere vertices,
   caelumque nunc lucem tenebris
      nunc tenebras variare luce,   **8**
qui temperatae sceptra modestiae
dat et protervae frena superbiae,
   qui lacrimis foedat triumphos,
      et lacrimas hilarat triumphis.   **12**
exempla longe ne repetam, en iacet,
fractusque et exspes, quem gremio suo
   Fortuna fotum nuper omnes
      per populos tumidum ferebat.   **16**
nec tu, secundo flamine quem super
felicitatis vexerat aequora,
   Henrice, virtus, nesciisti
      imbriferae fremitum procellae.   **20**
sed pertinax hunc fastus adhuc premit
urgetque pressum, et progeniem sui
   fiducia pari tumentem
      clade pari exagitat Philippum.   **24**
te, qui minorem te superis geris
culpamque fletu diluis agnitam,
   mitis parens placatus audit
      et solitum cumulat favorem,   **28**
redintegratae nec tibi gratiae
obscura promit signa. sub algido
   nox Capricorno longa terras

The Scotsman George Buchanan's

Miscellaneous Poems

1 *To the most invincible king Henry II of France, after the capture of Calais*

It is not Fate, aware of what is ordained, nor the unstoppable wheel of slippery Fortune, nor the course of the stars, but the creator of the universe alone who governs the world. He commands the earth to stand inert in its place, the sea to roll its timeless waves, and the sky to alternate light with darkness, darkness with light. He grants sovereignty to restrained moderation, and curbs wanton pride; He mars triumphs with tears, and tears He gladdens with triumphs. Not to seek examples from far off, see how he lies broken and in despair who was cherished by Fortune in her bosom, and but recently swept, swollen with pride, through all the nations. Not that you, Henry, whose valour had conveyed you with a favourable breeze over the seas of good fortune, have not experienced the roaring of the torrential gale. But headstrong pride still afflicts him and forces him on; and his child, Philip, puffed up with equal boldness, is harassed with equal disaster. But you, who behave as an inferior to the gods and wash away your acknowledged guilt with your tears, are heard by our gentle father who is thereby placated and heaps His accustomed goodwill upon you. And far from obscure are the tokens of restored grace which he discloses to you. The long night was covering the earth with its endless

133

perpetuis tenebris premebat;   32
rigebat auris bruma nivalibus,
amnes acuto constiterant gelu,
  deformis horror incubabat
    iugeribus viduis colono: 36
at signa castris Francus ut extulit
ductorque Franci Guisius agminis,
  arrisit algenti sub Arcto
    temperies melioris aurae.   40
hiems retuso languida spiculo
vim mitigavit frigoris asperi;
  siccis per hibernum serenum
    nube cava stetit imber arvis.   44
stravit quietis aequora fluctibus
Neptunus, antris condidit Aeolus
  ventos, nisi Francas secundo
    flamine qui veherent carinas.   48
per arva nuper squalida, et ignibus
adhuc Britannis paene calentia,
  cornu benigno commeatus
    Copia luxurians profudit.   52
idem ut reductas abdidit oppidis
Francus cohortes, mitis hiems modo
  se rursus armavit procellis
    et positas renovavit iras.   56
stant lenta pigro flumina marmore
canisque campi sub nivibus latent,
  diverberatum saevit aequor
    horriferis Aquilonis alis.   60
ergo nec altis tuta paludibus
tulere vires moenia Gallicas,
  nec arcibus tutae paludes
    praecipitem tenuere cursum.   64
Loraene princeps, praecipuo Dei
favore felix, praecipuas Deus
  cui tradidit partes, superbos
    ut premeres domitrice dextra,   68
unius anni curriculo sequens
vix credet aetas promeritas tibi

darkness at the winter solstice, the winter was glacial with snow-laden winds, the streams had ceased to flow with the bitter frost, and ugly bristling cold brooded over fields deserted by farmers. But as François de Guise, leader of the French army, led the standards out from camp, the mildness of a more favourable breeze smiled beneath the chilling Bear. Sluggish winter, its barbs made blunt, softened the force of its sharp chill. In a clear winter's sky, the rain stood still in its enveloping cloud over dry fields. Neptune calmed the sea with gentle waves, Aeolus enclosed the winds in their caves except those which would carry French ships with a favourable breeze. Through-out fields which were recently neglected, and still almost warm with English flames, abundant Plenty poured out provisions from her lavish horn. As soon as this same François led back his troops and gave them retirement in the towns, the mild winter re-armed itself with stormy winds, and renewed the angry blasts which it had laid aside. Slow-moving rivers stand still with sluggish marble-like surfaces, fields lie hidden beneath white snow, and the ocean seethes, lashed by the dreadful wings of the North Wind. So neither could walls protected by deep marshes resist the strength of France, nor marshes protected by strong defences hold back their headlong course. Prince of Lorraine, happy in the special favour of God, you to whom God entrusted a special role, to crush the proud with conquering arm, a subsequent age will scarcely believe that, in the course of one short year, so many victories were won by you,

tot laureas, nec si per auras
Pegasea veherere penna.   72
cessere saltus ninguidi et Alpium
inserta caelo culmina, cum pater
  Romanus oraret propinquae ut
    subiceres humeros ruinae.   76
defensa Roma et capta Valentia,
coacta pacem Parthenope pati,
  fama tui Segusianus
    barbarica face liberatus.   80
aequor procellis, terra paludibus,
armis Britannus, moenia saeculis
  invicta longis, insolentes
    munierant animos Caletum.   84
Loraena virtus, sueta per invia
non usitatum carpere tramitem,
  invicta devincendo, famam
    laude nova veterem refellit.   88
ferox Britannus, viribus antehac
Gallisque semper cladibus imminens,
  vix se putat securum ab hoste
    fluctibus Oceani diremptus.   92
regina, pacem nescia perpeti,
iam spreta maeret foedera, iam Dei
  iram timet sibi imminentem,
    vindicis et furiae flagellum.   96
cives et hostes iam pariter suos
odit pavetque, et civium et hostium
  hirudo communis, cruorem
    aeque avide sitiens utrumque.   100
huic luce terror Martius assonat
diraeque caedis mens sibi conscia,
  umbraeque nocturnae quietem
    terrificis agitant figuris.   104
sic laesa poenas Iustitia expetit,
fastus superbos sic Nemesis premit,
  sic mitibus iustisque praebet
    mitis opem Deus atque iustus.   108

not even if you were carried through the air on Pegasus' wings. The snowy mountain passes and the summits of the Alps rising to the sky gave way, when our father in Rome prayed you to set your shoulder against the collapse that was near at hand. Rome was defended, Valenza captured, Naples forced to endure peace, and the Lyonnais freed from the barbarian's firebrand through your renown. The sea with its storms, the land with its marshes, the Englishman with his arms, and ramparts unconquered for long generations had all fortified the insolent spirits of the inhabitants of Calais. The courage of Lorraine, accustomed to picking an untrodden path through pathless regions, unconquered by dint of conquering, outstripped his former renown with new glory. The wild Englishman, who was formerly always threatening the French with force and disaster, scarcely thinks he is safe, separated though he is from the enemy by the waves of the ocean. His queen, unable to bear peace, is now sorry that treaties have been disdained, now fears the wrath of God hanging over her, and the scourge of His avenging fury. Now she hates and fears equally her subjects and enemies, being a leech common to both subjects and enemies, thirsting equally greedily for the blood of both. By day, martial terror sounds in her ears, and her mind is conscious of her cruel murders, and the shadows of night disturb her sleep with terrifying apparitions. Thus Justice, if outraged, seeks retribution; thus Nemesis crushes arrogant pride; thus a mild and just God provides help to the mild and just.

2 *In Castitatem*

    Castitas blandi domitrix amoris,
    Castitas vitae specimen prioris,
    labe cum puras suboles colebat
        aurea terras,   4
    Castitas vitae specimen futurae,
    Morte cum victa sociata membris
    pura mens puris radiantis aulam
        incolet aethrae,   8
    una nec certam Veneris sagittam
    iura nec fati metuis severi,
    quippe quae rursus moriente maior
        Morte resurges,   12
    pura cum puris agites ut aevum
    angelis, quorum studium secuta
    colliges fructus socios secundae
        reddita vitae.   16

3 *De amore Cossaei et Aretes*

    Quo te sub antro, quo nemorum avio,
    aestus levantem frigore languido
      Cossaeus aspexit, profanis
        cerni oculis, Arete, insolentem?   4
    tu cura es illi, seu roseo dies
    arridet ortu, seu medio dies
      incandet aestu, sive caelum
        nox tacitis operit tenebris.   8
    tu si vocaris, per iuga Caucasi
    te belluosi, torrida solibus
      per tesqua Maurorum, per aequor
        puppibus indomitum sequetur.   12
    non tecta tectis, praedia praediis,
    aurumve stratis cogere montibus,
      non certat Eoum decoris
        Oceanum spoliare gemmis,   16
    non otiosa lentus inertia
    vitae fugacis ver breve carpere,
      somnoque iucundo molestas
        aegri animi relevare curas.   20

2   *To Chastity*

Chastity, conqueror of alluring love, Chastity, the token of a former

way of life when a golden race inhabited a world free from stain,

Chastity, the token of a future life, when Death has been conquered,

and the pure soul united with a pure body will inhabit the courts of

the radiant heavens, you alone fear neither the sure arrow of Venus

nor the laws of stern Fate, for you will rise up once again greater at

the death of Death, to spend eternity in pureness with the pure

angels, whose endeavours you will follow as you gather the fruits in

partnership with them, duly delivered to a second life.

3   *On the love of Cossé and Arete*

In what grotto, in what woodland wilderness did Cossé see you, Arete,

relieving the midday heat in the drowsy cool, you who are not usually

seen by profane eyes? You are his loved one, whether the day smiles at

rosy dawn, or glows hot at midday, or night envelops the sky with

silent darkness. If you have called, he will follow you across the peaks

of the monster-teeming Caucasus, across the deserts of the Moors, swel-

tering in the heat of the sun, across the ocean unconquered by ships. He

does not strive to accumulate houses, estates, or gold by levelling

mountains, or to strip the seas of the Orient of their fine jewels, or

slothfully, in idle laziness, to enjoy the short springtime of a fleeting life,

or to relieve the troublesome cares of a weary mind in pleasant sleep.

unam irretorto lumine te videt,
unam inquieta sollicitudine
   te spectat absentem invocatque,
      te dominam veneratur unam.   24
non ille compta molle nitens coma
te nec Sabaeis ambit odoribus;
   non improbus captat dolosis
      illecebris animum rebellem,   28
sed luce ferri luctifica minax
pectusque squamis asper aeneis,
   aut spumeos frenos fatigans
      quadrupedis praeeuntis Euros,   32
qualis virentem Mars prope Strymona
exercet acrem quadriiugum fugam,
   seu Parthiae cladem feroci
      seu gelido meditatur Istro.   36
nec tu labores despicis anxios,
te nacta dignam scilicet indolem,
   nec credulum pascens amorem
      spe sterili crucias amicum.   40
seu per procellis feta nivalibus
praerupta et Alpes agmen agit feras,
   seu per tumentes imbre fluctus,
      seu validas labefactat arces,   44
tu dux per Alpes pandis iter feras,
amnes frementes pontibus alligas;
   tu claustra portarum revellis,
      et peragis sine caede bella.   48
quacumque iustas, te duce, verterit
Cossaeus iras, luridus anteit
   Pallor Tremor Terror Pavorque
      depositis male fortis armis.   52
tu dura Rheni pignora et asperos
Lari colonos, tu Ligurem levem
   et Cantabrum exarmas docesque
      indocili iuga ferre collo.   56
quacumque amicos, te duce, verterit
vultus, per agros pax nitet aurea,
   pax laeta securas per urbes

You alone he looks upon with unswerving gaze, and in your absence has regard for and calls for you alone with anxious concern; you alone he worships as his mistress. He does not seek to win you looking effeminately sleek with well coiffured hair and Sabaean perfumes; he does not, cunning with treacherous allurements, entice your mind against its will, but menacing with the ill-boding glint of his sword, his breast rough with bronze scale-armour, or urging on ceaselessly the foamy bit of his horse as it outstrips the East Winds, just as Mars by the green banks of the Strymon urges on the swift path of his chariot, whether he plans disaster for fierce Parthia or for the cold Danube. Neither do you scorn his anxious toil, since you have obtained a nature worthy of yourself, nor feeding a credulous love do you torment a friend with barren hope. Whether he leads his army across rugged paths abounding in snow-laden gales, and through the wild Alps, or across rivers swollen with rain, or causes strong citadels to shake, you are his leader, laying open a path through the wild Alps, crossing seething streams with bridges; you tear away the bolts of gates, and wage bloodless war. Wherever Cossé under your leadership turns his righteous anger, he is preceded by ghastly Pallor, Trembling, Terror and Fear, weakly laying down their arms. You disarm the tough offspring of the Rhine and the wild settlers of lake Como, the nimble Piedmontese, and the Cantabrian, and teach them to bear the yoke on their untamed necks. Wherever, under your leadership, he turns a friendly face, golden Peace shines through the countryside, joyful Peace pours forth wealth and easy sleep through safe cities;

fundit opes facilemque somnum;   60
hostes quietis fraus male callida
et vis facessunt; cana iterum Fides
    terras revisit Veritasque,
Iustitiae reducis sorores.   64
o diva, custos pacis amabilis
bellique formidabilis arbitra,
    quae iura fatorum superba
    non metuis dominasque Parcas,   68
fac ne maligni iniuria temporis
tot vestri amoris pignora deleat,
    aut obruat caecae sepulta
    sub tenebris taciturnitatis.   72

4 *Ad Franciscum Olivarium Franciae Cancellarium,* Εὐχαριστικόν
Si quod sub antro Castalio latet
carmen repostum quod fera robora,
    quod saxa ducat, fluminumque
    praecipites remoretur undas,   4
nunc prome, sacri Calliope chori
regina, Olivari et memora piam
    mentem Camenarum erga alumnos,
    et memori refer ore grates;   8
qui, quamquam ab alto culmine Gallicae
rei gubernet munia publicae et
    a Rege permissas habenas
    imperio moderetur aequo,   12
nec fasci iniquo subditus ingemit
nec re secunda turgidus intumet,
    utraque fortuna peraeque
    infragilisque animique rectus.   16
interque curae pondera publicae
Martisque vixdum compositas minas,
    non neglegit, ceu se minores,
    vulgi humiles tenuis querelas.   20
et quamquam honoris contigit hunc gradum
quo celsius nil ambitio impotens
    sperare possit pectorisve
    compositi moderamen optet,   24

the enemies of peace, cunning deceit and violence, depart, venerable

Faith and Truth, the sisters of restored Justice, return again to the

Earth. Goddess, the guardian of delightful Peace, and arbiter of ter-

rifying war, who do not fear the haughty laws of destiny or the

powerful Fates, do not allow the damage of evil times to destroy the

many pledges of your love, or to overwhelm them, buried in the dark-

ness of obscure silence.

4   *Poem of thanks to François Olivier, chancellor of France*
If there is any poem lying hidden in the Castalian cave which can

cause wild oak-trees and rocks to move, and the swift-flowing river

waters to stand still, produce it now, Calliope, queen of the sacred

band, and call to mind Olivier's heart which remains dutiful towards

the nurslings of the Muses, and give thanks with grateful lips. For

although he controls from his lofty height the functions of the French

commonwealth, and handles with just authority the reins entrusted

to him by the king, he does not groan when he has to shoulder an

unfair load, nor grow arrogant, puffed up by success, being equally

unbreakable and upright in mind in both kinds of fortune. And

amidst the burdens of public cares and the threats of war which have

scarcely yet been allayed, he does not neglect like his inferiors the

humble complaints of the poor citizenry. And although he has

reached such a position of honour that raging ambition cannot hope

for, nor the restraint of a peaceful heart desire, anything higher,

olim in iuventa Pieridum comes
clarus per illas redditus ac potens,
    agnoscit acceptos honores,
        Pieridum pater ac patronus.   28
quod si ad Garumnae litora Vasconis
abs te impetrato perfruar otio,
    liberque curis entheoque
        Pieridum furiatus oestro,   32
si nostra cultus indiga splendidi
Camena, silvis aptior asperis,
    aulae reformidet nitorem
        et dociles melioris urbes,   36
Echo loquaci te scopulo latens
amnisque densa cinctus arundine
    fontesque, Olivari, sonabunt
        et virides nemorum recessus.   40

5 *In Polyonymum*

Lusitanicus unus es mare ultra et
citra Algarbicus Indicusque Arabsque,
Persicus Guineusque et Africanus
Congusque et Manicongus et Zalophus;
nec tuis titulis abest superbis   5
Aethiops nimio perustus aestu,
nec circum triplicem refusus orbem
cunctarum Oceanus parens aquarum;
nec portus neque merx neque insula ulla est,
lucelli unde levis refulget aura,   10
quae te non titulo augeat. tot ergo
cui sunt nomina, nonne iure Regem
multis nominibus vocabo magnum?
sed Rex nominibus tot ille magnus,
si belli furor aut mare aestuosum   15
occludat piperariam tabernam,
[famam fenore pransitabit emptam]
versuram faciet vel esuribit.

once, in his youth, as a companion of the Muses, he was made famous and powerful through them, and now recognises the honours he has received by being the father and protector of the Muses. And if, by the banks of the Gascon Garonne, I enjoy leisure granted by you, free from cares and inspired by the divine fury of the Muses, if our Muse, lacking splendid apparel and more suited to the wild woods, shuns the splendour of the court and cities that are quick to learn better poetry than mine, Echo hiding in the chattering crag, the stream surrounded by thick reeds, the pools of water, and the verdant recesses of the woods will celebrate you, Olivier.

5   *To Polyonymus*
Being a single Portuguese, you are known on either side of the sea as ruler of the Algarve, of India, Arabia, Persia, Portuguese Guinea, Africa, the Congo, the Kongo Kingdom, and Sofala, and your proud titles include that of the ruler of Ethiopia parched with excessive heat, and of Ocean the father of all waters, flowing round the threefold globe; and there is no port, trade, or island from which a slight gleam of profit shines which does not enhance you with a title. Since you have so many names, shall I not be right in calling you the Great King of Many Names? But if the fury of war or the raging sea shuts down the pepper stall, that great King of so many names will [lunch on the reputation purchased with borrowed money; he will] borrow money, or go hungry.

6   *In Leonoram*

Cum faciem nimbo madidam, Leonora, viderem,
  et cerussatas arte nitere genas,
pingere credideram solum te scire: probavi
  ex facie doctam terque quaterque manum.   4
at simul aurato mihi fulserat anulus aere
  quaeque nitet digitis vitrea gemma tuis,
non animo tantum didici te fingere, verum
  certant cum vafris aemula signa dolis.   8
fictum animum pictamque cutem fraudesque latentes
  aes breve tam certis exprimit indiciis
ut te non melius potuisset pingere Apelles,
  fingere vel fuso doctius aere Myron.   12

7   *Ad Peiridem lenam*

Lena tibi est genitrix, tu matris filia paelex,
  et tua suscipiet filia matris onus.
cumque tibi fratrem prudens natura negasset,
  in monachis fratrum tu quoque nomen amas.   4
quam bene quod primis pater est tibi mortuus annis,
  ne natae iam plus quam pater ille foret.
exulat extremos tibi vir depulsus ad Indos,
  proque viro lixas diligis atque coquos.   8
consobrina suos tecum partitur amores,
  et tibi crissanti est Aethiopissa tribas.
nescio quid monstri celas, Leonora, reclusi,
  quando tibi solum monstra pudenda placent.   12
impietas odisse suos est maxima, verum
  impietas sic est maior amare suos.

8   *Ad Henricum II Franciae Regem de soluta urbis Mediomatricum obsidione*

Caelo vetustas intulit Herculem,
  mirata monstris letiferam manum,
    flammisque stellatus refulget
      saxificae domitor Medusae.   4
si poscat aequo nuda sub arbitro
  virtus honores, impiger Hercules,
    Henrice, concedet priores
      iure tibi volucerque Perseus.   8

6 *On Leonora*

When I saw your face, Leonora, dripping with perfume and the shine on your cheeks, artfully coloured with white-lead, I only thought that you knew how to paint. I approved your thrice and four times skilful hand on looking at your face. But as soon as your ring had gleamed at me with its gilded copper, and the glass gem that shines on your fingers, I learnt that it is not only in your mind that you are deceitful, but external signs vie in rivalry with cunning guiles. A little copper expresses a deceitful mind, painted skin, and hidden deceit with such reliable indications that Apelles would have been unable to paint better than you, or Myron to work more skilfully in melted bronze.

7 *To the bawd Peiris*

Your mother is a bawd, you are the promiscuous daughter of your mother, and your daughter will take on her mother's job. And although Nature wisely denied you a brother, you love even the name of brother amongst the monks. It's a good thing your father died in your early youth so that he should not now be more than a father to his daughter. Your husband is an exile, driven to the furthest corner of India, and in place of your husband you love sutlers and cooks. A female cousin shares her love with you, and you are brought to orgasm by a black lesbian. You are hiding some sort of unleashed monster, Leonora, since you only like shameful monsters. It is the height of sinfulness to hate one's relatives, but it is more sinful to love them thus.

8 *To Henri II, king of France, on the relief of the siege of Metz*

The ancients placed Hercules in the heavens, marvelling at his arm which dealt death to monsters, and the tamer of petrifying Medusa shines out with his flames after being placed among the stars. If unadorned worth demands its honours under a fair judge, Henry, the tireless Hercules and winged Perseus will rightly concede greater honours to you.

nam multiformi tu numerosius
Hydra, Medusa pestiferum magis,
   monstrum repressisti impetusque
      prodigii retudisti inanes.   12
Occasum et Arcton iam comitem trahens,
et arma Eoae Carolus Austriae,
   torrentis hiberni petebat
      more furens populator urbes.   16
sub semimauro Caesare, pro pudor!
Germana virtus cesserat, Italum
   indocta libertas tyranni
      ferre iugum tacite fremebat.   20
spes inquietae blanda cupidinis
nutrix in orbem vota tetenderat,
   rerumque fastus somniabat
      imperium, male certus augur.   24
tu bellicosae dux bone Galliae
sperare promptam cuncta superbiam
   compescuisti, tu dedisti
      indomito laqueos furori.   28
quis vultus illi, qui dolor intimis
arsit medullis, spiritus impotens
   cum claustra spectaret Mosellae
      et iuvenum intrepidam coronam?   32
sic unda rupes saevit in obvias,
clausus caminis ignis inaestuat,
   Hyrcana sic tigris cruento
      dente suas furit in catenas.   36
sed nota Marti dextra Bironii
murisque virtus impatiens tegi
   ut fulsit, et pulsi procella
      cornipedum tremuere campi,   40
ceu nocte suetae degeneres ferae
vexare caulas, in timidum pecus
   fortes, ad aspectum leonem
      in latebras pavidae recurrunt,   44
sic ille, nuper spe insatiabili
complexus orbem, robora Galliae
   spectare vix ausus recurrit
      ad solitas male cautus artes.   48

For you have checked a monster more prolific than the manifold Hydra, more destructive than Medusa, and have beaten off the ogre's empty onslaughts. Charles was now dragging in tow the West and North, and the armies of Eastern Austria, and the raging plunderer was attacking cities like a winter torrent. The valour of Germany had yielded, oh shame! under a half-caste emperor; the freedom of Italy, unused to bearing a tyrant's yoke, muttered in silence. Hope, the gentle nurse of restless ambition, had extended his prayers to the world, and pride, an unreliable prophet, was dreaming of universal dominion. You, good leader of warlike France, have restrained an arrogance ready to hope for all things, you have put in bonds uncontrolled frenzy. How did he look, what pain burnt deep in his heart, when his uncontrollable spirit looked on the barrier of the Moselle and the undaunted ring of warriors? In this way the waves rage against the projecting cliffs, fire enclosed in furnaces seethes, the Hyrcanian tigress chafes at her chains with bloody tooth. But when the right arm of Biron, well known to Mars, and his valour, impatient at being protected by ramparts, shone out, and the plain quaked, trampled by a storm of horses, just as ignoble wild animals, which usually harass the sheep-pens at night, being bold against the timid flock, scurry back in fear to their hiding-places on seeing a lion, so he who recently embraced the world with unquenchable hope, scarcely daring to look on the might of France, scurries back unwarily to his old wiles.

9   *Ad iuventutem Burdegalensem*

Vasconis tellus, genitrix virorum
fortium, blandi genitrix Lyaei,
cui parens frugum favet et relictis
    Pallas Athenis,   4
te licet claris decoret triumphis
Martius belli labor et vetusti
nominis splendor seriesque longum
    ducta per aevum,   8
ni tamen doctas foveas Camenas
et bonas artes opera fideli,
spes tuas vano studio in futuros
    porrigis annos.   12
non enim moles Pariae columnae,
Phidiae aut vivax ebur, aut Myronis
aera mansurae poterunt sacrare
    nomina famae.   16
obruet longos cita mors labores,
obruet claros titulos opesque;
saxa findentur vitiata serae
    dente senectae.   20
Mulciber quamvis et iniqua Iuno
verterint urbem Priami superbam,
illa Smyrnaeis inimica pensat
    fata Camenis,   24
nec suo mallet cineri superstes
Ilium Eois dare iura terris
qua patent nigros Rhodope ab nivosa
    usque sub Indos.   28
sola doctorum monumenta vatum
nesciunt fati imperium severi,
sola contemnunt Phlegethonta et Orci
    iura superbi.   32

10   *Marco Antonio Monlucio*

Monluci, armatae regeres ut frena cohortis
   supra annos virtus consiliumque dedit.
supra annos animi vis Martia perdidit ausum
   obvia fulmineo pectora ferre globo.   4
quem super astantem muros prius horruit hostis
   postea defuncti vindicis ossa colit.

9   *To the youth of Bordeaux*
Aquitaine, mother of brave heroes, mother of delightful Bacchus,
favoured by the mother of harvests and by Pallas, forsaking Athens,
although you are distinguished through the martial toil of war, by
glorious victories and by the splendour of an ancient name and a line
of descent that extends through long ages, unless you nurse the
learned Muses and their excellent arts with faithful aid, you are
wasting your time in trying to extend your hopes to future years. For
neither the mass of Parian columns, nor the living ivory of Phidias,
nor the bronze statues of Myron will be able to enshrine names in
lasting fame. Swift death will overwhelm years of work, renowned
titles, and wealth; stones weakened by the tooth of advanced old age
will be split. Although Vulcan and cruel Juno overturned the proud
city of Priam, Troy wins compensation for the hostility of fate
through the poetry of Homer, and Troy would not prefer to survive
its ashes and rule the lands of the Orient, as far as they extend from
snow-covered Rhodope right to the swarthy Indians. Only the
writings of the learned bards ignore the sway of harsh Destiny, they
alone scorn Phlegethon and the laws of proud Orcus.

10   *To Marc-Antoine Monluc*
Valour and wisdom beyond your years enabled you, Monluc, to keep
armed troops under control. Martial courage beyond your years
destroyed you when you dared to expose your breast to the cannon
ball. The enemy trembled at first to see you standing on the ramparts,
and afterwards respects the bones of the dead defender.

11 *Calendae Maiae*

Salvete sacris deliciis sacrae
Maiae Calendae, laetitiae et mero
  ludisque dicatae iocisque
    et teneris Charitum choreis.   4
salve voluptas et nitidum decus
anni recurrens perpetua vice
  et flos renascentis iuventae
    in senium properantis aevi.   8
cum blanda veris temperies novo
illuxit orbi, primaque saecula
  fulsere flaventi metallo
    sponte sua sine lege iusta,   12
talis per omnes continuus tenor
annos tepenti rura Favonio
  mulcebat et nullis feraces
    seminibus recreabat agros.   16
talis beatis incubat insulis
felicis aurae perpetuus tepor
  et nesciis campis senectae
    difficilis querulique morbi.   20
talis silentum per tacitum nemus
levi susurrat murmure spiritus,
  Lethenque iuxta obliviosam
    funereas agitat cupressos.   24
forsan supremis cum Deus ignibus
piabit orbem, laetaque saecula
  mundo reducet, talis aura
    aethereos animos fovebit.   28
salve fugacis gloria saeculi,
salve secunda digna dies nota,
  salve vetustae vitae imago
    et specimen venientis aevi.   32

12 *Alexandro Cocburno*

Ingratis vexata hominum Natura querelis,
  et sterilis lassis credita visceribus,
Cocburnum in lucem dedit et rude pignus alendum
  Mnemosynes natis tradidit et Sophiae;   4

11   *May Day*

Hail, May Day, sacred to sacred delights, dedicated to joy and wine, games, jesting, and the delicate dances of the Graces. Hail pleasure, and bright glory of the year returning in an eternal cycle, and bloom of reviving youth, hastening towards time's old age. When spring's pleasant warmth shone upon a new world, and the first generations gleamed with golden metal, naturally righteous without any laws, an uninterrupted course like this through all the years caressed the countryside with a warm West Wind, and renewed the fertile fields without seeds. Such is the endless warmth from delightful breezes which lies over the Isles of the Blessed, and over the fields which know not crabbed old age or complaining disease. Such a breath murmurs in a gentle whisper through the quiet grove of the Silent ones, and stirs the deathly cypress trees beside Lethe, river of forgetfulness. Perhaps when God purifies the world in the final conflagration and brings back happy ages to the universe, such a breeze will refresh the heavenly spirits. Hail, glory of a fleeting age, hail, day worthy of a favourable mark, hail, picture of a former life, and token of an age to come.

12   *To Alexander Cockburn*

Harassed by men's ungrateful complaints, and believed to be barren with her womb exhausted, Nature gave birth to Cockburn, and handed the tender child over to the daughters of Mnemosyne and to Wisdom to be nurtured.

Sors, ubi maturis accessit robur ab annis,
    addidit et dotes ambitiosa suas.
sed, sibi praeferri Virtutem irata, doloris
    exegit poenas vindice morte sui.   8
si numeres annos, cecidit florente iuventa,
    si studia et mores et benefacta, senex.

13 *Ad Thomam Cromelium Anglum*

Portus et afflictis statio tutissima rebus
    et nostro miseris sola sub axe salus,
vindice quo floret pietas rediviva parentum
    sanctaque cum nivea simplicitate fides,   4
illius haud duro munuscula suscipe vultu
    mente tuus tota qui cupit esse cliens;
qui vagus exul inops terra iactatur et unda
    per mala quae fallax omnia mundus habet,   8
dum ferus hinc saevit veterani exercitus hostis,
    dum tonat horrificas Principis aula minas,
dum nivibus canent impervia culmina montes,
    dum valles nimiis impediuntur aquis.   12
post mala tot fessus velut Atthida stratus ad aram
    ante tuos supplex offero dona pedes,
ingenii sterilis tenui de messe maniplos,
    quos dat non fallax, sed male cultus, ager.   16
si placeant, librum, si non, amplectere mentem;
    maius erit voto, si sit utrumque, meo.

14 *Epitaphium Nicolai Baconis Procancellarii Angliae*

Hic Nicolaum ne Baconem conditum
existima, illum tam diu Britannici
regni secundum columen, exitium malis,
bonis asylum; caeca quem non extulit
ad hunc honorem sors, sed aequitas, fides,   5
doctrina, pietas, unica et prudentia.
neu morte raptum crede, qui unica brevi
vita perennes emerit duas: agit
vitam secundam caelites inter animus;
fama implet orbem, vita quae illi tertia est.   10
hac posita in ara corpus animi olim domus,
ara dicata sempiternae memoriae.

When strength had come from mature years, ambitious Fate also added her gifts. But annoyed that he preferred Virtue to herself, she punished him with death to avenge her own chagrin. If you count his years, he fell in the bloom of youth; but if you count his studies, character, and good works, he was an old man.

13   *To Thomas Cromwell, Englishman*
Haven and safest of anchorages in distress, and only salvation for the wretched in this realm, under whose protection the revived religion of our ancestors flourishes, and holy faith along with simplicity shining white, accept with kind countenance the gifts of one who longs with all his heart to be under your protection, who wandering, exiled, and needy, is tossed about on land and sea by all the evils a deceitful world contains, while on one side the savage army of an old enemy rages, while a prince's court thunders dreadful menaces, while the mountain peaks are impassable and white with snow, and valleys are obstructed by floods. Weary after so many misfortunes, like one stretched out before the Athenian altar, in supplication I offer gifts at your feet, bundles from the poor harvest of my sterile mind, provided not by a deceitful but an ill cultivated field. If they are pleasing, accept the book; if not, my intention. If you do both, it will be more than I hope for.

14   *Epitaph for Nicholas Bacon, Vice-Chancellor of England*
Do not think that Nicholas Bacon is buried here, for so long the second prop of the English realm, the destruction of the evil, and the refuge of the good; who was not raised to this position by blind chance, but by justice, faith, learning, piety, and a unique wisdom. And do not think he was snatched away by death, who through one short life has bought two eternal ones. His soul lives a second life among the saints; his fame fills the world, which is his third life. Once the home of his soul, his body is placed in this monument, a monument dedicated to his everlasting memory.

15 *Ad Henricum VIII, Angliae Regem*
     Fama levis (si certa fides adhibenda poetis)
     ex humili enascens paullatim assurgit et alto
     vertice caeruleo sese inserit ardua caelo.
     quippe velut tenui nascens de fomite rivus
     per tacitas primum nullo cum murmure valles   5
     serpit et, ut patrii se sensim e margine fontis
     largius effudit, pluvios modo colligit imbres,
     nunc lacubus sese pigrisque paludibus auget;
     at postquam spatio vires accepit et undas,
     spumeus effractis prorumpit in aequora silvis: 10
     sic primo summissa metu vaga fama susurrat;
     mox vulgo insinuat se; postquam audacia crevit,
     torva oculos vultuque minax atque ore procaci
     certa auget dubiis, miscet mendacia veris.
     illa sed in cunctos nimium Dea prodiga, facti   15
     infectique loquax, in te tamen invida laudis,
     parca sui, studioque animi deprensa maligno est.
     nam licet ingenti praeconia fuderit ore
     speque tui adventus animos implerit et aures,
     laudibus inferior tanto est virtute tuique   20
     dotibus ingenii quanto se attollere vero
     altius et vano solita est splendescere fuco.
     illa quidem haud falso mentis celebravit acumen
     ingeniumque capax et primis semper ab annis
     pectora Cecropiae studiis addicta Minervae;   25
     nec tacuit recti memorem sanctaeque tenacem
     iustitiae mentem, miserisque in rebus egenis
     praesidium, poenamque malis, nulloque favore
     ancipites inter corda inclinantia lites.
     magna (nec infitior) sunt haec, sed summa tuarum   30
     non ibi consistit laudum nec terminus haeret.
     scilicet in tanto sortis splendore secundae
     nosse modum, quantoque supra virtutibus omnes
     omnibus emineas, tanto submissius aequo
     te gerere in cunctis, tetrico nec honore severum   35
     nec fracta gravitate levem, non ore superbum,
     non tristem aspectu vultusque horrore minacem;
     sed comem placidumque bonis, placabilis irae,

15   *To Henry VIII, king of England*

Fickle Rumour (if firm credence is to be placed in the poets), born from a humble position, gradually rises up and insinuates herself aloft, with head held high, in the azure sky. For just as a stream, welling up from an insubstantial source, first of all meanders noiselessly through silent valleys and, as it gradually pours forth more abundantly from the edge of its parent source, at one time it gathers showers of rain, at another increases in size from lakes and sluggish marshes; but when in time it has gained strength and floods of water, breaking through the woodlands, it pours out foaming into the sea. So wandering Rumour at first whispers, submissive with fear; soon she creeps into the mob; after her boldness has increased, wild-eyed and with threatening face and shameless mouth, she embellishes certainty with doubt, and mixes lies with truth. But this goddess who is excessively profuse to all, chattering of what has happened and what has not happened, has nevertheless in your case been found to be grudging of praise, sparing of herself, and niggardly at heart. For although she has poured out fulsome praises of you and filled our minds and ears with hope of your coming, she is as much below the mark in her praise of your virtue and the gifts of your intellect as she usually soars above the truth and shines with empty deceit. She did indeed truthfully celebrate the acuteness of your mind, your capable intellect, and your heart which from your earliest years has been devoted to the cares of Athenian Minerva; nor did she fail to mention your mind, which remembers what is right and upholds holy justice, the protection you afford to the unfortunate in time of need, your punishment of the wicked, and your lack of partiality in deciding doubtful quarrels. These things, I do not deny it, are great, but the sum of your praises does not stop here, nor is the boundary fixed here. For there is your observance of moderation in the great splendour of your good fortune, your behaviour in all things which is as submissive to justice as you are pre-eminent over all others in all virtues, being neither stern with severe dignity, nor frivolous with gravity impaired, nor proud in word, sullen in look, nor threatening with dreadful countenance; but courteous and kindly to the good, of easily appeased temper,

quique magistratus largissima frena remittas
sponte tua, salva quoad maiestate liceret.   40
haec tua te virtus diis immortalibus aequum
efficit atque hominum supra fastigia tollit.

16 *Mutuus Amor*

Armata telis dexteram,
laevam veneno, saeviat
mors; cuncta tempus demetat
falce aut senecta deterat: 4
non mortis hoc propinquitas,
non temporis longinquitas,
solvet fides quod nexuit
intaminata vinculum.   8
mors et senectus obruit
cum Scipione Laelium,
canam fidem non obruit,
non pectorum constantiam.   12
durabit usque posteris
intaminata saeculis
sincera quae Britannidas
nectit fides Heroidas.   16
rerum supremus terminus
ut astra terris misceat,
regina Scota diliget
Anglam, Angla Scotam diliget.   20

17 *In Leonoram*

Sicine de nostra numquam egrediere culina,
pinguibus et fies semper amica coquis?
utque coquum coquus expellit, fit protinus heres
successorque tuo fit nova praeda toro.   4
iamque etiam hesternas deglubere coeptat ofellas,
crescit et in mores filia parva tuos;
lingit et algentes concreto iure patellas,
nudaque ieiunae praeripit ossa cani.   8
sic tener et firmis nondum satis unguibus ursus
magnanimo lambit vulnera facta patri.
munus obire potest, Leonora, decentius istud

most generously relaxing of your own will the reins of office, as far as is possible without violation of your majesty. This virtue of yours makes you equal to the immortal gods, and raises you above the heights of mortal men.

16   *Mutual Love*
Let death rage, her right hand armed with weapons, her left with poison. Let time harvest all things with his scythe, or old age wear them away. Neither the proximity of death nor length of time will undo this bond which undefiled fidelity has tied. Death and old age overwhelmed Laelius along with Scipio, but they do not overwhelm venerable faith nor the constancy of hearts. The fidelity which binds together the heroines of Britain will always endure undefiled and unimpaired throughout future generations. Though the final end of the universe confounds the heavens with the earth, the Queen of Scots will love the English Queen, the English Queen the Queen of Scots.

17   *On Leonora*
So, will you never get out of our kitchen, and will you always become the girl-friend of fat cooks? As cook drives out cook, there is an immediate heir, and the successor becomes fresh booty for your bed. And now, your little daughter is also beginning to suck(?) yesterday's titbits, and she is growing up into your habits. She licks pans which are cold with congealed soup, and snatches bare bones away from a starving dog. Just so, a young bear whose claws are still too soft licks the wounds inflicted by its courageous father. Your white-haired mother,

longaeva senior cana parens Hecuba,   12
efferat annosos rabies cui spumea rictus,
    et latrat, patulo dum cupit ore loqui;
et stipis exiguae si spes accessit, adulat,
    nec quicquam in dura fronte pudoris habet.   16
illa analecta legat, dentes illi ossa fatigent,
    cum canibus certet de dape paene canis:
tu iuvenum potius validis obnitere nervis,
    et facie atque annis concipe digna tuis.   20
filia parva aviam spectet matremque et utrimque
    spem capiat vitae consiliumque suae.

18 Ad eandem

Vive male, monachique tui lixaeque coquique,
    mater edax, illex filia, nigra tribas.
ne tamen interea vestri immemor arguar esse,
    vos penes hoc nostri pignus amoris erit.   4

19 In Leonoram

Mendicis aetas monachis tibi prima dicata est,
    iam tibi maturae sola culina placet.
divinare licet, sed non libet, et pudet, aevo
    excipies quales deteriore viros.   4

20 In Neaeram

Cum pulchram roseus dies Neaeram
ostendit mihi, sic miser furore
inquietus agor trahor peruror
ut rursus tacitas amem tenebras,
ceu mali medicina sint tenebrae.   5
at cum nox tenebris opaca caecis
iam solis iubar aureum fugavit,
et solis iubare aureo refulgens
iubar splendidiusque puriusque,
formosam mihi sustulit Neaeram,   10
iam rursus tenebras malas perosus,
pulchram cernere quae negant Neaeram,
noctem deprecor et diem reposco,
quae pulchram mihi referat Neaeram,

older than long-lived Hecuba, can undertake this job more fittingly, whose mouth-foaming insanity makes her ancient grin look wild and who barks as she tries to speak with gaping mouth. And if the hope of a small donation comes along, she fawns, and has no trace of shame on her hard face. Let her as maid-servant gather up the crumbs, let bones tire out her teeth, let her, almost dog-like, fight with dogs for a meal. You should rather press against the strong members of young men, and conceive things worthy of your face and years. Let your little daughter look on her grandmother and mother, and from both sources draw hope and advice for her life.

18   *On the same*
Fare you ill, along with your monks and sutlers and cooks, voracious mother, seductress daughter, and black lesbian. But in case, meanwhile, I am accused of being forgetful of you, this token of our love will be in your possession.

19   *On Leonora*
Your youth was devoted to the mendicant friars, and now that you are mature, only the kitchen pleases you. One can foresee, although it isn't pleasant or decent, what sort of men you will welcome in your declining years.

20   *On Neaera*
When rosy day reveals fair Neaera to me, restless with frenzy, poor creature, I am so driven and dragged and consumed with fire that I love again silent darkness, as if darkness were a remedy for my ill. But when shady night with its gloomy darkness has now put to flight the golden splendour of the sun, and has removed from me beautiful Neaera, a splendour shining more brilliantly and clearly than the golden splendour of the sun, loathing once more the evil darkness which prevents my seeing fair Neaera, I curse the night, and ask again for the daylight to restore fair Neaera to me,

ceu mali mihi causa sint tenebrae.   15
quis vitae manet ordo me modusque?
cui vota ut tribuant dei faventes,
cum votis neque dii dabunt faventes
ne miserrimus esse perseverem.
hoc Venus probat, et probat Cupido   20
diis votisque potentior secundis.

21 *In Iulium II Pontificem*
Genua cui patrem, genitricem Graecia, partum
   pontus et unda dedit, num bonus esse potes?
fallaces Ligures, et mendax Graecia, ponto
   nulla fides. in te singula solus habes.   4

22 *De Nicotiana falso nomine Medicaea appellata*
Doctus ab Hesperiis rediens Nicotius oris
   Nicotianam rettulit,
nempe salutiferam cunctis languoribus herbam,
   prodesse cupidus patriae.   4
at Medice Catharina, κάθαρμα luesque suorum,
   Medea saeculi sui,
ambitione ardens, Medicaeae nomine plantam
   Nicotianam adulterat;   8
utque bonis cives prius exuit, exuere herbae
   honore vult Nicotium.
at vos auxilium membris qui quaeritis aegris,
   abominandi nominis   12
a planta cohibete manus, os claudite, et aures
   a peste taetra occludite;
nectar enim virus fiet, panacea venenum,
   Medicaea si vocabitur.   16

23 *Ad Carolum Cossaeum Brixiaci Dynastam, post captas Vercellas*
Quis me nivosos Alpium trans vertices
   curru volucri deferet?
quis nube saeptum me remotis Pegasus
   sistet iugis Oenotriae?   4
non ut parentum laude Romam vel sua
   virtute Venetum nobilem

as if darkness were the cause of my ill. What system or method of living is in store for me? Even though the favouring gods may grant me my prayers, not even the favouring gods will grant me, together with my prayers, the boon of not continuing to be utterly wretched. Venus approves of this, as does Cupid, who is more powerful than favourable gods and prayers.

21   *On Pope Julius II*
Your father was from Genoa, your mother from Greece, and the waves of the sea gave you birth. How can you be good? Italians are false, Greeks liars, and no-one can trust in the sea. You alone have each of these things in you.

22   *On Tobacco, wrongly called the 'herbe médicée'*
The learned Nicot, returning from the western shores, brought back tobacco [*Nicotiana*], without doubt a plant to cure all illnesses, anxious as he was to be of service to his country. But Catherine de Médicis, the dregs and plague of her people, the Medea of her generation, burning with ambition, defiles the tobacco plant with the name of 'herbe médicée'. And as previously she stripped her citizens of their goods, she wishes to deprive Nicot of the honour of his plant. But you who seek help for sick limbs, keep your hands from a plant of ill-omened name, close your mouths, and shut your ears from the foul plague. For nectar will become venom and panacea poison if it is named after Médicis.

23   *To Charles de Cossé, comte de Brissac, after the capture of Vercelli*
Who will transport me across the snowy summits of the Alps in a winged chariot? What Pegasus will set me down, enclosed in a cloud, on the distant mountains of Italy? Not that I may see Rome, famous through the praise of our ancestors, or Venice, famous through its own worth,

fratrisve flammis et sororum lacrimis
    Padum calentem conspicer,   8
sed te, beatae lux beata Galliae
    Cossaee, propius ut colam,
te mirer Italum, te Pelasgum gloriam
    splendore fuscantem novo,   12
ceu Sol Dianam, ceu Diana ceteras
    obscurat astrorum faces.
nec pectus hac mi perculit cupidine
    florentis aevi gloria;   16
seu pertinacem cum Batavum impelleres,
    saeva tremendus cuspide,
qualis columbas spargit imbelles fuga
    ales minister fulminis;   20
seu cum decoro squalidum te pulvere
    mirata quondam est Ruscino,
solum feroces bellicosae Iberiae
    parma morantem exercitus,   24
tunc cum tuorum fida castrorum comes
    attonita Virtus par novum
spectavit, hinc virum, inde bellum, et horruit
    quod fecerat spectaculum.   28
Vercella pectus una sollicitat meum,
    Vercella sola macerat,
Vercella victa, Galliis, dum vincitur,
    felicior victricibus;   32
virtute tanta comminus cui perfrui
    indulsit astrorum favor,
inusitato quam theatrum caelites
    elegerint spectaculo,   36
cum, te chorago, pace cum placida feram
    Mars copulavit dexteram,
Bellona mitis frena legum pertulit,
    innoxioque foedere   40
vis aequitati iuncta, ius licentiae,
    secura pressit compita,
salvoque recti et improbi discrimine
    castris forum se miscuit.   44
quem nuper inter arma fossarum morae

or the Po, glowing with a brother's flames and sisters' tears, but to be nearer as I honour you, Cossé, blessed light of blessed France, to admire you, obscuring the glory of Italy and of Greece with a new brilliance, just as the sun obscures the moon, and the moon the other lights of the stars. The glory of your flourishing life did not strike my heart with this desire either when, terrifying with your cruel spear, you drove back the stubborn Dutch, just as the winged bearer of the lightning scatters in flight the unwarlike doves; or when Perpignan once wondered at you, grimy with seemly dust, the only one who could delay the wild armies of warlike Spain with your shield; or when the faithful companion of your camp, Virtue, was astonished to see a new pair of combatants, on one side a man, on the other an army, and shuddered at the spectacle she had created. Vercelli alone moves my heart, Vercelli alone pains it, conquered Vercelli, more fortunate in its defeat than conquering France. The favour of the stars allowed her to enjoy at first hand your great virtue, being chosen by the gods as the stage for a rare spectacle, when, with you as stage-manager, Mars linked his fierce arm with gentle peace, Bellona, become gentle, accepted the law's restraint, force united with justice in a harmless bond and law united with freedom thronged the safe crossroads and the market-place mingled with the camp, with the distinction between right and wrong preserved. The army which recently was not frightened in battle by the obstacles of trenches,

celsaeque pinnarum minae,
tot stricta tela plumbeaeque grandinis
   procella non exterruit,   48
idem, urbe capta, fronte non tristi ferox,
   non impotens victoria,
non ira et odio saevus implacabili,
   non efferatus caedibus,   52
perambulavit liberas metu vias,
   ceu pace festa, exercitus.
non insolentis militis formidine
   matrona cultus exuit,   56
non officina clausa merces abdidit,
   non hospes aurum credidit
solo refosso, non pudori filiae
   parens, maritus coniugi   60
vim expavit ullam. subitus oppressae sonus
   urbis, tubarum et cornuum
clangor, virorum clamor, armorum fragor,
   vulgi insidebant auribus.   64
caedes ob oculos et fuga et ferrum madens
   cruore nondum frigido.
volvebat animus quid facere victor, pati
   victus soleret. tot tamen   68
inter timores vim timere, te duce,
   nemo sibi permiserat,
cum tu tot animos militum, tot ensium
   sic temperares impetum   72
ceu versat animus corpus unum et corpore
   enata ab uno bracchia.
Natura genitrix, tam novam discordium
   rerum videns concordiam,   76
leges stupebat non minus vinci suas
   quam vatis olim Thracii
ad carmen amnes stare, silvas currere,
   cervo leonem, ovi lupum   80
mitem accubare, et acribus lepusculum
   latus Molossis iungere.
ego hunc triumphum, hac te decorum gloria,
   Cossaee, malim cernere   84

the lofty threatening battlements, so many unsheathed swords, and the barrage of a hail of lead, that very army, now that the city is captured, is not fierce with grim face, or uncontrollable in victory, or savage with wrath and implacable hatred, or wild from slaughter, but it has walked through streets free from fear, as though in joyful peacetime. The married woman has not laid aside her finery for fear of the immoderate soldier; no shop has shut and hidden its wares, no host has entrusted his gold to a hole in the ground; no parent has feared any violence for his daughter's honour, no husband for his wife. The sudden sound of a captured city, the noise of trumpets and horns, the shouting of men, the clashing of arms, were firmly fixed in the ears of the mob. They visualised slaughter, flight, and swords dripping with still warm blood. Their minds were reflecting on the usual conduct of victors and the usual suffering of the vanquished. But amidst all these fears, nobody had allowed himself to fear violence under your leadership, since you restrained the passions of so many soldiers and the attack of so many swords in the same way as the mind moves a single body, and the limbs which come from that body. Mother Nature, seeing such a novel concord of discordant things, was no less surprised that her laws were being overcome than she was surprised that, once upon a time, at the song of the Thracian poet, rivers stood still, woods moved swiftly, the lion lay down with the deer and the gentle wolf with the sheep, and the little hare lay side by side with the keen Molossian hounds. *I* would rather see this triumph, and you honoured with this glory, Cossé,

quam spolia regum dirutarumque urbium
  gazaeque pompam barbarae,
victaeque turbae fletibus plaudentium
  contaminatum gaudium.   88
sed quando tanto dissitis caelo et solo
  sors invida id praecluserit,
te prosequemur mente grata, qua licet,
  et vota nuncupabimus;   92
haustusque dulcis Liberi libabimus
  heroas inter sospites;
canetque victor pariter et victus tuum
  hic robur, hic clementiam.   96

24 *Ioannis Calvini epicedium*
  Si quis erit nullos superesse a funere manes
  qui putet, aut si forte putet, sic vivit ut Orcum
  speret et aeternas Stygio sub gurgite poenas,
  is merito sua fata fleat, sua funera ploret
  vivus, et ad caros luctum transmittat amicos.   5
  at nos, invitis quamquam sis raptus amicis
  ante diem, magnis quamvis inviderit ausis
  mors, te flere nefas, Calvine, et funera vanae
  ludibrio pompae et miseris onerare querelis.
  liber enim curis, terrenae et pondere molis,   10
  astra tenes, propiusque Deo, quem mente colebas,
  nunc frueris, puroque vides in lumine purum
  lumen, et infusi satiatus numinis haustum
  exigis aeternam sine sollicitudine vitam;
  quam neque deiciunt luctus nec tollit inani   15
  ebria laetitia spes exanimantve timores,
  quaeque animo offundit morbi contagia corpus.
  hanc ego, quae curis te lux exemit acerbis,
  natalem iure appellem, qua raptus in astra
  in patriam remeas, et post fastidia duri   20
  exilii, mortis iam mens secura secundae,
  fortunae imperio maior, primordia longae
  ingreditur vitae. nam ceu per corporis artus
  cum subiit animus, pigrae vegetatque movetque
  molis onus, funditque agilem per membra vigorem;   25

than the spoils of kings, the display of cities destroyed and foreign treasure, and the rejoicing of applauding men, defiled by the tears of the conquered masses. But since envious Fate has prevented me from doing so, separated as I am from you by such an expanse of sky and land, I shall honour you with gratitude, with which I *can* honour you, and I shall make my vows. I shall pour libations of draughts of sweet wine in the company of safe heroes; and both the victor and the vanquished will sing your praises, the one for your strength, the other for your mercy.

24   *Elegy for Jean Calvin*
If there is anyone who thinks that no spirits survive after death, or if perhaps he thinks they do, and lives in such a way as to expect Hell and eternal punishment in the Stygian flood, he would be justified in weeping for his fate and bemoaning his death while he is alive, and passing on his grief to his dear friends. But although you have been snatched away prematurely from your friends against their will, although death has envied you your great achievements, Calvin, it would be wrong for us to weep for you, and to weigh down your death with the mockery of empty pomp and pathetic laments. For, free from cares and the burden of your earthly mass, you dwell in heaven, and now enjoy at close quarters the sight of God, whom you worshipped in your mind; in pure light you see pure light, and filled with a draught of godhead which has been poured into you, you live an eternal life free from worry, which is neither cast down by grief, nor raised up by hope, inebriated with groundless joy, nor prostrated by fears and the infection of disease which the body spreads over the soul. That day which has freed you from bitter cares I would justifiably call a birthday when, carried off to the heavens, you return to your home-land, and after the unpleasantness of a hard exile, your mind, now free from the fear of second death and superior to the rule of Fate, enters on the beginning of a long life. For just as when the soul passes through the limbs of the body, and animates and moves the weight of its sluggish mass, and perfuses its members with quickening life;

cum fugit, exanimum iacet immotumque cadaver,
nec quicquam est luteae nisi putris fabrica massae:
sic animi Deus est animus, quo si caret, atris
obruitur tenebris, specieque illusus inani
fallaces rectique bonique amplectitur umbras.   30
ast ubi divini concepit numinis haustum,
diffugiunt tenebrae simulacraque vana facessunt,
nudaque se veri facies in luce videndam
exhibet aeterna, quam nullo vespere claudit
saepta caput furvis nox importuna tenebris.   35
hunc ergo in portum caelo plaudente receptus
tu licet in placida tranquillus pace quiescas,
non tamen omnino potuit mors invida totum
tollere Calvinum terris: aeterna manebunt
ingenii monumenta tui, et livoris iniqui   40
languida paullatim cum flamma resederit, omnes,
religio qua pura nitet, se fundet in oras
fama tui. ut nuper falso te nomine Clemens,
te Pauli duo, flagitiis et fraude gemelli,
te Iuli timuit rabies, te nobilis una   45
fraterna impietate Pius: sic nominis umbram
ingeniique tui effigiem post fata timebit
vana superstitio; quique olim in sede Quirini
triste furens flammaque minax ferroque tyrannus
transtulit inferni cuncta in se munia regni,   50
imperio Pluto, foedis Harpyia rapinis,
Eumenis igne, Charon naulo, triplicique corona
Cerberus, immissi stupefactus lumine veri,
terrificoque tuae deiectus fulmine linguae,
transferet infernas in se post funera poenas: 55
inter aquas sitiens, referens revolubile saxum,
vulturibus iecur exesus, cava dolia lymphis
frustra implens, Ixioneum distentus in orbem.

25 *Ioanni Areskino, Comiti Marriae, Scotorum Proregi*
Si quis Areskinum memoret per bella ferocem,
pace gravem nulli, tempore utroque pium;
si quis opes sine fastu, animum sine fraude, carentem
rebus in ambiguis suspicione fidem;   4

when it departs, the corpse lies lifeless and immobile, and there is nothing left but the rotting structure of a mass of clay; so God is the soul of the soul, without which it is overwhelmed with black darkness, and fooled by empty appearances it accepts deceiving shadows of what is right and good. But when it has received a draught of the divine godhead, the darkness dissolves, empty phantoms depart, and the unadorned face of truth displays itself to be seen in eternal light, which no night, its head enveloped in swarthy darkness, cruelly brings to a close with evening shadows. So, although you have been welcomed with the applause of heaven to this port, and quietly take your rest in calm peace, envious death could not remove Calvin entirely from the earth. Eternal will remain the monuments of your genius; and when the flame of unfair envy has gradually grown faint and abated, your fame will spread to all shores where the true religion shines. As recently the falsely named Clement, two Pauls, alike in sin and deceit, the insanity of Julius, and Pius famous only for his unbrotherly impiety, feared you, so empty superstition after your death will fear the ghost of your name and the image of your genius. And he who once raged cruelly on the seat of Romulus, a tyrant menacing with fire and sword, and took on himself all the functions of the king of Hell, a Pluto with his power, a Harpy with his foul plundering, a Fury with his fire, a Charon with his passage-money, and a Cerberus with his triple crown, stunned by the light of inrushing truth and cast down by the terrifying thunder of your tongue, will take on himself after death the punishments of Hell: thirsting in the midst of water, bringing back the rolling stone, his liver devoured by vultures, vainly filling pierced pitchers with water, racked on Ixion's wheel.

25   *To John Erskine, Earl of Mar, Regent of Scotland*
If anyone speaks of Erskine as bold in wartime, harsh to no-one in peacetime, a good Christian in both; if he speaks of wealth without pride, a mind without deceit, and loyalty free from suspicion in changeable fortunes;

  si quod ob has dotes saevis iactata procellis
      fugit in illius patria fessa sinum;
  vera quidem memoret, sed non et propria: laudes
      qui pariter petet has unus et alter erit.   8
  illud ei proprium est, longo quod in ordine vitae
      nil odium aut livor quod reprehendat habet.

26 *Matthaeo Stuarto, Leviniae Comiti, Scotorum Proregi*
        Regis avus, Regis pater, alto e sanguine Regum
            imperio quorum terra Britanna subest,
        Matthaeus: genuit Levinia, Gallia fovit,
            pulso Anglus thalamum remque decusque dedit.   4
        coepi invicta manu; famam virtute refelli,
            arma armis vici consilioque dolos.
        gratus in ingratos, patriam iusteque pieque
            cum regerem, hostili perfidia cecidi.   8
        care nepos, spes una domus, meliore senectam
            attingas fato, cetera dignus avo.

27 *Annae Valsingamiae, Thomae Randolphi uxori*
        Anna hic Randolphi iaceo cum prole sepulta,
            et genitrix uno et mortua et orba die.
        et genus et facies populo sunt nota, sed uni
            sat mihi sit mores complacuisse viro;   4
        quos gemitu probat et lacrimis curaque fideli,
            nec patitur famam me moriente mori.

28 *Ad Camillam Morelliam*
            Camilla, multo me mihi carior,
            aut si quid ipso est me mihi carius,
            Camilla, doctorum parentum
                et patriae decus et voluptas,   4
            ni Gratiae te plus oculis ament,
            ni te Camenae plus oculis ament,
            nec Gratias gratas, nec ipsas
                esse rear lepidas Camenas;   8
            quae virgo nondum nubilis, artibus
            doctis Minervam, pectine Apollinem,
            cantu Camenas, et lepore

if he recalls that, because of these gifts, our homeland which had been tossed around in raging storms fled weary to his bosom, he would indeed be speaking the truth, but not of his peculiar qualities; more than one person will likewise lay claim to these praises. What is peculiar to him is that, in the long course of his life, hatred and envy have nothing to rebuke him with.

26 *To Matthew Stewart, Earl of Lennox, Regent of Scotland*
I am Matthew, grandfather of a king, father of a king, of the lofty blood of kings under whose command the land of Britain lies. Lennox bore me, France nurtured me, in exile England gave me a marriage, wealth, and honour. I undertook feats that are unbeaten; I surpassed my reputation with my courage; I overcame arms with arms, and deceit with good counsel. Although I was grateful to ingrates and ruled my country justly and piously, I fell to an enemy's treachery. Dear grandson, only hope of our family, may you reach old age with a better fate, but in other respects worthy of your grandfather.

27 *To Anne Walsingham, wife of Thomas Randolph*
Here I lie, Anne, the wife of Randolph, buried with my child, a mother, a corpse, and childless on one and the same day. My family and appearance are known to the people, but let it be sufficient for me that my ways pleased one man, of which he shows his approval by his moans and tears and faithful love, nor does he allow my fame to die at my death.

28 *To Camille de Morel*
Camille, much dearer to me than I am myself, or than anything which is dearer to me than myself, Camille, the glory and delight of your learned parents and your country, if the Graces do not love you more than their eyes, if the Muses do not love you more than their eyes, I would not think the Graces are graceful, or the very Muses charming. Although you are still a maiden not yet of marriageable age, you would outstrip or equal Minerva in the learned arts, Apollo on the lyre, the Muses in singing, and the Graces in charm.

vel superes Charites vel aeques.   12
hos ferre fructus, Utenhovi, decet
laurum vireto quae teneram comam
nutrivit et ramos refudit,
Castalio saturata rore.   16

29 *In rusticum*

Rusticus 'hem' cunctos cum congeminaret ad ictus,
   hiberno properans findere ligna foco,
syllaba quid toties iuvet 'hem' geminata 'laborem'
   quaerenti uxori rettulit ille 'iuvat;   4
nempe simul toto contentis corpore nervis
   in rimam cuneum fortius ictus agit.'
illa memor, Veneris media inter gaudia, telum
   ut penetret magis, 'hem' congeminare iubet.   8
'nil opus est' inquit 'nunc hoc conamine, coniunx;
   findere te sane nolo, forare volo.'

30 *E Graeco Simonidis*

Homo cum sis, nihil assere stabile,
nec ubi videris hominem, certa
spatia aetatis promitte; etenim
muscae volucris res in morem
inconstantia rotat humanas.   5

31 *Ex eodem*

Ut arma fugias, fata non fugies tamen.

32 *Ex eodem*

De luce cassis cor memoriam non supra
unum tenebit, si cor habeamus, diem.

33 *Ad Henricum Scotorum Regem*

Caltha suos nusquam vultus a sole reflectit,
   illo oriente patens, illo abeunte latens:
nos quoque pendemus de te, sol noster, ad omnes
   expositi rerum te subeunte vices.   4

It is fitting that these fruits, Utenhove, should be borne by the laurel tree which fed its tender leaves in a grassy place, and, soaked in Castalian dew, drenched its branches in turn.

29 *On a peasant*
When a peasant was repeating 'hem' at each blow as he was hurrying to split logs for the winter fire, and his wife asked why he liked to repeat the syllable 'hem' all the time, he replied to her: 'It helps the work. For once my muscles are strained throughout my body, the blow drives the wedge into the crack more powerfully.' She remembers this in the midst of the joys of love and tells him to repeat 'hem' so that his weapon will go in further. 'There is no need', he says, 'for such effort, dear wife. I don't want to split you, just pierce you.'

30 *From the Greek of Simonides*
Since you are a man, do not claim that anything is constant. And when you see a man, do not promise a certain span of years. For inconstancy turns human fortunes around like a winged fly.

31 *From the same*
Although you may flee from battle, you still will not escape fate.

31 *From the same*
Our hearts will not remember the dead for more than one day, if we have any sense.

33 *To Henry, king of Scotland*
Nowhere does the marigold turn its face away from the sun, opening when it rises and closing when it sets. We also depend on you, our sun, and are exposed to all the vicissitudes which you undergo.

34 *Ad Carolum Utenhovium*

Morte carent superi: superis par cetera diva est
Saxonidas iusto quae regit imperio.
at morte ut careat mortali stirpe creata,
    non dare Lysippus Praxitelesve potest: 4
Musa potest fati domitrix, quae pectora vatum
enthea fatidico plena furore quatit.
te manet, Utenhovi, decus hoc, decus hoc manet illam,
    ut celebris numeris fiat uterque tuis;   8
solus enim vates es tali Heroide dignus,
haec sola ingenio est area digna tuo.

35 *Ad Salutem in nuptiis Reginae*

Alma Salus, reduci tibi Nymphae haec vota dedere
quattuor, ut dominae conciliere suae,
eius et aeternam statuas in pectore sedem:
    non alia poteris sanctius aede coli.   4

36 *Hymnus in Christi ascensionem*

Io triumphe, Ecclesia,
iam victor hostium tuus
dux templa scandit aetheris,
adversa patri vulnera
it et coronam ostendere,   5
qualis redit de proelio
tabo decoro sordidus.
demissa nubes se explicat
sub Imperatoris pedes;
reclusa caeli ianua   10
invitat omnem exercitum;
vox Angelorum cantibus
venire Regem nuntiat;
aether nitescit gaudio,
timore pallent Tartara,   15
mundus stupet spectaculo
suspensus ante incognito;
Mors victa flet, spes praemii
levat labores militum.
cum Patre Proles unica,   20

34   *To Charles Utenhove*
The gods above are deathless; in all other respects, equal to the gods is
the goddess who rules over the Saxon race with legitimate authority.
But neither Lysippus nor Praxiteles can ensure that a creature of
mortal stock should be deathless. The Muse, conqueror of Fate, can
do so, who, full of prophetic fury, causes the inspired hearts of poets
to beat fast. This glory awaits you, Utenhove, and it awaits her, that
you should both become famous through your verse; for you are the
only bard worthy of such a heroine, and she is the only subject
worthy of your genius.

35   *To Health, on the Queen's wedding*
Bountiful Health, to you on your return four Nymphs made this
prayer, that you should be favourably disposed to their mistress, and
establish an everlasting home in her breast. In no other temple can
you be worshipped more piously.

36   *Hymn on the Ascension of Christ*
Hosanna, oh Church, now your leader, victorious over his enemies,

rises up to the vaults of heaven; he goes to show the wounds on his front

and his crown to the Father, like one who returns from battle, grimy

with seemly gore. The cloud drops and unfolds beneath the sovereign's

feet. The gate of Heaven opens up and invites the whole host in. Angel

voices announce with their singing the coming of the King. Heaven

shines with joy, Hell grows pale with fear, the anxious World is amazed

at this previously unknown sight. Vanquished Death weeps, the hope of

recompense eases the soldiers' travail. Only Son with the Father,

et ex utroque Spiritus,
adeste sic pugnantibus
ut sint triumphi compotes.

37   *E Graeco Stobaei de brevitate vitae*
Rebus in humanis nulla est constantia certa.
  veridico vates Chius ut ore canit,
'non minus est foliis hominum gens fluxa caducis.'
  pauci ubi ceperunt auribus ista suis   4
pectoribus fixere; animis namque indita quondam
  spes teneris blande credula corda fovet.
et dum laeta viret iucundo flore iuventa,
  percursant animos irrita multa leves;   8
nec senium mortemve pavet, neque corpore sano
  provida venturi cura doloris adest.
o male stultorum mens credula, qui brevis aevi
  tempora non norint quam fugitiva volent!   12
at tu praemonitus nigrae ad confinia mortis
  laetus age, et genio gratificare tuo.

38   *Apud Clementem Alexandrinum, Strom. lib. 6*
Muliere nulla res viro praestantior
bona evenire, nil mala peius potest.

and Spirit deriving from both, aid the combatants so that they may

partake of the triumph.

37   *From the Greek of Stobaeus on the shortness of life*
There is no reliable constancy in human affairs. As the Chian bard
sang with truthful lips, 'Mankind is no less fleeting than falling leaves.'
Few men, on hearing this, have implanted it in their hearts; for hope,
once placed in young minds, seductively wheedles credulous hearts.
And so long as joyful youth flourishes in delightful bloom, many
vanities pass through carefree minds. It does not fear old age or
death; nor, while the body is sound, is there any far-seeing concern
for future pain. Oh stupidly credulous minds of fools, who do not
know how fleetingly a short lifetime flies by! But you who are fore-
warned, live joyfully right up to the brink of death, and indulge your
inclinations.

38   *From Clement of Alexandria, Stromata book VI*
Nothing more outstanding can happen to a man than a good wife, and
nothing worse than a bad one.

Commentary

The following abbreviations have been used:
McFarlane   I. D. McFarlane, *Buchanan* (London, 1981)
OLD   Oxford Latin Dictionary
O.O.   Buchanan, *Opera omnia* (Leiden, 1725)
TLL   Thesaurus Linguae Latinae

1   *Ad invictissimum Franciae Regem Henricum II post victos Caletes*

This ode was written on the occasion of the capture from the English of
Calais by François, duc de Guise, in January 1558. The poem was published
in two separate editions soon afterwards, by both Robert and Charles
Estienne (see McFarlane, p. 507), and is part of the flurry of poetic activity
which surrounded this event (see Saulnier's list of 'Les Poètes de la prise de
Calais (1558)' in 'Deux œuvres inconnues de Jean Sève et une édition
inconnue de Baïf'). The poem demonstrates Buchanan's total sympathy at
this time with the French cause as represented by the Guises (cf. 65–8),
although the ending does contain a warning against *hybris*. The poem is
written in the alcaic metre.

1.	cf. Virgil, *Aeneid* 4.519 sq. 'conscia fati/sidera', copied by Manilius 1.1 sq.
3.	cf. 'siderum lapsu' Virgil, *Aeneid* 4.524, Lucan 2.268, Statius, *Thebaid* 1.499.
4.	cf. Ovid, *Metamorphoses* 1.79 'ille opifex rerum'; Lucan 10.266 sq. 'ille creator/atque opifex rerum'.
5.	cf. Horace, *Odes* 3.4.45 sq. 'qui terram inertem, qui mare temperat/ventosum'. Buchanan, who had started his work on the *De sphaera* by this time, asserts his belief in the Ptolomaic system here, which has the earth as immobile, in the centre of the universe.
6.	cf. Horace, *Odes* 2.9.22 'minores volvere vertices'.
7–8.	Buchanan varies the length of the second syllable of *tenĕbris* and *tenĕbras* here, cf. his treatment of *lăcrimis* and *lăcrimas* in 11 and 12.

10. Buchanan follows Greek rather than normal Horatian usage in allowing a short opening syllable in the first three lines of the alcaic stanza, cf. 29 and 41.

13. The subject of 'iacet' is Britannus, the English (nation), not mentioned specifically until 50.

20. Compound adjectives are a hallmark of Buchanan's style in the 1550s, cf. also *horrifer* (60) and *terrificus* (104).

23. Buchanan follows Alcaeus rather than Horace in allowing a short syllable (*pări*) as the fifth syllable of the first three lines, cf. 35 and 95.

24. Philip II of Spain had married Mary Tudor in 1554.

25. cf. Horace, *Odes* 3.6.5 'dis te minorem quod geris'.

30. The abrupt transition from the introductory section of the ode to the narration of the central event is typical of Horace.

34. cf. Horace, *Odes* 1.9.3 sq. 'geluque/flumina constiterint acuto'.

37–8. There is a pun on Francus (= Francis and French).

39. cf. Pontanus 'algentem festinant in arcton' cited in Ravisius Textor, *Specimen epithetorum*, and Horace, *Odes* 1.26.3 for *sub Arcto* in this metrical position.

44. *nube cava*, a common combination in Latin poetry, e.g. Virgil, *Aeneid* 1.516 and 5.810.

46–7. cf. Virgil, *Aeneid* 1.52–4 'hic vasto rex Aeolus antro/luctantis ventos . . ./imperio premit'. Aeolus was the god of the winds.

51–2. cf. Horace, *Odes* 1.17.14 sqq. 'hic tibi copia/manabit ad plenum benigno/. . . cornu'; id., *Epistles* 1.12.28 sq. 'aurea fruges/Italiae pleno defudit Copia cornu'. A brimming horn was the attribute of the deified abstraction Copia.

53. cf. Horace, *Odes* 3.4.38 'fessas cohortes abdidit oppidis'.

58. cf. Horace, *Satires* 2.5.41 'cana nive', and other passages listed in *TLL* 3.296.37.

60. Aquilo, the North Wind, was associated with wet, stormy weather; cf. Cicero, *Aratea* fragment 34, line 13 (Traglia) 'horrisonis Aquilonis tangitur alis', quoted by Cicero himself, *De natura deorum* 2.111, as 'horriferis Aquilonis tangitur auris'.

65. Another reference to François, duc de Guise, the brother of the cardinal de Lorraine, and a very successful soldier at this time (cf. 69–71).

69. The year in question is 1557–8.

72. cf. Ludovicus Bigus 'Paegaseis divina sequi vestigia pennis' (cited in Textor), Catullus 58b.2 'non si Pegaseo ferar volatu', and Propertius 2.30.3 'non si Pegaseo vecteris in aere dorso'.

73. *ninguidus*, a post-classical word used by Ausonius and Prudentius.

74–5. Pope Paul IV managed to persuade Henri II to enter into a treaty in 1556, which resulted in Guise's being sent at the head of an army to capture Naples. After initial successes, the Naples adventure was something of a fiasco.

79.   The Segusiavi were a Gallic tribe which, in Caesar's day, occupied the country near Lyons. The spelling of the name is guaranteed by inscriptions, but in manuscripts it is often corrupted to Segusiani, the form which got into early editions of Latin authors such as Buchanan used. The area around Lyons was being attacked in 1557 by the duc de Savoie after his successes at Saint-Quentin, but Guise managed to drive him out.

82–3. Calais had been held by the English since 1347.

87.   It was generally accepted in Neo-latin poetry that final *o* was common (cf. *De prosodia libellus, O.O.* II.715), hence *devincendŏ* and *hirudŏ* (99).

88.   An odd use of *refello*, 'I refute', but cf. also 26.5.

93.   Mary Tudor had declared war on France in 1557. Buchanan must be referring here (97–100) to her repressive religious policy, which earned her the epithet Bloody.

106.   Nemesis, the goddess of justice who punishes *hybris*. In *Silvae* 5, the 'Deploratio status rei Gallicae, sub mortem Francisci Secundi Regis', Buchanan saw her turning her attention to France.

2 In Castitatem

This poem, along with 16, 'Mutuus Amor', was written for use at the Scottish court during the Shrovetide festivities of February 1564, for details of which see above, p. 107 and McFarlane, p. 232. The poem is in the sapphic metre.

1.   cf. Lucretius 1.19 'blandum . . . amorem', and other examples listed in *TLL* 2.2038.6.
       Domitrix is quite rare in classical Latin poetry, but a favourite word of Buchanan's.

2 & 5. *specimen*, cf. 11.32.

3–4.   The *topos* of the Golden Age and lost innocence was popular in France in the 1550s, cf. Elizabeth Armstrong, *Ronsard and the Age of Gold* (Cambridge, 1968). The theme of man's deterioration harmonises well with the Christian concept of original sin, which seems to be beneath the surface of this poem. On Chastity's links with the Golden Age, cf. Juvenal 6.1 sqq. where she is called Pudicitia.

6.   cf. 11–12 'moriente . . ./Morte' and 36.18 'Mors victa' for the theme of death being conquered, and also I Corinthians 15.26 'novissima autem inimica destruetur mors' and 54 'absorpta est mors in victoria'.

12.   cf. I Corinthians 15.51 'omnes quidem resurgemus' and 52 'canet enim tuba, et mortui resurgent incorrupti'. Cf. also Shelley, *Adonais* 41 'he lives, he wakes; 'tis Death is dead, not he'.

3 *De amore Cossaei et Aretes*

This poem must have been written soon after Buchanan's return to Paris in 1552 when he was seeking the patronage of Charles de Cossé, comte de Brissac, the marshal in charge of the French expedition to Italy. The first edition of the *Jephthes* (1554) is dedicated to him, and Buchanan subsequently became tutor to his son, Timoléon, to whom the *De sphaera* is dedicated, see above p. 8. This ode is in the alcaic metre.

Title. Arete, the Greek word for Virtue, is used allegorically in the poem, which with its bucolic setting is in many ways reminiscent of Virgil, despite its Horatian form. The whole poem seems to be modelled to some extent on Horace, *Odes* 4.14, where the Roman poet sets out to immortalise the name of Augustus.

1.   cf. Ovid, *Metamorphoses* 1.479 'nemorum avia lustrat' (a reading now discredited), Lucan 1.569, and Statius, *Thebaid* 5.564. Ancient Latin uses only the plural *avia* (not the singular *avium*) as a substantive; hence the emendation *nemore* reported by Burman.

2.   *languido* more normally refers to drowsiness, sleep, cf. Virgil, *Aeneid* 12.908, Lucan 5.504. It is much more appropriate to *aestus* than to *frigore*; hence *languidos* (a variant reported by Burman) seems a certain emendation.

4.   *cerni . . . insolentem*: Buchanan is unlikely to have encountered *insolens* construed with an infinitive in ancient Latin.

5.   *roseo*, common epithet for dawn since Homer.

7.   *incandeo* is first attested in sixth century AD (Gregory the Great); the ancient form is *incandesco*.

9.   cf. Claudian 11.31 (p. 88 Koch) 'per iuga Caucasi'.

10.   *belluosus* comes from Horace, *Odes* 4.14.47.

13–16. Buchanan condemns the acquisitiveness of others, for example the Portuguese, elsewhere, cf. *Miscellany* 5 and *De sphaera* 1.181 sqq. Notice here a favourite device of Buchanan's, the juxtaposition of the same word in different cases (polyptoton or traductio).

14.   *aurumve stratis*: in accordance with Neo-latin practice, but contrary to ancient usage, Buchanan makes no attempt to avoid short vowel endings before words beginning with *s* plus consonant; cf. also 30 and 33.

18.   The traditional *carpe diem* theme, but for once not advocated by the poet.

19.   cf. [Virgil], *Culex* 93, 'iucundoque . . . somno'.

21.   cf. Horace, *Odes* 2.2.23 'oculo inretorto'. *inretortus* is a coinage of Horace's which no ancient writer imitated. It ought to mean 'not cast *back*'; i.e. *oculo inretorto* ought to mean 'without a *backward* glance', but this does not fit our passage. Buchanan evidently took it to mean 'with unswerving gaze', as Ruddiman argues in his long note on *Psalms* 33.18 (where the same phrase is used).

24.   cf. the opening lines of the *Te Deum*, 'te Dominum confitemur,/te aeternum patrem omnis terra veneratur'.

26.   Saba was the south-west corner of Arabia, the biblical Sheba, modern Yemen, famous for its myrrh and frankincense.

29.   *luctifica*: another compound adjective to heighten the tone. There is an anacoluthon in this stanza, which contains three adjectives/participles (*minax, asper, fatigans*) but no main verb.

30.   cf. Virgil, *Aeneid* 11.487–8 'aënis/horrebat squamis'.

32.   *Euros*, the East or South-East Wind, renowned for its strength, cf. Horace, *Odes* 2.16.23 sq. 'agente nimbos/ocior Euro'. *praeeuntis*: the opening diphthong, preceding another vowel, is shortened.

33.   The river Strymon formed the boundary between Macedonia and Thrace. It is the latter country which is referred to here; Mars was invested by Roman poets with many of the attributes of the Greek god Ares, one of which was a strong association with Thrace; cf. Virgil, *Aeneid* 3.35 'Gradivumque patrem [i.e. Mars], Geticis [i.e. Thracian] qui praesidet arvis'. For Mars riding by the banks of the Strymon see Statius, *Silvae* 1.1.18 sqq.

39–40. cf. Ovid, *Metamorphoses* 1.496 'et sterilem sperando nutrit amorem', and id., *Heroides* 6.21 (= *Metamorphoses* 7.826) 'credula res amor est'.

41–4.   A reference to Cossé's successful campaigns in Piedmont.

47.   *claustra portarum*: cf. passage listed in *TLL* 3.1319.67 sqq.

50–1.   cf. Ovid, *Metamorphoses* 4.267 'luridus . . . pallor'. For the personification of 'Pallor Tremor Terror Pavorque', cf. Virgil, *Aeneid* 6.273 sqq.

53–6.   A reference to Cossé's various victories throughout the 1540s and 1550s.

55–6.   cf. Horace, *Odes* 3.3.14 sq. 'indocili iugum/collo trahentes'.

58.   *aurea* 'golden', i.e. 'of great excellence', 'splendid' (*OLD* sense 5), but
        not without reference to the Golden Age.
60.   *facilemque somnum* in this metrical position Horace, *Odes* 2.11.8; cf.
        also ib. 3.21.4, Ovid, *Heroides* 11.29. In descriptions of the simple
        life, one of the regular features is sleep that comes readily to a man
        when his mind in not troubled by anxieties nor his body by indi-
        gestion due to excessive or over-rich food.
62.   cf. Virgil, *Aeneid* 1.292, 'cana Fides'. In this passage of Virgil, Jupiter
        prophesies an age of peace in Rome. Buchanan is again using the
        Golden Age theme here; for the departure of Iustitia from the
        world, cf. Ovid, *Metamorphoses* 1.149 sq.
65-6.   *amabilis* and *formidabilis* may be either genitives or nominatives.
67-8.   cf. Ovid, *Tristia* 5.3.17 'dominae fati . . . sorores' (the Parcae).
70.   *vestri* apparently for *tui*, a usage which is very rare (and mostly
        disputed) in ancient Latin.

4   *Ad Franciscum Olivarium Franciae Cancellarium,* Εὐχαριστικόν

This ode, written in the alcaic metre, dates from some time after May 1545,
when Olivier became Chancellor of France (cf. 9–12). Previously he had
been attached to the court of Marguerite de Navarre at Nérac, when
Buchanan no doubt became acquainted with him. He seems to have been a
fair man, opposing excessive taxes and religious persecution, while trying
to curb the expenditure of the court. This poem, probably dating from
1545, may well be in response to the request addressed to Olivier in *Elegy* 5.
(For an alternative suggestion, see McFarlane, pp. 114–15.)

1.   Castalia was a fountain on mount Parnassus which was associated
        with Apollo and the Muses.
2-4.   A reference to the powers of the poet Orpheus, cf. Horace, *Odes*
        1.12.9–12 'arte materna [his mother was Calliope] rapidos
        morantem/fluminum lapsus celerisque ventos,/blandum et auritas
        fidibus canoris/ducere quercus'.
5-6.   cf. Horace, *Odes* 3.4.2 'regina . . . Calliope'.
7.   cf. Ausonius, *Epistulae* 6.3 sq. (p. 229.1 sq. Peiper) 'Paule, Camena-
        rum celeberrime Castaliarum/alumne quondam, nunc pater'.
9-12.   Olivier became chancellor of France in May 1545 and held the post
        until January 1551.
13.   cf. Virgil, *Georgics* 3.347 'iniusto sub fasce'.
14.   There is no good evidence for *intumeo* (=*intumesco*) in ancient
        Latin.

17. cf. Lucan 9.951 'curarum . . . pondera'.

18. Probably an allusion to the treaty of Crépy, established between François Ier and Charles V in September 1544, also referred to in *Elegy* 5.17–20.

28. cf. 'Camenarum . . . nunc pater' in the passage of Ausonius quoted on line 7 above.

29–30. This no doubt refers to Buchanan's time in Bordeaux just before his departure for Coimbra, but after the first sojourn there which ended in 1543.

31–2. On this imagery, and the theme of divine fury, see above p. 68.

33–5. In fact, few extant works can be attributed with any certainty to this period. Perhaps there were indeed pastoral poems which are now lost.

33. *indiga splendidi*: short *a* before *s* plus consonant.

5 *In Polyonymum*

A satirical poem, presumably dating from just after Buchanan's return from Portugal and aimed at Dom João III. *Polyonymus*, or 'having many names', is an epithet frequently found of deities in the Orphic Hymns, to which both Marullus and Ronsard had turned their attention, although here it is put to a very different use, referring to Portugal's colonial expansion. (On this theme, cf. *Fratres fraterrimi* 29 and 30, and *De sphaera* I.181 sqq.) The metre is the hendecasyllable, in which Buchanan follows the practice of Catullus in allowing a certain amount of variety in the opening foot but with a predominance of spondees.

4. Manicongo or Kongo Kingdom was a Bantu kingdom on the Congo, taken over by the Portuguese in 1484 and converted to Christianity. Zalophus may be a reference to Sofala (cf. also *De sphaera* I.223), a trading port in Mozambique, colonised by the Portuguese in 1508, and an important centre for gold. The governor of Sofala had a virtual trading monopoly as far as the Cape of Good Hope. (Mr Stephen Parkinson of the University of Aberdeen kindly provided this suggestion.)

7. cf. Ovid, *Metamorphoses* 12.40 'triplicis confinia mundi', so-called because it is made up of sky, land, and sea.

8. cf. Virgil, *Georgics* 4.382 'Oceanumque patrem rerum'.

10. Buchanan clearly has in mind Virgil, *Aeneid* 6.204 'discolor unde auri per ramos aura refulsit'; here *auri aura* is a very bold phrase to which the ancient commentator Servius gave the meaning 'gleam of gold' ('splendor auri'); this is the view followed by Buchanan.

13.   *vocabo*: short final *o*, cf. 1.87.

17–18. It would appear that these lines were alternative versions of a closing line, both of which were preserved in printed versions of the poem by mistake. In BN MS lat. 8141 fo. 1ʳ, line 18 is missing.

6 *In Leonoram*

One of the elegiac poems making up the Leonora cycle, for a discussion of which see above, pp. 87–9. Buchanan deals with the theme of cosmetics and falsehood in *Elegy* 8 and *Epigrams* I.16, 17, 22, 28 and 52.

1.   *nimbo*, a cloud of perfume, *OLD* sense 3.
2.   *cerussatus* is practically confined to Martial, who uses it three times. White-lead was used both by painters and by women for whitening their skin.
10.   *indiciis*: tetrasyllabic endings to the pentameter were used occasionally by Buchanan, although they were on the whole avoided by the ancient elegiac poets, especially Ovid.
11.   Apelles, a famous painter of the time of Alexander the Great.
12.   Myron, a famous Attic sculptor of the fifth century BC.

7 *Ad Peiridem lenam*

Another elegiac poem in the Leonora cycle, containing a wealth of details about the unfortunate Leonora's past history and concentrating on her sexual tastes, with the *pointe* alluding to her incestuous tendencies.

8.   Cooks are particularly seen as figures of fun in Roman comedy.
10.   *crisso* is to move the haunches during intercourse; *tribas* is used by Martial 7.67.1 and 7.70.1.
12.   *quando*: final short *o*, cf. 1.87.

8 *Ad Henricum II Franciae Regem de soluta urbis Mediomatricum obsidione*

An alcaic ode, written shortly after Buchanan's return to France from Portugal. According to the *Vita*, this poem was written in rivalry with Mellin de Saint-Gelais's poem on the same subject. The relief of the siege of Metz took place in January 1553. For a longer discussion of this poem and the text of Mellin's poem, see Ford, 'George Buchanan's Court Poetry and the Pléiade', pp. 142–7. The poem was translated into French by du Bellay (Chamard, ed. cit., V.280 sqq.).

1.   Horace, *Odes* 3.5 likewise begins with *caelo* and a mythological allusion. Hercules was deified as a reward for his services to mankind in ridding the earth of monsters in the course of his twelve labours. Horace is fond of using Hercules as a prototype of the emperor Augustus.

2.   cf. Ovid, *Metamorphoses* 12.606 'letifera . . . dextra'.

3.   *flammisque stellatus*: short final vowel before *s* plus consonant, cf. l.31. *stellatus*, 'placed in the heavens as a constellation', a meaning found only in Cicero, *Tusculan Disputations* 5.8 and possibly Manilius 1.341.

4.   An allusion to Perseus, cf. Ovid, *Metamorphoses* 4.699 'Gorgonis anguicomae Perseus superator'. *saxificae*: this compound adjective is almost a standing epithet of the Gorgon Medusa in Roman poetry, and is probably used only of her.

6.   cf. Horace, *Odes* 4.8.30 'impiger Hercules'.

8.   Perseus is called *volucer* by Statius (*Silvae* 2.1.95, *Thebaid* 10.892) because of the winged sandals which helped him in his mission to slay Medusa.

11.   *monstrum* refers to the Holy Roman Emperor, Charles V, who had been a long-standing opponent of François Ier.

17.   Ronsard refers to the Spaniards as 'my-Mores' in 'La Harangue de tres-illustre Prince François, duc de Guise, aux soldats de Metz', Laumonier V.204. The line is modelled on Horace, *Odes* 3.5.9 and 7.

18–19. Charles V had captured Rome in 1527.

20.   *ferre iugum* in this metrical position Horace, *Odes* 1.35.28.

21.   *inquieti* in this metrical position Horace, *Odes* 3.3.5; cf. also *Fratres fraterrimi* 28.4 'bonarum blanda nutrix artium'.

25.   cf. Horace, *Odes* 4.5.37 'dux bone' (of Augustus).

31.   Metz stands on the Moselle.

35.   cf. Virgil, *Aeneid* 4.367 'Hyrcanaeque . . . tigres'. Hyrcania was a country on the south-east side of the Caspian sea.

37.   Originally this read 'dextera Guysii', but this was replaced after Buchanan's break with the Guises, see Ford, art. cit., on Buchanan's court poetry, p. 152, n. 13. Arnaud de Gontaut, baron de Biron, fought in Italy under Cossé.

40.   cf. Virgil, *Aeneid* 11.875 'quadripedumque putrem cursu quatit ungula campum'.

41–3.   cf. Virgil, *Aeneid* 9.59 sqq. for a similar comparison: 'ac veluti pleno lupus insidiatus ovili/cum fremit ad caulas ventos perpessus et imbris/nocte super media . . .'.

45.   *spe*: unusual elision of monosyllable, cf. 23.61.

9 *Ad iuventutem Burdegalensem*

This sapphic ode, presumably dating from the 1540s when Buchanan was teaching in Bordeaux, celebrates the power of poetry and its immortalising abilities, a theme that would be dear to the heart of Ronsard in the 1550s. Horace deals with a similar theme in *Odes* 4.8.

2.   *Lyaei*, cult-title of Bacchus, often used by metonymy to mean 'wine'.

3.   *parens frugum*, antonomasia for Ceres, goddess of agriculture.

4.   Pallas used for Minerva.

13.   Paros was famous for its white marble. Cf. Juvenal 8.102 sq. 'et cum Parrhasii tabulis signisque Myronis/Phidiacum vivebat ebur' and Horace, *Odes* 4.8.6 'quas aut Parrhasius protulit aut Scopas'. Phidias was a famous Athenian sculptor of the fifth century BC, as was Myron (see 6.12).

17.   *cita mors* in this metrical position Horace, *Odes* 2.16.29.

20.   *dente senectae*, cf. Ovid, *Metamorphoses* 15.234 sqq. 'tempus edax rerum, tuque, invidiosa vetustas,/omnia destruitis vitiataque dentibus aevi/paulatim lenta consumitis omnia morte'.

21   *Mulciber*, an alternative name for Vulcan; cf. Ovid, *Tristia* 1.2.5–6 'Mulciber in Troiam, pro Troia stabat Apollo:/aequa Venus Teucris, Pallas iniqua, fuit'. For Juno's hostility to Troy cf. Horace, *Odes* 3.3.18 sqq.

23.   *illa Smyrnaeis*: short final *a* before *s* plus consonant. *Smyrnaeus* is used as an epithet for Homer because he was said to have been born on the island of Smyrna (among other places, cf. 37.2); cf. Lucan 9.984.

27–8.   Rhodope, a mountain range in Thrace, signifies the far north; therefore *Indi* must signify the far south (not the far east); Roman poets (e.g. Virgil, *Georgics* 4.293) sometimes used *Indi* to mean the Ethiopians, and this must be what Buchanan has in mind.

31.   Phlegethon was one of the rivers, Orcus the god, of the underworld.

10 *Marco Antonio Monlucio*

This epigram, written in elegiac couplets, is an epitaph to Marc-Antoine Monluc (*c.*1527–57). A French captain serving in Italy, he was mortally wounded on the way back from Ostia, but managed to report to marshal Strozzi before dying. This poem would date from the year of his death. Du

Bellay composed two Latin epitaphs for Monluc; see *Poésies françaises et latines*, edited by E. Courbet, 2 vols (Paris, 1918), II.515-16.

3-4.   Du Bellay refers to Monluc as a latter-day Protesilaus, the first Greek warrior to be killed at Troy.

5.   Apparently all editions read *hostem* (instead of *hostis*) at the end of the line. With this reading Ruddiman, missing a subject for *horruit* and *colit*, proposed to alter *postea* to *Ostia*. But (i) *postea* is necessary for the contrast with *prius*; (ii) even if Ostia had got hold of Monluc's bones, it is difficult to suppose that it was already worshipping them when Buchanan wrote this epigram, presumably shortly after Monluc's death. The emendation adopted here is much more plausible. The couplet may well have a general reference: 'an enemy earlier trembles at a man as he stands above their walls (i.e. in storming their city), but later they worship the bones of the dead champion.' Buchanan may be thinking of the Spartan general Brasidas (Thucydides 5.11): killed at Amphipolis, he was worshipped as a hero and honoured as a second founder by the inhabitants of that city.

6.   Buchanan knew that the last vowel of *postea* is long, but he thought it was sometimes shortened; see the *De prosodia libellus* (*O.O.* II.715). As evidence for the shortening he quotes Ovid, *Fasti* 1.165, where modern texts read not *posteā* but *post ĕă*.

11 *Calendae Maiae*

On the probable dating of this fine alcaic ode in the 1550s, see McFarlane, p. 114. The poem presents a mixture of the pagan and the Christian, typical of the Renaissance. However, instead of coming to a 'carpe diem' conclusion (cf. *Elegy* 2), Buchanan looks forward to the joys of the after life. He expressed similar sentiments in poem 2.

3.   As has frequently been pointed out, there is a false quantity in the *i* of *dicatae*.

6.   May day, the beginning of spring, marks the start of the yearly cycle of the seasons.

10-12.   An allusion to the Golden Age (see note on 3.62); cf. Ovid, *Metamorphoses* 1.89 sq. 'aurea prima sata est aetas, quae vindice nullo,/sponte sua, sine lege fidem rectumque colebat'.

13-16.   cf. Ovid, *Metamorphoses* 1.107 sq. 'ver erat aeternum, placidique tepentibus auris/mulcebant zephyri natos sine semine flores'.

19–20. cf. Horace, *Ars poetica* 173 on the *senex* who is 'difficilis, querulus'.
21.   cf. Virgil, *Aeneid 6.386* '*per tacitum nemus*'.
22.   *murmure spiritus*: short final *e* before *s* plus consonant.
24.   Cypresses are still associated with death in Mediterranean coun-
        tries, where they are planted in cemeteries; cf. also Virgil, *Aeneid*
        3.63 sq. 'stant manibus arae,/caeruleis maestae vittis atraque
        cupresso' and Lucan 3.442 'luctus testata cypressus'.
30.   cf. Horace, *Odes* 1.36.10 'Cressa [=white] ne careat pulchra dies
        nota'.
31–2.   cf. 2.2 and 5.

12 *Alexandro Cocburno*

Alexander Cockburn, a pupil of John Knox, died in 1564 at the age of
twenty-eight. He was a learned man, with a knowledge of Latin, Greek,
Hebrew, and French, and was the author of a number of works including a
book of *Elegiae*, and works based on his extensive travels in Europe.
Buchanan wrote another epitaph for him (*Epigrams* II, 'Iusta' 26).

1–2.   cf. Pliny, *Epistulae* 6.21.1 'neque enim, quasi lassa et effeta, natura
        nihil iam laudabile parit'.
        visceribus: on the tetrasyllabic ending to the pentameter, cf. note on
        6.10.
4.   Mnemosyne, Memory, the mother of the Muses, cf. Ausonius,
        Epistulae 14.64 (p. 247 Peiper) 'Mnemosynes natae'.
        Sophiae: trisyllabic endings to the pentameter are relatively
        uncommon in Roman poetry and were proscribed in the Renais-
        sance verse manuals (cf. Despauterius, ed. cit., fo. IX^r). However,
        Greek usage was much freer, and the presence of the two Greek
        names in this line evidently influenced Buchanan here.
8.   For *vindex* used adjectivally cf. Catullus 64.192 'multantes vindice
        poena'.
9.   *florente iuventa* in this metrical position Horace, *Ars poetica* 115.

13 *Ad Thomam Cromelium Anglum*

Buchanan probably addressed this elegiac poem to Thomas Cromwell,
Henry VIII's chancellor, in 1539 after his escape from Scotland and before
his departure for Paris later the same year. Cromwell, who had presided
over the dissolution of the monasteries and was responsible for the Act of

Supremacy, had also set about certain other Church reforms, but he was executed in 1540 and died professing the Catholic faith.

1.   cf. Ovid, *Epistulae ex Ponto* 2.8.68 'vos eritis nostrae portus et ara fugae'.

3 sq.   A reference to Cromwell's Church reforms.

6.   *cliens*, a person who attached himself to a *patronus*, a man of greater political influence, to gain protection and advancement.

7.   cf. Virgil, *Aeneid* 1.3 'et terris iactatus et alto'. Both *vagus exul* and *exul inops* are common combinations in ancient Latin.

9–10.   An allusion to Buchanan's troubles with the authorities in Scotland which led to his exile (see McFarlane, pp. 66–77). Buchanan was later to claim before the Portuguese Inquisition that the break with James V was simulated to enable him to spy on the English.

11–12.   Buchanan's journey from Scotland seems indeed to have been hazardous, cf. Thomas Randolph's letter (*O.O.* II.746) and McFarlane, p. 73.

13.   *Atthida stratus*: short final *a* before *s* plus consonant. As Ruddiman explains (*O.O.* II.416), this refers to the Ara Misericordiae in Athens, described by Statius (*Thebaid* 12.481 sqq.).

14.   *offero*: short final *o*, cf. note on 1.87.

16.   cf. Ovid, *Ars amatoria* 1.401 'fallacibus arvis'.

14   *Epitaphium Nicolai Baconis Procancellarii Angliae*

This epitaph, written in iambic trimeters, marks the death in 1579 of Sir Nicholas Bacon, father of the famous essayist. He was related by marriage to William Cecil and was the husband of Ann Cooke, daughter of Sir Anthony Cooke, who survived him.

2–3.   cf. Silius Italicus 15.385 'Ausonii columen regni' (in 1553, Bacon had become Lord Keeper of the Seal).

        columen: 'the horizontal ridge-pole that supported the roof, hence the person who was the "key-stone" or "corner-stone" of his group', Nisbet–Hubbard on Horace, *Odes* 2.17.4.

8.   *duas: agit*: Roman lyric writers are averse to ending the trimeter with two iambic words, but Buchanan seems to have been unaware of this.

9.   *inter animus*: dactyls are not normally found in the fifth foot of an iambic trimeter in Roman lyric usage, although Buchanan considered it to be permissible (cf. also 12). See Buchanan's scheme for the iambic trimeter in the *De prosodia libellus* (*O.O.* II.718).

11–12. Bacon was buried in a tomb in St Paul's Cathedral on 9 March 1579.
        Ruddiman suggested replacing *posita* (agreeing with *domus*) by
        positum (agreeing with *corpus*); this restores normal usage.

15 *Ad Henricum VIII, Angliae Regem*

This hexameter poem, which contains fulsome praise of Henry VIII, must
date (like 13) from Buchanan's stay in England in 1539.

1.   Ruddiman points to the opening of Ausonius, *Epistulae* 6.1 (p. 228
        Peiper) 'si qua fides falsis umquam est adhibenda poetis'. For
        classical poets' treatment of Fama, cf. in particular Virgil, *Aeneid*
        4.173 sqq. and Ovid, *Metamorphoses* 12.39 sqq.

2–3.   cf. Virgil, *Aeneid* 4.176 sq. 'parva metu primo, mox sese attolit in
        auras/ingrediturque solo et caput inter nubila condit'.

4.   *fomes*, 'tinder-wood', first in Christian Latin used of the place in
        which a river rises; cf. *fomes* used as a source of lies in *Fratres
        fraterrimi* 2 'fomes et parens mendacii'.

4–10.   For a similar comparison tracing the course of a river cf. Catullus
        68.57 sqq.

10.   cf. Silius Italicus 1.646 sq. 'spumeus hic, medio qui surgit ab
        aequore, fluctus/ . . . vestras effringet in urbes'.

11.   cf. Virgil, *Aeneid* 4.176 (cited in note on 2–3).

15–16. cf. *Aeneid* 4.190 'facta atque infecta canebat'.

18.   cf. for similar sentiments Paris's words to Helen in Ovid, *Heroides*
        16.141 'magna quidem de te rumor praeconia fecit'.

20.   cf. *Heroides* 16.145 'minor est tua gloria vero'.

25.   Henry did indeed have a reputation as a scholar and poet.

31.   *terminus haeret* in this metrical position Virgil, *Aeneid* 4.614.

38.   cf. Ovid, *Tristia* 3.5.31 'magis est placabilis irae'.

40.   Outside the dramatic poets *quoad* is very rare in Latin verse and
        where it does occur it is always scanned as a monosyllable, and was
        probably pronounced as such in Roman speech.

41.   *diis* is scanned as a monosyllable by synezesis.

16 *Mutuus Amor*

Like 2, this poem on the mutual love of Mary Stuart and Elizabeth I was
written for the Shrovetide festivities of the Scottish court in 1564. The
metre is iambic dimeter.

3–4.   A child, in the character of Time, appeared with the third course of the meal at the Court celebrations when this poem was performed.

10.   The friendship of Gaius Laelius and Scipio Africanus (second century BC) was proverbial, and it is after Laelius that Cicero's treatise on friendship is named.

11.   cf. note on 3.62.

17–18. An allusion to the Last Judgement.

17 *In Leonoram*

Another elegiac poem from the Leonora cycle, containing a number of words with sexual meanings or implications (cf. *deglubere* (5), *lingit* (7), *nuda* (8), *lambit* (10), *obnitere nervis* (19), *concipe* (20)).

1.   A reminiscence of the opening lines of Plautus' *Mostellaria*: 'exi e culina . . . ; egredere . . . ex aedibus.'

5.   cf. Plautus, *Persa* 77 'hesternas reliquias'. *deglubere* means 'peel', 'skin', 'flay', but Buchanan has in mind the use of the word by Ausonius, *Epigrammata* 79.7 (p. 341 Peiper), of a woman masturbating men; Ausonius is following the use by Catullus (58.5) of the simple verb *glubere* in the same obscene sense. (Recent discussions of the meaning of *(de)glubere* will be found in *Liverpool Classical Monthly*, IV (1979), 85 sq., 87 sqq.) Whether Buchanan understood the word correctly seems doubtful; his use of it here rather suggests that he thought it denoted some activity of the mouth.

7.   cf. Terence, *Eunuchus* 939 (describing prostitutes) 'quo pacto ex iure hesterno panem atrum vorent'.

9.   The source of this simile is Statius, *Thebaid* 11.29 sqq.: (after a lion has killed some cattle) 'rauci tunc comminus ursi,/tunc avidi venere lupi, rabieque remissa/lambunt degeneres alienae vulnera praedae'; inferior animals like bears and wolves lick up the blood from the wounds of the prey killed by another animal (the lion). So Buchanan means that a young bear, not yet able to hunt for its own food, licks up the blood on the wounds dealt by its valiant father in the course of killing his prey.
        unguibus ursos in this metrical position Ovid, *Metamorphoses* 10.540.

12.   *cana parens*, Leonora's mother, compared to Hecuba who (a) was proverbial for old age, (b) was in the end metamorphosed into a bitch; cf. Ovid, *Metamorphoses* 13.568 sq. 'rictuque in verba parato/latravit conata loqui'. On the trisyllabic ending, see 12.4.

15.   *adulant* (of dogs) in this metrical position Lucretius 5.1070.
17–18. cf. Martial 7.20.16 sq. 'colligere longa turpe nec putat dextra/
        analecta quidquid et canes reliquerunt'.

18 Ad eandem

This elegiac poem on Leonora, alluding to a number of themes already dealt
with in the cycle, may have served as a concluding poem.

2.   *nigra tribas*, cf. 7.10. There may have been other poems on this
        theme which have not survived.

19 In Leonoram

Another elegiac poem on Leonora, again referring to her penchant for
monks and cooks.

20 In Neaeram

A hendecasyllabic poem addressed to Neaera, and written in the Neo-
catullan style. After the opening with its traditional *aubade* theme (1–5),
Buchanan goes on to deal with the irreconcilability of two contrasting
pleasures, a subject which may well have been suggested by Joannes
Secundus, *Basia* 7.

1.   cf. 3.5.
3.   cf. Marullus, *Epigrams* 1.37 'iactor, dispereo, crucior, trahor huc
        miser atque huc'.
7–8.   cf. Ovid, *Metamorphoses* 7.663 'iubar aureus extulerat Sol'.
10.   cf. Secundus, *Basia* 7.11 'o formosa Neaera'.
12.   cf. *Basia* 7.16 sqq. 'non datur tua cernere/labra, non roseas genas/
        ocellosque loquaculos/molles nec mihi risus'.
14.   Buchanan has a false quantity in the first syllable of *referat*, which
        should be short.
16.   *ordo*: short final *o*, cf. note on 1.87.
18.   *dii* scanned as a monosyllable by synezesis, cf. *diis* (21), and note on
        15.41.

21   *In Iulium II Pontificem*

Although included in the Miscellaneous poems, this piece is not by
Buchanan, appearing as it does in *Pasquillorum tomi duo* (Bâle, 1544), where
it is attributed to C. G.; it had previously appeared in J. Lascaris, *Epigrammata* (Paris, 1542). For further details see McFarlane, p. 309.

22   *De Nicotiana falso nomine Medicaea appellata*

This poem is one of a series directed against Catherine de Médicis after the
Saint Bartholomew massacre in 1572. Tobacco was first called *nicotiana* in
1570 by the Liebault brothers, and was not called the *herbe médicée* until
1572 in Gohory's translation of Nicolò Monardes's *Historia medicinal de las
cosas que sirven al uso de medicina* (Seville, 1565). For further details, see
Count Corti, *A History of Smoking*, translated by P. England (London, 1931),
pp. 58 sqq. Buchanan's poem is written in couplets of alternating hexameters and iambic dimeters.

1.   Jean Nicot (*c.*1530–1600) was a diplomat by profession.
3.   cf. Statius, *Achilleis* 1.117 'salutiferas . . . herbas' in this metrical
          position. Charles Clusius, in his Latin translation of Monardes,
          refers to tobacco as a *panacea*, cf. l.15.
6.   Medea contains a pun on the name Médicis, although the com-
          parison is an apt one since Catherine was infamous for her interest
          in drugs, poisons, and magic potions.
7–8.   In fact, the term *herbe médicée* seems to have been coined by
          Gohory in a bid to win the queen's favour.
13.   Ruddiman suggests that *nares* would make better sense in this line
          than *et aures*, a reading that could easily be due to a typographical
          error.
15.   cf. *Hendecasyllables* 6.18 sqq. 'ut sit nectare suavius venenum,/vita
          mors potior, labor quiete,/sanitate furor, salute morbus'.
16.   *Medicaea*: an opening anapaest is rare in the classical lyric dimeter,
          although Buchanan considered it perfectly permissible; cf. *De
          prosodia libellus* (*O.O.* II.718).

23   *Ad Carolum Cossaeum Brixiaci Dynastam, post captas Vercellas*

This is a poem in alternating iambic trimeters and iambic dimeters in cele-
bration of Cossé's capture of Vercelli in 1553, and may well have been
written by Buchanan to woo his future patron. Buchanan exhibits a

strongly Erasmian attitude in his emphasis on Cossé's clemency and ability to bring peace to an area he has conquered, cf. 55–61. The poem is in three main sections: 1–28, announcing the subject of the poem; 29–82, concentrating on Vercelli and the events surrounding its capture; and 83–96, which praise Cossé for his *robur* and his *clementia*. For a more detailed discussion, see above, pp. 92–3.

2. cf. Horace, *Odes* 1.34.8 'volucremque currum'.

3. cf. Virgil, *Aeneid* 1.439 'saeptus nebula'.

4. Oenotria originally denoted the region in the toe of Italy but gradually came to be used in poetry to denote the whole of Italy.

6. Buchanan has a tribrach as the second foot of this line, of which there is only one instance in Horatian iambic dimeters, but which Buchanan considered to be permissible (cf. *De prosodia libellus*, *O.O.* II.718).

7–8. A reference to the legend of Phaëthon who was thrown from the chariot of the Sun into the Po when Jupiter struck him down with a thunderbolt to prevent his doing any further damage. His sisters, the Heliades, were turned into poplars, and continued to weep for him on the banks of the Po with tears of amber (see Ovid, *Metamorphoses* 2.319–66).

11. *Italum* and *Pelasgum* are both genitive plurals.

17. *Batavum*: probably an allusion to Cossé's action at Landrecies, which in 1543 was being besieged by Charles V. Although he was surrounded by the enemy, he managed to get out of the situation brilliantly, and was made a *chevalier de l'ordre du roi* as a result.

18. cf. Horace, *Odes* 4.6.7 sq. 'tremenda/cuspide pugnax'.

19. cf. Horace, *Odes* 4.4.31 sq. 'imbellem . . . / . . . columbam', and ib. 1.37.17 sq. 'accipiter velut/molles columbas' (*sc.* adurget).

20. cf. Horace, *Odes* 4.4.1 'ministrum fulminis alitem', the eagle.

21. cf. Horace, *Odes* 2.1.22 'non indecoro pulvere sordidos'.

23. Ruscino, now Perpignan. Cossé took part in the siege of 1542, where he was wounded protecting the artillery during a sortie made by the defenders.

26. Virtus, also personified in 3 as Arete, Cossé's faithful companion. Buchanan starts the dimeter with a dactyl, unusual in ancient poetry although Buchanan found it acceptable (*O.O.* II.718).

27–8. Buchanan's source is Lucan 6.191 sq. 'parque novum Fortuna videt concurrere, bellum/atque virum'. *par* is a pair of combatants, *spectaculum* a public (e.g. gladiatorial) show, *bellum* a warring army.

29–30. cf. Terence, *Andria* 886 sq. 'quor me macero?/quor meam senectutem . . . sollicito?'.

35–7.   A striking theatrical metaphor by Buchanan. The *choragus* was the man who supplied 'a dramatic company with all the equipment it required' (*OLD*).

39.   Bellona, goddess of war.

42.   *compita*, 'crossroads', where crowds met.

43.   cf. Quintilian 12.3.7 'in recti pravique discrimine'.

47–8.   cf. Ovid, *Metamorphoses* 3.534 sq. 'quos non bellicus ensis,/non tuba terruerit, non strictis agmina telis'.

51.   cf. 15.38.

55.   cf. Horace, *Odes* 1.16.21 'exercitus insolens'.

61.   *vim*: unusual elision of monosyllable, cf. 8.45.

62–3.   cf. Virgil, *Aeneid* 2.313 (= 11.192), 'clamorque virum clangorque tubarum'.

73–4.   cf. similar comparison in 24.23 sqq.

75.   cf. Horace, *Epistles* 1.12.19 'rerum concordia discors'; also Ovid, *Metamorphoses* 1.433, Lucan 1.98.

78.   *vatis . . . Thracii*, antonomasia for Orpheus, cf. note on 4.2–4, and also Isaiah 11.6, 'habitabit lupus cum agno, et pardus cum haedo accubabit; vitulus et leo et ovis simul morabuntur'.

80.   cf. note on 14.8.

82.   The Molossi were a tribe in Epirus famous for a breed of large dogs.

89.   *quando*: short *o*, cf. note on 1.87.

93.   *Liberi*, another name of Bacchus, here used by metonymy for 'wine'.

24   *Ioannis Calvini Epicedium*

Calvin, whom Buchanan may well have known in his early days in Paris in the 1520s, died in 1564, no doubt the year of composition of this elegant and solemn hexameter composition.

6.   Buchanan produces a ponderous spondaic line to reflect the friends' grief here.

10.   *liber . . . curis*, cf. 4.31.

13.   Ruddiman's conjecture *haustu* (for *haustum*) seems certain. Burman's defence of *haustum* as a Graecism is hardly convincing.

        On the light and the draught of revivifying water awaiting the righteous in heaven, cf. Revelation 21.23–4 'et civitas non eget sole neque luna, ut luceant in ea; nam claritas Dei illuminavit eam, et lucerna eius est Agnus. et ambulabunt gentes in lumine eius'; and ib. 22.1, 'et ostendit mihi fluvium aquae vitae, splendidum tamquam crystallum, procedentem de sede Dei et Agni'.

27.   On man's creation from clay by Prometheus, cf. Horace, *Odes*
        1.16.13 sqq. and Juvenal 6.13.
32.   cf. Ovid, *Amores* 1.6.9 'simulacraque vana' in this metrical position.
37.   cf. Virgil, *Aeneid* 1.249 'nunc placida compostus pace quiescit'.
43.   *Clemens*, Clement VII, pope 1523–34; cf. *Fratres fraterrimi* 13,
        where Buchanan says 'contemnit foedera Clemens'.
44.   *Pauli duo*: Pope Paul III (1534–49), who promoted the Council of
        Trent, described as a venal pederast by Buchanan (*Fratres frater-
        rimi* 4, 12, and 13); and Paul IV (1555–9).
45.   *Iuli*: Pope Julius III (1550–5), whom Buchanan lampooned in *Fratres
        fraterrimi* 11 and 13.
46.   *Pius*: Pope Pius IV (1559–65), mentioned in *Fratres fraterrimi* 10.
        nominis umbra(m) in this metrical position Lucan 1.135, 8.449.
48.   *vana superstitio* in this metrical position Silius Italicus 5.126. *in sede
        Quirini*, cf. 'urbs Quirini' (Ovid, *Tristia* 1.8.37) for Rome. Quirinus
        was a name given to Romulus after his deification.
51.   *Harpyia* scanned as a trisyllable, as always; the middle syllable
        contains the Greek diphthong υι.
52.   *Eumenis igne*, an allusion to the Protestants who had been burnt at
        the stake for their beliefs; *Charon naulo*, a reference to the practice
        of charging money for indulgences; *triplicique corona/Cerberus*
        refers to the triple papal tiara, here likened to the three-headed dog
        of the underworld.
53.   Buchanan has in mind Virgil, *Aeneid* 8.246: (with the unlocking of
        the infernal regions) 'trepident immisso lumine manes', 'the shades
        tremble at the inrushing light'. Presumably he intended *immissi* to
        have the same sense as in Virgil, but by hypallage he has made it
        agree with *veri* instead of with *lumine*.
56.   *inter aquas sitiens* alludes to Tantalus' punishment in hell; *referens
        revolubile saxum* is Sisyphus' punishment; 'revolubile saxum' in this
        metrical position Silius Italicus 11.474.
57.   *vulturibus iecur exesus*, like Tityos, a giant who was so punished in
        the underworld for attempting to rape Latona.
        cava dolia lymphis/frustra implens: the Danaids were thus punished
        for murdering their husbands at their father's bidding, cf. Tibullus
        1.3.79 sq. 'Danai proles . . . /in cava Lethaeas dolia portat aquas'.
58.   Ixion was thus punished by Jupiter for attempting to violate Juno.

25 *Ioanni Areskino, Comiti Marriae, Scotorum Proregi*

John Erskine became regent on the death of Lennox (see 26) in September
1571, but he himself died in October 1572, and no doubt this epitaph dates
from shortly after this time. It is written in elegiac couplets.

26   *Matthaeo Stuarto, Leviniae Comiti, Scotorum Proregi*

Matthew Stuart (1516–71) became regent in 1570. In the disturbances of
1571, he was stabbed in the back and mortally wounded by Captain Calder,
and died in Stirling Castle, where he was buried in the Chapel Royal. Calder
was later interrogated by, among others, Buchanan (*Calendar of Scottish
Papers* III, 699). As well as this epitaph in elegiac couplets, Buchanan had
already devoted one of his *strenae* to him (*Epigrams* III.19).

1.   Lennox was father of Lord Darnley and therefore grandfather of
         James VI.
3.   He went to France in 1532 at the age of sixteen, and was naturalised
         in 1537.
4.   He married Lady Margaret, an English Catholic, in 1544, and was
         very much in favour during the reign of Mary Tudor.
5.   cf. note on 1.88.
8.   Unusual trisyllabic ending, cf. note on 12.4.
9.   *care nepos*, James VI, Buchanan's pupil.

27   *Annae Valsingamiae, Thomae Randolphi uxori*

Anne Walsingham, sister of Sir Francis Walsingham (1530?–90), married
Thomas Randolph (1523–90) in 1571. Since her father, William, died in
March 1534 n.s., she must have been in her late thirties on marrying, but
despite this had a son, Thomas, who succeeded his father as heir to the
estate. From Buchanan's epitaph it would seem that she eventually died in
childbirth.

1.   *Randolphi* sc. *uxor,*an ellipse which is well attested in ancient Latin.

28   *Ad Camillam Morelliam*

This alcaic poem, praising the precocious talents of Camille de Morel (born
1547), also contains a compliment to her tutor, Buchanan's friend and
'censor', Charles Utenhove, who taught the Morel children 1558–62. Its
style is distinctly Neo-catullan with its use of comparatives, indefinite
constructions, and repetition, and it presumably dates from Utenhove's
tutorship and Buchanan's final years in France (1558–61).

3.   *doctorum parentum*: Jean de Morel (1511–81) was a pupil of
         Erasmus and was married to Antoinette de Loynes.

5–6.   cf. Catullus 14.1 'ni te plus oculis meis amarem'.

9.   *virgo*, short *o*, cf. note on 1.87.

9–12.   A conventional humanist commonplace, cf. *Epigrams* I.11 on Marguerite de Navarre.

13–16. A complex metaphor in which *laurum* presumably stands for Camille, *fructus* her accomplishments mentioned in the previous stanza, *teneram comam* (and, by way of extra decoration, *ramos*) her youth or tender mind, and *Castalio rore* (cf. note on 4.1) the culture she has imbibed from her tutor.

29 *In rusticum*

On the fascinating history of this poem, see McFarlane, 'George Buchanan's *Franciscanus*: the History of a Poem', p. 127, n. 1. Buchanan's poem is written in elegiacs and is based on a *dizain* to be found in *La Fleur de vraye poesie françoyse* (Paris, *c*.1540), and may well date from the 1540s when Buchanan was in Bordeaux. The French text is as follows:

> Ung Mesnagier vieillard recreu d'ahan,
> Fendoit du boys, sa Femme estoit deuant,
> Qui luy a dict, pourquoy faictes vous han?
> Affin (dict-il) qu'il entre plus auant,
> Et tint ce mot; car la nuict ensuyuant
> En l'embrassant luy à dict: mon amy
> Coignez plus fort, pas il n'entre à demy
> Et faictes han premier que de descendre;
> Lors il luy dict: le han ne sert icy,
> Contentez vous, ce n'est boys que veuil fendre.

1.   cf. Virgil, *Aeneid* 12.713 sq. 'tum crebros ensibus ictus/congeminant'.

6.   Although here used in a literal sense, *rima* foreshadows the *pointe* of the epigram, being used of the female genitalia by Juvenal 3.97, Ausonius, *Epigrams* 87.6 (p. 344 Peiper); cf. Macrobius, *Saturnalia* 7.16.27.

7.   *telum* used of the penis by Martial 11.78.6, *Priapea* 9.14.

10.   *perforare* in this obscene sense *Priapea* 76.3.

30 *E Graeco Simonidis*

Buchanan presumably found the Greek text of this poem by Simonides of Ceos in the Stobaeus Anthology. This translation, together with 31, 32, 37, and 38, was published with the original Greek by Henri Estienne in *Pindari*

Olympia, Pythia, Nemea, Isthmia. Caeterorum octo lyricorum carmina, Alcaei, Sapphus, Stesichori, Ibyci, Anacreontis, Bacchylidis, Simonidis, Alcmanis (n.p., 1560), p. 282. It is fragment 6 in Diehl, *Anthologia lyrica graeca* (fasc. 5, p. 83). The first line of the Greek is echoed by Horace, *Odes* 1.9.13 'quid sit futurum cras fuge quaerere'. The metre of Buchanan's poem is anapaestic dimeter (*O.O.* II.618–19); Buchanan has no compunctions about having a dactyl preceding an anapaest, a combination which is rarely found in ancient Latin examples of this metre.

31   *Ex eodem*

Also by Simonides of Ceos, fragment 12 Diehl (fasc. 5, p. 85) and Estienne, p. 312. The line is an iambic trimeter. This line of Simonides is the origin of Horace, *Odes* 3.2.14 'mors et fugacem persequitur virum'.

32   *Ex eodem*

This poem is in fact by Semonides of Amorgos, and although the Renaissance did not always distinguish between Simonides and Semonides, Henri Estienne at least was aware of the existence of two poets, but believed his attribution of this poem to Simonides to be correct (Estienne, ed. cit., p. 429). For the original text, see Semonides, fragment 2 Diehl (fasc. 3, p. 51) or Estienne, p. 312. Buchanan's version, like the original, is in iambic trimeters.

1.   cf. Virgil, *Aeneid* 2.85 'cassum lumine'.
1–2.   *cor* is both the seat of the feelings and the seat of the intelligence.

33   *Ad Henricum Scotorum Regem*

Elegiac poem addressed to Henry, Lord Darnley, who married Mary Stuart in July 1565 and was murdered in 1567. Buchanan also addressed *Epigrams* III, 'Strenae' 1, to Darnley.

34   *Ad Carolum Utenhovium*

An elegiac poem containing fulsome praise of Elizabeth I, but emphasising the poet's unique ability to grant immortality to those of whom he sings.

Utenhove was in England between 1562 and 1565 where William Cecil acted as his patron. For further details, see Willem Janssen, *Charles Utenhove: sa vie et son œuvre (1536–1600)* (Maastricht, 1939).

4. Lysippus of Sicyon, a sculptor famous for his work in bronze, the only sculptor whom Alexander the Great allowed to portray him. Praxiteles, Athenian sculptor of the fourth century BC, especially famous for his work in marble.

5–6. Buchanan is clearly referring here to the Platonic theory of divine *mania*, cf. *Phaedrus* 245a.

10. *area*, 'field of activity', here 'subject for poetry' as in Ovid, *Amores* 3.1.25 sq. 'cane facta virorum:/"haec animo" dices "area facta meo est" '.

35 *Ad Salutem in nuptiis Reginae*

This elegiac quatrain was spoken by the four Maries to Health on the third day of the festivities held to mark Mary Stuart's marriage to Darnley in 1565.

1–2. *Nymphae . . . /quattuor*, the four Maries, Mary Fleming, Mary Seton, Mary Beaton, and Mary Livingstone, who had all accompanied Mary Stuart to France in 1548, and had been her companions since then. The Queen's health had not been good at this time, hence the address to Salus.

36 *Hymnus in Christi ascensionem*

This hymn is written in iambic dimeters.

3. *caeli templa*, an Ennian phrase, used several times by Lucretius. What sense Buchanan attached to it is uncertain; for modern views see C. Bailey's note (in his edition, Oxford, 1947) on Lucretius 1.120.

4. cf. Cicero, *De oratore* 124 'iudicibus cicatrices adversas . . . ostendere'.

5. *coronam*, the crown of thorns.

7. cf. note on 23.21.

15. *timore pallent*, cf. Ovid, *Fasti* 2.467 sq. 'timore/pallet'.

18. *Mors victa*: cf. note on 2.6.

37   *E Graeco Stobaei de brevitate vitae*

Translation of an elegiac poem on the *carpe diem* theme, taken from the
Stobaeus Anthology and included in Estienne, pp. 318–19. There is no
agreement about the authorship of the original Greek verses. Stobaeus
ascribes them to Simonides, and some modern scholars follow this view.
Many, however, have ascribed them to Semonides of Amorgos; so Diehl
(fasc. 3, p. 63), who prints them as fragment 29. See H. Lloyd-Jones, *Females
of the Species: Semonides on Women* (London, 1975), 96 sq.

2.   *vates Chius* refers to Homer, who was reputed to have been born
        on the island of Chios (but cf. 9.23).
3.   For this beautiful simile, see Homer, *Iliad* 6.146, 'Even as are the
        generations of leaves, such are those also of men'.

38   *Apud Clementem Alexandrinum, Strom. lib. 6*

For the original text of this epigram, see chapter 3, note 15 and Estienne,
p. 315. The original iambic couplet is by Semonides of Amorgos; it is
fragment 6 in Diehl (fasc. 3, p. 52). It echoes two lines of Hesiod (*Works and
Days* 702 sq.); see Lloyd-Jones, op. cit., p. 92.

Select Bibliography

Works on Buchanan

Aitken, J. M., *The Trial of George Buchanan before the Inquisition* (Edinburgh and London, 1939)

Bögl, E. W., *George Buchanans Satire Franciscanus und Fratres in philologischer Betrachtung* (Innsbruck, 1954)

Brown, P. Hume, *George Buchanan: Humanist and Reformer* (Edinburgh, 1890)

Chaney, Virginia Miles, 'The Elegies of George Buchanan in Relation to those of the Roman Elegists and to the Latin Elegies of John Milton' (Ph.D. thesis, Vanderbilt University, 1961)

Dorez, Léon, 'Le MS original des Elégies, Sylves, et Hendécasyllabes de George Buchanan (1566)', *Revue des bibliothèques* (1903), 262–7

Durkan, John, 'George Buchanan: Some French Connections', *Bibliotheck*, IV (1963), 66–72

Ford, P. J., 'George Buchanan et ses paraphrases des Psaumes', in *Acta conventus neo-latini turonensis*, edited by J.-C. Margolin, 2 vols (Paris, 1980), pp. 947–57

'George Buchanan's Court Poetry and the Pléiade', *French Studies*, XXXIV (1980), 137–52

'Leonora and Neaera: a Consideration of George Buchanan's Erotic Poetry', *BHR*, XL (1978), 513–24

Fries, Carl, 'Quellenstudien zu George Buchanan', *Neue Jahrbücher für das klassische Altertum, Geschichte und deutsche Litteratur und für Pädagogik*, VI (1900), 177–92, 241–61

George Buchanan: Glasgow Quatercentenary Studies, 1906 (Glasgow, 1907)

Grant, W. Leonard, 'The Shorter Latin Poems of George Buchanan, 1506–1582', *Classical Journal*, XL (1945), 331–48

Lebègue, Raymond, *George Buchanan: sa vie, son oeuvre, son influence en France et au Portugal* (Coimbra, 1931)

Lindsay, W. M., 'Buchanan as a Latin Scholar', in *George Buchanan: a Memorial*, edited by D. A. Millar (St Andrews and London, 1907), pp. 204–11

McFarlane, I. D., *Buchanan* (London, 1981)

'George Buchanan's *Franciscanus*: the History of a Poem', *Journal of European Studies*, IV (1974), 126–39

'George Buchanan's Latin Poems from Script to Print', *The Library*, XXIV (1969), 277–332

'The History of George Buchanan's *Sphaera*', in *French Renaissance Studies 1540–70: Humanism and the Encyclopedia*, edited by Peter Sharratt (Edinburgh, 1972), pp. 194–212

'Notes on the Composition and Reception of George Buchanan's Psalm Paraphrases', in *Renaissance Studies*, edited by I. D. McFarlane, A. H. Ashe, D. D. R. Owen (Edinburgh and London, 1972), pp. 21–62

Martyn, J. R. C., 'George Buchanan's *Franciscanus*', in *Acta conventus neo-latini Amstelodamensis*, edited by P. Tuynman, G. C. Kuiper, E. Kessler (Munich, 1979), pp. 721–46

Millar, D. A. (ed.), *George Buchanan: a Memorial* (St Andrews and London, 1906)

Naiden, James R., 'The *Sphera* of George Buchanan (1506–1582)' (Ph.D. thesis, Columbia State University, 1948)

Neilson, George, 'The *Franciscan*: some Footnotes', in *George Buchanan: Glasgow Quatercentenary Studies, 1906* (Glasgow, 1907), pp. 297–332

Phillips, James E., 'George Buchanan and the Sidney Circle', *Huntington Library Quarterly*, XII (1948–9), 23–55

Santos, Domingos Maurício Gomes dos, 'Buchanan e o ambiente coimbrão no século XVI', *Humanitas*, XV and XVI (1963–4), 261–327

Utenhovius, Carolus, (ed.), *Georgii Buchanani Scoti poetae eximii Franciscanus et Fratres, quibus accessere varia eiusdem et aliorum poemata* (Bâle, [1568])

Wall, John, 'The Latin Elegiacs of George Buchanan (1506–1582)', in *Bards and Makars*, edited by A. A. Aitken, M. P. McDiarmid, D. S. Thomson (Glasgow, 1977), pp. 184–93

General Works

Alexander de Villa-Dei, Das Doctrinale des, edited by Dietrich Reichling (Berlin, 1893)

Armstrong, Elizabeth, *Ronsard and the Age of Gold* (Cambridge, 1968)

Bolgar, R. R., *The Classical Heritage and its Beneficiaries* (Cambridge, 1954)

    (ed.), *Classical Influences on European Culture: AD 1500–1700* (Cambridge, 1976)

Bradner, Leicester, *Musae Anglicanae: a History of Anglo-Latin Poetry 1500–1925* (Wisconsin, 1940)

Brink, C. O., *Horace on Poetry: the 'Ars Poetica'* (Cambridge, 1971)

Buisson, F., *Répertoire des ouvrages pédagogiques du seizième siècle* (Paris, 1886)

Calendar of the State Papers relating to Scotland and Mary, Queen of Scots 1547–1603, edited by Joseph Bain (Edinburgh, 1898)

Calepinus, Ambrosius, *Dictionarium* (Paris, 1518)

Carvalho, Joaquim de, *Notícias chronológicas da Universidade de Coimbra escriptas pelo beneficiado Francisco Leitão Ferreira* (Coimbra, 1937–44)

Cave, Terence, *The Cornucopian Text: Problems of Writing in the French Renaissance* (Oxford, 1979)

Chamard, Henri, 'Le Collège de Boncourt et les origines du théâtre classique', in *Mélanges offerts à Abel Lefranc* (Paris, 1936), pp. 246–60

Histoire de la Pléiade, 4 vols (Paris, 1939–40)

Cohen, Abraham, (ed.), *The Psalms: Hebrew Text, English Translation and Commentary* (Hindhead, Surrey, 1945)

Coleman, Dorothy, *The Gallo-Roman Muse: Aspects of Roman Literary Tradition in Sixteenth-Century France* (Cambridge, 1979)

Corti, Count, *A History of Smoking,* translated by P. England (London, 1931)

Craufurd, Thomas, *History of the University of Edinburgh from 1580 to 1646* (Edinburgh, 1808)

Curio, Caelius Secundus, *Pasquillorum, tomi duo* (Bâle, 1544)

Despauterius, Joannes, *Ars versificatoria* (Paris, 1520)

Dictionary of National Biography (London, 1908–9)

Dorat, Jean, *Les Odes latines,* edited by Geneviève Demerson (Clermont-Ferrand, 1979)

du Bellay, Joachim, *La Deffence et illustration de la langue francoyse,* edited by Henri Chamard (Paris, 1904)

Œuvres poétiques, edited by Henri Chamard, 7 vols (Paris, 1908–31)

Poésies françaises et latines, edited by E. Courbet, 2 vols (Paris, 1918)

Dunbar, The Poems of William, edited by W. Mackay MacKenzie (London, 1960)

Erasmus, Desiderius, *De duplici verborum ac rerum copia* (Paris, 1512)

De recta latini graecique sermonis pronuntiatione dialogus (Bâle, 1528)

Encomium Moriae (Paris, 1511)

Estienne, Henri (ed.), *Dauidis Psalmi aliquot latino carmine expressi a quatuor* [sic] *illustribus poetis quos quatuor regiones Gallia, Italia, Germania, Scotia genuerunt* (n.p., 1556)

(ed.), *Pindari Olympia, Pythia, Nemea, Isthmia. Caeterorum octo lyricorum carmina, Alcaei, Sapphus, Stesichori, Ibyci, Anacreontis, Bacchylidis, Simonidis, Alcmanis* (n.p., 1560)

Forcadel, Etienne, *Recréation et passetemps des Tristes* (Paris, 1573)

Gaertner, Johannes A., 'Latin Verse Translations of the Psalms 1500–1620', *Harvard Theological Review,* XLIX (1956), 271–305

Gaguin, Robert, *Ars versificatoria* (Paris, 1505)

Gaisford, Thomas, *Scriptores latini rei metricae* (Oxford, 1837)

Gesner, Conrad (ed.), *Sententiae ex thesauris Graecorum delictae* (Bâle, 1549)

Glareanus, Henricus, *De ratione syllabarum brevis isagoge* (Bâle, 1516)

Gmelin, Hermann, 'Das Prinzip der Imitatio in den romanischen Literaturen der Renaissance', *Romanische Forschungen,* XLVI (1932), 83–360

Gualtherus, Rodolphus, *De syllabarum et carminum ratione, libri duo* (Zürich, 1542)

Hill, George Birkbeck (ed), *Boswell's Life of Johnson,* 6 vols (Oxford, 1934–50)

Hulubei, Alice, *L'Eglogue en France au XVIe siècle: époque des Valois (1515–1589)* (Paris, 1938)

Hutten, Ulrich von, *Rudimenta poëtices: carmen her[oicum] ab adulescente quondam ipso compositum* (Strasbourg, 1523)

Hutton, James, *The Greek Anthology in France and in the Latin Writers of the Netherlands to the Year 1800* (Ithaca, 1946)

IJsewijn, J., *Companion to Neo-Latin Studies* (Amsterdam, New York, Oxford, 1977)

Janssen, Willem, *Charles Utenhove: sa vie et son oeuvre (1536–1600)* (Maastricht, 1939)

Jeanneret, Michel, *Poésie et tradition biblique au XVIe siècle* (Paris, 1969)

Lebègue, Raymond, *La Tragédie religieuse en France: les débuts (1514–1573)* (Paris, 1929)

McFarlane, I. D., *A Literary History of France: Renaissance France 1470–1589* (London and Tonbridge, 1974)

'Poésie néo-latine et poésie de langue vulgaire à l'époque de la Pléiade', in *Acta conventus neo-latini Lovaniensis*, edited by J. IJsewijn and E. Kessler (Louvain and Munich, 1973), pp. 389–403

'Reflections on Ravisius Textor's *Specimen epithetorum*', in *Classical Influences on European Culture: AD 1500–1700*, edited by R. R. Bolgar (Cambridge, 1978), pp. 81–90

Renaissance Latin Poetry (Manchester, 1980)

Marullus, Michael, *Carmina*, edited by Alessandro Perosa (Zürich, 1951)

Micyllus, Jacobus, *De re metrica, libri tres* (Frankfurt, 1539)

Montaigne, Michel de, *Oeuvres complètes*, edited by Albert Thibaudet and Maurice Rat, Bibliothèque de la Pléiade (Paris, 1962)

Morrison, Mary, 'Catullus and the Poetry of the Renaissance in France', *BHR*, XXV (1963), 25–56

'Ronsard and Catullus: the Influence of the Teaching of Marc-Antoine de Muret', *BHR*, XVIII (1956), 240–74

Muret, Marc-Antoine, *Catullus et in eum commentarius* (Venice, 1554)

Iuvenilia (Paris, 1552)

Murmellius, Joannes, *Tabulae in artis componendorum versuum rudimenta* (Paris, 1539)

Nausea, Fridericus, *In artem poeticen, carminumque condendorum primordia* (Venice, 1522)

Nichols, Fred J. (ed.), *An Anthology of Neo-Latin Poetry* (New Haven and London, 1979)

Postgate, J. P., *Prosodia Latina: an Introduction to Classical Latin Verse* (Oxford, 1923)

Putschius, Helia, *Grammaticae latinae auctores antiqui* (Hanover, 1605)

Quicherat, J., *Histoire de Sainte-Barbe*, 3 vols (Paris, 1860)

Raven, D. S., *Latin Metre* (London, 1965)

Ravisius Textor, Joannes, *Specimen epithetorum* (Paris, 1518)

Robertson, Joseph, *Inuentaires de la Royne Descosse Douairiere: Catalogues of the Jewels, Dresses, Furniture, Books, and Paintings of Mary Queen of Scots, 1556–1569* (Edinburgh, 1863)

Ronsard, Pierre de, *Oeuvres complètes*, edited by Paul Laumonier, 20 vols (Paris, 1914–1975)

Sainct-Gelays, Oeuvres complètes de Melin de, edited by Prosper Blanchemain, 3 vols (Paris, 1873)

Salmon Macrin, Jean, *Le Livre des épithalames (1528–1531); les Odes de 1530 (livres I & II)*, edited by Georges Soubeille (Toulouse, 1978)

Sandys, J. E., *A History of Classical Scholarship*, 3 vols (Cambridge, 1931)

Saulnier, V.-L., *Maurice Scève*, 2 vols (Paris, 1948)

'Les Poètes de la prise de Calais (1558)', in 'Deux oeuvres inconnues de Jean Sève et une édition inconnue de Baïf', *Bulletin du bibliophile* (June 1949), 265–79

Scaliger, Julius Caesar, *Poetices libri septem* (Lyons, 1561)

Schottus, Petrus, *Epitome de syllabarum mensura* (Strasbourg, 1500)

Silver, Isidore, *The Intellectual Evolution of Ronsard*, vol. I, *The Formative Influences* (St Louis, 1969)

Soubiran, Jean, *L'Elision dans la poésie latine* (Paris, 1966)

Sutherland, Robert Garioch, *Buchanan's Jephthah and The Baptist: Translatit frae Latin in Scots* (Edinburgh and London, 1959)

Collected Poems (Loanhead, Midlothian, 1977)

Tahureau, *Poésies de Jacques*, edited by Prosper Blanchemain, 2 vols (Paris, 1870)

Tieghem, Paul van, 'La Littérature latine de la Renaissance', *BHR*, IV (1944), 177–418

Viau, Théophile de, *Le Parnasse satyrique du sieur Théophile avec le recueil des plus excellens vers satyriques de ce temps*, 2 vols (Paris, 1861)

Vida, *The 'De arte poetica' of Marco Girolamo*, edited by R. G. Williams (New York, 1976)

Voragine, Jacobus de, *Legenda aurea*, edited by T. Graesse (Leipzig, 1850)

Index